DISCARDED

Spanish-Speaking People in the United States

Proceedings of the 1968 Annual Spring Meeting
of the American Ethnological Society

June Helm, Editor

William Madsen, Program Chairman

AMERICAN ETHNOLOGICAL SOCIETY

Distributed by the University of Washington Press

Seattle and London

PREFACE

The 1968 Annual Spring Meeting of the American Ethnological Society was held in Detroit on May 3 and 4. The program of papers on SPANISH-SPEAKING PEOPLE IN THE UNITED STATES was arranged by William Madsen. The Society met in conjunction with the Central States Anthropological Society. Arnold R. Pilling was in charge of local arrangements.

Lynn A. Robbins, University of Oregon, won the Elsie Clews Parsons Prize for student papers. His paper, "Economics, Household Composition, and the Family Cycle: The Blackfeet Case," is published in this issue of the Proceedings. Other student papers chosen for presentation were by Woodrow W. Denham, Jr., University of Washington; Miss Suad Joseph, Columbia University; Mr. Philip F. McKean, Brown University; and Mr. Davyd J. Greenwood, University of Pittsburgh. Roger Owen arranged the student paper session.

Emily Meeks has served as Editorial Assistant in preparing the papers of this volume for publication.

June Helm, Editor

University of Iowa

CONTENTS

SAMPLING AND GENERALIZATION IN ANTHROPOLOGICAL RESEARCH ON SPANISH-SPEAKING GROUPS

Thomas Weaver
University of Pittsburgh

Anthropologists, as a rule, study groups of less than several thousand persons during a relatively short period of time. Yet, they generalize from their data to a much larger group, usually to the whole society of which the community is only a small part and over a longer time span. Thus, generalizations are made about certain cultural attributes of Spanish-speaking people, Latin Americans, Mexican Americans, Negroes, North American Indians, California Indians when, in fact, the basis of the generalization is one or a few ethnographies. This problem is not unique to anthropologists working in the United States but also characterizes generalizing about other cultures. Generalization from such a small base fails to account for status, stratification, subcultural, economic and other differences present in the society as a whole.

Non-anthropologists also make unwarranted generalizations from our work, and usually we have not provided the necessary guide lines which allow the reader to identify the segment of the total population to which our generalizations or descriptions apply. It could be argued that our ethnologies are entitled <u>Moche</u> and <u>Tzintzuntzan</u>, and so on, but our readers tend to generalize far beyond the limits of the materials presented. Disclaimers could also be provided that generalizations from the descriptions of single villages, communities or towns to whole cultures and societies are to demonstrate a concept, theory or point. Of course, the anthropologist could also claim that travel through the larger society or brief visits among them qualify his intuitive notions about the larger group.

What assurances do we have that our generalizations apply to larger groups? How much can the anthropologist generalize from Tepoztlan to Mexicans, from Moche to Peruvians or from both to Latin Americans, or in an area more closely related to the present paper-- from the studies of Clark, Madsen and Romano to Mexican Americans, from Leonard and Loomis to Spanish Americans, and from Senior, Padilla and Lewis to Puerto Ricans? What specific techniques have we devised or utilized to assure ourselves that the generalizations derived from these studies apply to the 5.1 million Spanish-speaking persons living in the U. S. and who represent many different national origins and subcultures?

These questions become particularly important as increasing numbers of anthropologists turn to the study of complex societies, large communities, cities, and ethnic minorities and subcultural groups and as administrators and politicians make increasing use of our data. The importance of the problem becomes apparent even before. When a generalization is made about large minority or subcultural groups the anthropologist has already left the area of small isolated and self-sustaining community studies and has entered the area of complex societies.

As long as anthropologists view the subject of their study in terms of community, whether peasant or aboriginal, they will fail to recognize the need for sampling technique in their work. At the same time, though, even if he views his material in terms of small communities but then also proceeds to generalize about larger populations, such as the total society or a large minority group, one can say that it has already become a problem of dealing with a large scale complex society. In order to do this accurately he must use sampling technique in conjunction with standard anthropological research techniques. Put another way, the anthropologist's avoidance of sampling because he has claimed to work in small closed groups has been a fiction since he has always generalized to larger groups.

The general problem involves assuring representativeness and generalizability. To assure representativeness at the community level means that a sufficient number of people have been interviewed so that the data represents all social and cultural variation within the whole community. This applies whether the community is small or large, rural or urban, whether it is a relatively self-sufficing and closed system or one which is open and part of a larger system. The same problem characterizes the matter of generalizability, which refers to establishing the limits of applicability of generalizations of the single study to other similar units in the total society. However, a distinction must be made between generalizability of a part of a society to the whole society, which is what is referred to here, and cross-cultural comparison. In the latter case a greater concern is felt for finding appropriate categories for comparison between different cultures.

The problem of the generalizability of small anthropological studies raises the question of demographic accommodation. If the county is to be used as the unit of comparison an intermediate step is needed before you move from the community to the larger unit. This relates to choosing a community which is representative of the county. In other words, the anthropologist must not only accommodate his techniques to the nature of the culture he is studying but also, at another level, he must accommodate the unit he studies to the demographic environment in order to use demographic data. That is, he must choose a community in that county or larger unit which is representative of the larger unit.

As far as methodology is concerned, whether opportunistic

sampling is used in small communities or random table sampling for larger communities or sub-societies, sampling of some type will solve the problem of representativeness. In the same manner the generalizable limits of the study in question can be established through the use of various demographic, or population statistics in conjunction with sampling techniques.

This paper explores these two problems within the context of available published material on Spanish Americans in New Mexico. I hope to demonstrate some of the limitations of drawing inferences about large groups from the available literature and to provide some suggestions for making more useful generalizations from small ethnographic samples.

Sampling

Anthropologists usually have not been concerned with problems of formal sampling; where they have it has been a matter of opportunistic rather than random sampling methods. Holmes, perhaps, represents the general attitude of anthropologists regarding sampling:

> It is seldom that an anthropological field worker must proceed in the manner of the sociologist--ascertaining the composition of the population and making up a representative sample. In a small primitive community composed of say three hundred people almost any intelligent knowledgeable person will know much of the way of life of his community and will represent to a certain extent a representative sample of the people (1965:327).

Holmes states later in the same source that

> The success of the research does not depend so much on how many informants are used but rather on their proper selection (p. 328).

This would seem to argue for a more directed and planned use of sampling techniques.

Other anthropologists, such as Honigmann, however, have recognized the need for representativeness in selecting informants. In this sense, then, the problem has been recognized although not implemented by other anthropologists. Paul, for example, describes opportunistic sampling:

> Ideally, informants should be so selected as to comprise a panel representative of the major social subdivisions and categories recognized within the community.... Within the range of practical choices the field worker makes his selection in such a way as best to approximate the ideal requirements of representativeness, moving further in the desired direction as his circle of acquaintanceship expands (1953:443).

Paul approximates the position suggested here.

In large communities socio-economic mapping and use of

random-number tables to select households or subjects may prove desirable for purposes of statistical control (1953:444).

Oscar Lewis studied Tepoztlan, with its population of approximately 3,500, utilizing standard anthropological techniques. But because of its relatively large size and complexity he used sampling and other quantitative techniques. He described his methodology as follows:

> ...the traditional anthropological reliance upon a few informants for obtaining a picture of the culture was obviously inadequate in this situation. Sampling and securing data and informants representative of all the significant differences in the village seemed just as important here as in a study of a modern urban community. We therefore employed quantitative procedures wherever possible, utilizing census data, local government records and documents, schedules, and questionnaires. Numerous surveys were made with the assistance of local informants and a small staff of field workers (1951:xiv).

> As a preliminary to obtaining families that would represent the various socio-economic groupings in the village, several informants ranked the families in each of the barrio lists according to relative wealth and social position. The criteria used in this tentative classification were the ownership of (1) a house, (2) land, or (3) cattle. In this way we obtained a rough idea of the relative economic standing of all the families in the village. On the basis of this, three families, each representing different socio-economic levels, were tentatively selected for study in each of the seven barrios (1951:xvii).

However, he does not explain why he chose ownership of house, land or cattle as determinants of socio-economic standing nor why three families constitute an adequate sampling of the different socio-economic levels in each of the social and political divisions of the village. In spite of these deficiencies, Lewis is one of the few anthropologists who has been actively concerned with the application of sampling to anthropological field work, and as will be seen later also with the problem of generalizability of his community to other Mexican communities.

There are several reasons why anthropologists have not been overly concerned with sampling. One reason, undoubtedly, has been the small size of the community and society studied which has allowed the sample to encompass the whole community or most of it. A second reason is the general anthropological bias against anything that approaches quantitative technique. Third, societies which have been the subject of study for anthropologists have not been differentiated greatly in terms of a wide divergence of class and status. Fourth, only recently have anthropologists recognized that what they believed were small closed systems are in fact parts of larger societies which cannot be adequately considered in isolation.

One of the problems of the change in research interest of the anthropologist from the small-scale peasant and primitive environment to the complex societal setting is one of applying all of his abilities to this endeavor. These are generally recognized as participant observation, intensive interviewing, functional analysis, a systems approach and a holistic approach. With regard to holism, the anthropologist has been at a distinct disadvantage in the city. His techniques, however insightful and valuable in small societies, are of little value to the construction of the anthropological viewpoint if holism is ignored. One way in which holism can be utilized is the accommodation of sampling and quantitative techniques to the anthropological viewpoint to insure coverage of all aspects of the large society. It is no longer sufficient to interview a few informants intensively and expect an adequate representation of the large scale society.

Generalizability

The problem of generalizability is an extension of ascertaining representativeness within a single community. The difference involves a matter of scale; that is, the concern is with how much a small community, neighborhood, or ethnic group can be said to represent the entire society rather than how closely informants represent the community-based culture.

Oscar Lewis was not only concerned with the problem of selecting informants who would provide him with data from the different socio-economic strata in Tepoztlan, but he was also concerned with how representative his community was of other parts of Mexico. He described the problem in the following manner:

> The anthropologist must be sufficiently versed in the more important historical, geographical, economic, and cultural characteristics of the region and nation to be able to place his community in relation to each of them, and to indicate just what the community is representative of in the larger scene. Like the sociologist, the anthropologist must become skilled in the use of census data and comparative statistics to relate and compare population trends, standards of living, health and education, and types of agricultural problems. In the matter of cultural characteristics the anthropologist must know what is unique to his community and what it shares with broader areas, what is new and what is old, what is primitive and what is modern...one of the questions to

5

be considered in this study, therefore, is: What is Tepoztlan representative of in rural Mexico (1951:xxi)?

Oscar Lewis uses geography, history, population trends, agrarian problems, and other aspects of culture to indicate the ways in which Tepoztlan is representative of the nation. Of particular interest to the subject of this paper is Lewis' use of population statistics and measurements on land use and types, distribution of population by age group, birth and mortality rates, average mortality rate by age group, and measurements of language and literacy. He has, however, some qualifications about the comparability of Tepoztlan to Mexico.

Obviously, in a country of such diversity as Mexico it would be impossible to find any single village or municipio which would represent the entire range of variations and differences. Tepoztlan is not here presented as _the_ synthesis of Mexico but rather as _one_ synthesis (1951:xxvii).

Spanish Americans in New Mexico

The material presented below expands on the contribution by Lewis: additional population characteristics are utilized, and an attempt is made to compare the community with other similar political units as well as with the total national group as exemplified by Lewis.

Variation of Spanish-Speaking Groups

A quick perusal of population statistics available indicates a wide variation among persons who are Spanish speaking in New Mexico. Such indicators as rural-urban, nativity or parentage, school years completed, school enrollment and occupational indices, all point to this wide variation.

Rural-Urban. Of the 269,122 persons of Spanish surname listed in the U. S. Census report of 1960 for New Mexico about 57.4 percent are classified as urban dwellers, that is, living in places of 2,500 or more inhabitants. Of the rural population only 5.7 percent are rural farm and 36.6 percent are rural non-farm.

Nativity or Parentage. Eighty-seven and four-tenths percent of persons of Spanish surname are native born of native born parents, 8.6 percent are of foreign or mixed parentage, and 3.9 percent are foreign born, mostly in Mexico.

Median Age of Population. The median age of persons of native parentage is 17.0 years, 23.4 years for persons of mixed parentage, and 39.9 years for persons born in Mexico. This indicates that the median age for persons immigrating from Mexico is much greater than for persons born in New Mexico, a fact which has definite implications for their ability to acquire American culture and identification.

Years of School Completed. Median school years completed for natives of native parentage is 8.5 years for males and 8.6 years for females, both slightly higher in urban than rural areas (8.9 compared to 8.1 for males and 8.3 for females). Comparable figures for native born of foreign born parents is slightly lower at 8.3 and 8.2 years respectively, with a slightly greater variation in terms of urban-rural farm-rural-nonfarm habitation.

The differences are more revealing when the figures for foreign born in Mexico are considered: 3.9 years completed for males and females, slightly higher in the city and lower on the farm except for men who have a slightly higher (4.5) figure for residents of non-farm rural areas.

School Enrollment. The same gradient is apparent in the percentage of school children enrolled in school: for male children it is 59.5 percent for native born of native parentage, 46.3 percent for native born of mixed parents and 39.9 percent for those born in Mexico. Female children are a few percentage points lower in each category.

Occupation and Income. Approximately one half of the male labor force of the persons born in Mexico work as farm laborers or foremen compared to only 5.4 percent for persons of native birth, and 10.4 percent for persons of foreign or mixed parentage. The latter two categories are employed mostly in the more skilled manual occupations. This distribution in occupation is reflected in median income for all persons with income; $1923 annually for native born, $2209 for those of foreign or mixed parentage, and only $1538 for persons born in Mexico.

There are many other such demographic characteristics which could be cited to indicate the wide variation among segments of the Spanish-speaking population of the area. Enough has been said, perhaps, to substantiate the point.

How can one generalize about such a varied and large population? Can anthropologists furnish one or many "community" studies which will apply equally to all persons who are Spanish speaking? Are there differences between segments of this population which relate to national origin, i.e., Puerto Rican, Mexican, native born, in terms of values, religion, economic behavior, socialization patterns, kinship, political behavior, level of acculturation, and other cultural elements? Can the community study provide the kind of information required for understanding such a large population? What kinds of studies do anthropologists or sociologists have to describe and discuss the culture carried by these people? Do these studies represent the entire spectrum of differences represented by these groups?

There are problems in the use of demographic techniques because of their inadequate development. One of the problems is the difficulty in using demographic data for delimiting cultural or subcultural boundaries and a related problem of correlating these boundaries with political and census unit boundaries. Granting these deficiencies,

7

however, they can be a valuable adjunct research technique to the anthropologist.

Two points will be made below concerning the use of demographic data. The first relates to identifying subcultural differences and the second with assessing the representativeness of materials available on Spanish-speaking groups.

The general conclusions may be summarized as follows: subcultural areas of Spanish-speaking persons can be identified in New Mexico on the basis of demographic data. Secondly, these data appear to support a distinction on the basis of subcultural factors. Thirdly, with regard to representativeness, little can be said from the available data either about the total Spanish-speaking population or about other segments than the rural-farming-pastoral subculture.

Subcultural Areas

Several counties may be grouped in terms of similar demographic characteristics into subcultural regions. Although the primary characteristics which suggested the existence of this division in the beginning was the percentage of Spanish surname persons who are native born of native born parentage compared to those who are either born in Mexico or of Mexican parentage, there are other characteristics which distinguish the two regions.

The initial division of counties can be made on the basis of percent of persons of Spanish surname and percent born in Mexico. In this way a Core Spanish-American area may be identified and includes Rio Arriba, Taos, Mora, San Miguel, Guadalupe and Santa Fe counties, with the total population including from 55 to 86 percent persons of Spanish surname, or an average of 70 percent. This area also includes a population of Indians which is 3.3 percent of the total. Of the 70 percent Spanish name population only .6 percent were born in Mexico. All of the central and northern counties, except McKinley, have less than 3 percent of their Spanish surname population born in Mexico.

The second area which can be identified on the basis of Spanish-surname-nativity is the Core Mexican-American county area, mostly those southern counties which border Texas and Mexico. Persons of Spanish surname constitute 26.9 percent of the total population of the area, of which 10.9 percent were born in Mexico. Two and five-tenths percent of the total population is non-white, of which about half are Indians, mostly located in the Mescalero Apache Reservation area.

A more tenuous identification can be made of two other regions in the state: an Indian area and so-called "Little Texas." The Core Indian area includes San Juan, McKinley, and Sandoval counties, with 42.5 percent of the population being Indian, and 17 percent persons of Spanish surname, 2.4 percent of which were born in Mexico. "Little Texas" includes those counties which border Texas mostly in the southeast quadrant: Lea, Roosevelt, Curry, Quay, and possibly Harding and Union. They are characterized by a smaller population of Spanish Americans and Indians and a higher percentage of Spanish surname persons born in Mexico than the northern counties but not as high as for the Mexican-American counties. Many of the demographic characteristics discussed elsewhere in this article support the division into core areas which has been made in this section.

Subcultural Differences

There has been some discussion in the past as to whether persons in New Mexico who are Spanish speaking should be distinguished as Spanish Americans from the Mexican Americans or recent immigrants from Mexico. Many, I am certain, believe that the term Spanish-American is an affectation used to distinguish the native born person from the more culturally visible Mexican, and that in fact little can be found culturally which distinguishes the two groups. It is claimed that the term Spanish-American is sometimes also assumed to avoid the more overt prejudice linked with Mexicans.

The problem of naming this group has been discussed by many investigators, perhaps most notably by Saunders and Edmonson, both of whom support the distinction of the two populations in terminology at least. Persons of native birth or parentage maintain a similar position. Although they refer to themselves as _Mejicanos_ or _chicanos_, these terms are not directly translatable as "Mexican" as indicated by Saunders and Edmonson. New Mexican villagers distinguish themselves from Mexicans by referring to the latter group as _Mejicanos-Mejicanos_ or _Mejicanos de Mexico_, or in a less complementary fashion as _surumatos_.

The native New Mexican villager also makes cultural distinctions between himself and _Mejicanos de Mexico_. First he claims that the language spoken is so rapid, has such an unusual pronunciation and vocabulary that it is not understandable. Of course this is an exaggeration, but many a villager entertains his friends and relatives by imitating the more rapidly spoken Mexican dialect to demonstrate his point.

Other cultural distinctions obvious to the Spanish American include differences in dress. The farm laborer's, or _bracero's_ large straw hat and clothes of obvious Mexican manufacture are unknown in the northern counties of the state, possibly because of the lesser demand for _bracero_ labor. Although such things as folk music and moving pictures of Mexican origin are known through Spanish language radio and local theaters they are less appreciated in the northern than the southern counties. Few Spanish language publications reach the village, and no newspapers and only a few religious pamphlets of Protestant origin. Bibles printed in Spanish, however, are more frequently encountered.

The anthropologist can identify other cultural differences. Spanish Americans have no kinship ties to or relatives living in

9

Mexico and visits are not made to that country except as infrequent tourists. The history of the Mexican nation, its heroes and holidays are generally unknown to Spanish Americans. El Grito de Delores, Hidalgo, Cardenas, and Juarez are unknown names in northern New Mexico, although many people can identify Pancho Villa because his fame has been preserved in a popular folk song.

These are probably the main distinctions which can be made at the cultural level, but there are other differences which are reflected on the psychological level. To return to the factor of language, as an example, since there is little which reinforces the proper grammatical study of Spanish and because of the paucity of materials printed in Spanish, it is not surprising to find many persons, particularly younger people, who cannot read Spanish. The Spanish which is spoken in the village is mostly a household and farm-life language and it has become well laced with words of American English origin which are given a Spanish pronunciation.

Society is less imbued with class differences. The patron, today, is a mere shell of his former self; he wields political influence by virtue of what he can do for his friends rather than the more encompassing authority and power he once had. The values which keep him in this position of influence are no longer strictly Spanish-Colonial in origin, but a combination of being a good villager and knowing how to manipulate the Anglo power structure.

Other psychological conditions which are different between the Mexican American and the Spanish American are related to the position of each in Anglo society. The Mexican American as a relatively recent arrival and with the constant influence and reinforcement of Mexican national and cultural elements feels less at home in the Anglo world. Much of his loyalty still remains with Mexico and the Mexican. The Spanish American, on the other hand, cannot identify the Mexican flag. He has been raised as a part of the American culture. In school he learns about the Mayflower, Washington and Lincoln. His flag is the American flag; he has probably served, as have his relatives before him, in one of the recent three or four American war efforts. Some villagers can identify grandparents and parents who served in the Spanish-American and Civil Wars before the turn of the century. Although, like the Mexican American, he suffers the directed prejudice of the Anglo world, he identifies himself as a citizen of the U. S.

In summary, it can be said that there is evidence for distinguishing a Spanish-American from a Mexican-American subculture. But this would be a finely made distinction for the Mexican-American subculture overlaps a frontier-colonial base which is perpetuated by the close and continuing contacts with Mexico and the Mexican in the border area.

Adequacy of Available Studies

The data reported for New Mexico is varied in quality and kind.

Broadly speaking, studies of New Mexican culture can be divided into the following categories: (1) There are the early reports of travelers, trappers, traders, and soldiers who published general observations from an often value-laden point of view; (2) brief descriptions were contributed by early anthropologists as by-products of interests in other local groups such as Pueblo Indians; (3) studies of specific practices such as the penitente movement, folk tales, witchcraft, and music, but which were generally not reported in their "whole cultural" context; (4) sociological studies of the rural sociological tradition mostly related to agriculture or pastoralism, and some sociological community studies which lack the holistic concern of the anthropological approach; (5) recent anthropological and sociological community studies, mainly dissertations and other unpublished reports. The first four categories are important for comparative and background information but they often tell more about the reporter than the reported. The last category is most important for the purposes of this paper. These include the land tenure and economic studies of Leonard, the study of El Cerrito by Leonard and Loomis, Loomis' follow-up study on the same community, the study of Atrisco by Florence Kluckhohn, the description included in Vogt's Homesteaders, Edmonson's study, and the Johansen study of a rural community in Dona Ana County.

The problem of generalizability may best be highlighted by a series of questions regarding these studies. Basically, it is a matter of correlating the demographic and cultural characteristics of these studies with those of the population as a whole. The following questions may assist in doing this: What differences in terms of demography and subcultural variation are evident? What population in terms of numbers do the community studies involve? How does this compare to the total society? What are the various demographic characteristics of the community or next largest political unit in terms of rurality and urbanity, birth, mortality and morbidity rates, types of land use, education, occupational categories, ethnic composition, household characteristics, migration, etc.? How do these compare to similar characteristics of the larger group?

None of the studies of Spanish-American people has considered the problem of representativeness either to the county or population on which it has reported. For example, the Leonard and Loomis study in 1939 of El Cerrito in San Miguel county included about 150 persons, or about one percent of the 1960 Spanish surname population of the county. Johansen's study of eight hamlets and villages in Dona Ana county surpassed the one percent mark by a few hundred persons, and utilized the most extensive comparative demographic approach to date. Other studies, mostly dissertations, do not include demographic referrents of a nature which would make them comparable.

These studies have been on small rural farming-pastoral communities and do not account for the demographic and cultural variation present in the total population. To single out one of the most important variables is the previously mentioned fact that more than half of the total Spanish-speaking population in New Mexico lives in urban areas yet only two dissertations have directed attention to the urban environment, and they do not account for the vast majority of people who are employed in white collar, service, transportation, mining, and managerial occupations. Only a small percentage of the rural population is actually involved in farming-pastoral activities. Yet the assumption can be made from available reports that Spanish Americans are primarily occupied in these areas. For these reasons a good case can be made for questioning the representativeness of available studies.

The basic question I have raised in this paper regards the use of more rigorous and sophisticated sampling techniques in anthropological studies and the need for representing the total range of cultural variation present in such a complex group as the Spanish-speaking population of New Mexico. The use of demographic data constitutes a valuable adjunct to standard anthropological field techniques.

REFERENCES

Beagle, J. Allan, Harold F. Goldsmith and Charles P. Loomis
    1960   Demographic Characteristics of the U. S.-Mexican Border. Rural Sociology 25:107-162.
Clark, Mary Margaret
    1959   Health in a Mexican-American Community. Berkeley and Los Angeles, University of California Press.
Davis, Kingsley
    1959   The Sociology of Demographic Behavior. In Sociology Today: Problems and Prospects, Robert Merton and Leonard S. Cottrell, Jr., eds. New York, Basic Books, Inc. (Harper Torchbook edition, 1965.)
Edmonson, Munro S.
    1957   Los Manitos: A Study of Institutional Values. New Orleans, Tulane University. (Middle American Research Institute Publication 25:1-72.)
Eerden, Sister Lucia van der
    1938   Maternity Care in a Spanish-American Community of New Mexico. Washington, Catholic University of America, Anthropological Series No. 13.
Freedman, Ronald, Amos H. Hawley, Werner S. Landecker and Horace M. Miner
    1952   Principles of Sociology. New York, Henry Holt and Company.
Holmes, Lowell D.
    1965   Anthropology: An Introduction. New York, The Ronald Press Company.
Honigmann, John and Irma
    1955   Sampling Reliability in Ethnological Field Work. Southwestern Journal of Anthropology 11:282-287.

Hurt, Wesley R., Jr.
    1940   Witchcraft in New Mexico. El Palacio 47:73-83.
    1941   Manzano: A Study of Community Disorganization. Unpub-
           lished master's thesis. Albuquerque, University of New
           Mexico.

Johansen, Sigurd
    1942   The Social Organization of Spanish-American Villages.
           Southwestern Social Science Quarterly 23:151-59.
    1948   Rural Social Organization in a Spanish-American Culture
           Area. Albuquerque, University of New Mexico. Publica-
           tions in Social Sciences and Philosophy No. 1.

Kluckhohn, Florence R.
    1941   Los Atarqueños. Unpublished doctoral dissertation.
           Cambridge, Radcliffe College.
    1950   Dominant and Substitute Profiles of Cultural Orienta-
           tions: Their Significance for the Analysis of Social
           Stratification. Social Forces 28:376-393.

Kluckhohn, Florence R. and Fred L. Strodtbeck
    1961   Variations in Value Orientation. Evanston, Illinois,
           Row, Peterson and Company.

Lewis, Oscar
    1951   Life in a Mexican Village: Tepoztlan Revisited. Urbana,
           University of Illinois Press (paperback edition, 1963).
    1965   La Vida. New York, Random House.

Likert, Rensis
    1948   Public Opinion Polls. The Scientific American 179:7-11.
           (Reprinted in Principles of Sociology, Ronald Freedman,
           et al., eds. New York, Henry Holt and Company, 1952.
           Pp. 43-53.)

Leonard, Olen
    1943   The Role of the Land Grant in the Social Organization
           and Social Processes of a Spanish American Village in
           New Mexico. Ph.D. thesis. Baton Rouge, Louisiana,
           Louisiana State University. (Ann Arbor, Michigan, Ed-
           wards Brothers, Inc., 1948.)

Leonard, Olen and Charles P. Loomis
    1951   Culture of a Contemporary Rural Community: El Cerrito,
           New Mexico. Washington, Bureau of Agriculture and
           Economic Life Studies No. 1, U. S. Department of Agri-
           culture.

Loomis, Charles P.
    1958   El Cerrito, New Mexico: A Changing Village. New Mexi-
           can Historical Review 33:53-75.

Lundberg, George A.
    1946   Social Research: A Study in Methods of Gathering Data.
           New York and London, Longmans, Green and Company.

Madsen, William
    1964   Mexican-Americans of South Texas. New York, Holt,

Rinehart and Winston.

Mead, Margaret, ed.
1953   Cultural Patterns and Technical Change. Paris, UNESCO.

Mitchell, Robert Edward
1965   Survey Materials Collected in Developing Countries:
        Sampling, Measurement and Interviewing Obstacles to
        Intra- and Inter-National Comparisons. International
        Social Sciences Journal 17:665-685.

Moore, Frank C.
1947   San Jose, 1946: A Study in Urbanization. Unpublished
        master's thesis. Albuquerque, University of New Mexico.

Padilla, Elena
1958   Up From Puerto Rico. New York, Columbia University
        Press.

Paul, Benjamin
1953   Interview Techniques and Field Relationships. In
        Anthropology Today, A. L. Kroeber, ed. Chicago, Univer-
        sity of Chicago Press. Pp. 430-451.

Romano, Octavio I.
1960   Donship in a Mexican-American Community in Texas. Ameri-
        can Anthropologist 62:966-976.

Russell, John C.
1937   State Regionalism in New Mexico. Social Forces 14:268-
        271.

Samora, Julian
1962   Report on the Spanish-Speaking People of the U. S.
        Washington, D. C., U. S. Commission on Civil Rights
        (unpublished report).

Sanchez, George I.
1940   Forgotten People, A Study of New Mexicans. Albuquerque,
        University of New Mexico Press.

Saunders, Lyle
1954   Cultural Differences and Medical Care. New York,
        Russell Sage Foundation.

Senior, Clarence
1965   The Puerto Ricans: Strangers - Then Neighbors. Chicago,
        Quadrangle Books.

Senter, Donovan
1945   Acculturation Among New Mexican Villagers in Comparison
        to Adjustment Patterns of Other Spanish-Speaking Ameri-
        cans. Rural Sociology 10:31-47.

Sjoberg, Gideon
1947   Culture Change as Revealed by a Study of Relief Clients
        of a Suburban New Mexican Community. Unpublished master's
        thesis. Albuquerque, University of New Mexico.

Slonim, Morris James
1966   Sampling: A Quick, Reliable Guide to Practical Statis-
        tics. New York, Simon and Schuster.

Stephan, Frederick R. and Philip J. McCarthy
    1958   Sampling Opinions: An Analysis of Survey Procedure.
            New York, John Wiley and Sons, Inc.
U. S. Bureau of the Census
    1963   U. S. Census of Population: 1960 Subject Reports.
            Persons of Spanish Surname. Washington, U. S. Govern-
            ment Printing Office.
    1963   U. S. Census of Population: 1960, Vol. 1, Characteris-
            tics of the Population. Part 33, New Mexico. Washing-
            ton, U. S. Government Printing Office.
    1967   U. S. Census of Population: 1960. County and City
            Data Book: A Statistical Abstract Supplement. Washing-
            ton, U. S. Government Printing Office.
Vogt, Evon Z.
    1955   Modern Homesteaders: The Life of a 20th Century Frontier
            Community. Cambridge, Harvard University Press.
Waggoner, Laura
    1951   San Jose, A Study in Urbanization. Unpublished master's
            thesis. Albuquerque, University of New Mexico.
Walter, Paul, Jr.
    1938   A Study of Isolation and Social Change in Three Spanish-
            Speaking Villages in New Mexico. Unpublished doctoral
            dissertation. Stanford University.
Weaver, Thomas
    1965   Social Structure, Change, and Conflict in a New Mexican
            Village. Unpublished doctoral dissertation. Berkeley,
            University of California.
Zeleny, Carolyn
    1944   Relations Between the Spanish-Americans and Anglo-
            Americans in New Mexico. Unpublished doctoral disserta-
            tion. New Haven, Yale University.

APPENDIX

SAMPLING IN ANTHROPOLOGICAL FIELD WORK

Sampling has been defined as
...the use of a definite procedure in the selection of
a part for the express purpose of obtaining from it
descriptions or estimates of certain properties and
characteristics of the whole (Stephan and McCarthy
1958:23).
The adequacy of a sample is dependent upon the size and reliability of the sample. The extent to which a random sample will differ in its composition from that of the whole body of data will depend on the amount of homogeneity present and on the size of the
sample. Neither the actual size of the sample nor the size of the
probable error necessarily guarantees its representativeness. In

selecting a sample, Freedman states that:

> Since human populations are not distributed randomly in
> space, it is not always easy to choose a sample in an
> unbiased way, even with the best of intentions. An un-
> biased sample should be selected in such a way that
> every case in the population being sampled has an equal
> chance of inclusion in the sample (Freedman et al., pp.
> 11-12).

Biases may be introduced in the method of drawing the sample and in
the data gathering or survey techniques which follow the selection
of a sample.

The usefulness of sampling lies in working out a compromise
between the need for accuracy and economy. There are several
sampling methods utilized by sociologists which can serve the anthropological goal. Regardless of which is used it is probably wise to
use the advice of a sampling expert.

In most sample surveys a combination of sampling methods is used.
Types of sampling which are most applicable to the anthropological
approach include the following (Slonim 1966):

1. Simple random sampling requires the use of a table of random
numbers to derive the average of the units of the sample. An undesirable feature is that the selected average may not correspond to the
true average. Simple random sampling is not often used.

2. Stratified sampling involves a random proportional sample of
identified strata with an equal number of units sampled from each
stratum, usually with a predetermined weighting factor added. The
basis of stratification must be logically related to the items of information sought.

3. In cluster sampling clusters should contain a varied mixture of characteristics present in the whole. This method is generally less precise than a random sampling of the same size. In two
stage sampling, clusters are selected at random and a subsample is
chosen from each cluster at random.

4. Public opinion polls use samples based on the quota-controlled
method. In this method pollsters find the variables which have a high
correlation with voting behavior such as party affiliation, age,
economic status, etc. They then find how these variables are distributed in the whole population and finally assign to each interviewer
quotas based on this distribution of variables: the interviewer must
poll a certain number of persons in each age group, socio-economic
groups, etc. Several biases occur in this type of sampling, such as
when the interviewer fills his quota in the easiest manner possible.
In this way, it has been found, quota-samples tend to include few
respondents from high and low income families. The basic weakness
of the quota-controlled method, however, is that it does not employ
a random sample.

5. All indicators point to the necessity for a method which
rigorously follows random procedures for producing more accurate

samples. The result has been what is called <u>probability sampling</u>.
The fundamental requirement is that the persons polled are selected
by chance.

A method based on this principle is the area sample.
The first step is to make a purely random selection of
counties and metropolitan areas. Then within each of
these areas a sub-sample of small geographic segments
is selected, again by random methods. The final sample
may include all the dwellings in each selected segment,
or every k^{th} dwelling depending on the size of sample
desired. The selection of persons actually interviewed
in each dwelling will then depend on the purpose of the
survey; if its purpose is to predict an election,
the sample will consist of all the eligible voters
in the designated dwellings or certain voters selected
at random (Likert 1948).
Presumably if the purpose is an ethnographic survey or research on a
special problem of a particular group the sample will consist of each
member of the household selected.

The best method available to the anthropologist would seem to
involve an area sample of the total group which forms the basis of
his study. After selecting the areas and households the use of
standard anthropological techniques can be utilized according to
the nature of the problem or purpose of the study. This could be
referred to as the sample participant observation survey. By using
some type of sampling technique both on the community and area basis
complete representativeness could be accomplished, and anthropologists
could avoid those broad generalizations which are applicable only to
a small group or a few individuals.

Suggested Steps in Field Work on Complex Groups

1. Determine the population or universe to be studied. A preliminary field survey is often necessary.

2. Set up a sampling frame: list all units in the sampling
universe. The use of census materials may help in selecting the
population. Those variables which may be used to select a representative sample include rural-urban; community size variations; percentage of Spanish-speaking to other groups in each community; variations in occupational characteristics; lumbering, pastoral, farming,
day labor, service occupations, mining, etc.; education, fertility,
mortality, migration, household social and economic characteristics,
etc.

3. Choose the most efficient sample design for the degree of
precision needed. This requires the skill of a sampling technician.

4. Decide on the most efficient anthropological field techniques
required for researching the problem chosen, i.e., census forms, participant observation, etc.

5. If a questionnaire is to be used it should be developed and tested.

6. Conduct the field work.

SOCIAL CLASS, ASSIMILATION AND ACCULTURATION

Joan W. Moore
University of California-Riverside
and
Mexican-American Study Project, UCLA

Introduction

Spanish-speaking Americans are both one of the oldest and one of the newest of the ethnic groups in the United States. They include segments whose ancestors antedate the Plymouth colony, and segments of brand-new greenhorns from Mexico. The nation's second largest minority, they are concentrated in and scattered throughout a fairly small region of the country. It is also a region with few universities and with distinctive economic, social, political characteristics that have permitted them to go largely unnoticed in the intellectual and policy-making centers of the nation. The latter neglect--the political--is being remedied by a new aggressiveness on the part of ethnic leaders and a matching restlessness on the part of many Mexican Americans. The intellectual oversight, however, is probably going to take longer to overcome. Academics have less reason to be responsive to events and to people than politicians.

This is too bad, because analysis of the rich variety of internal diversity among the Mexican Americans could add greatly to our understanding of processes of acculturation and assimilation of ethnic groups. It could also add to a more general understanding of mobility and change in the society. The material I will present in this paper attempts to take advantage of some of that diversity, specifically with regard to questions of social class, assimilation and acculturation. I will present data illustrating inter-city diversity--comparing Los Angeles and San Antonio Mexican Americans. I will also present data illustrating intra-city diversity, suggesting that there are alternative modes of adapting to both poverty and upward mobility.

I will first discuss some general issues involved in analysis of social class and American ethnic groups. Second, I will describe the Los Angeles and San Antonio situations--and our samples. Third, I will present data on social class differences and in what might be called a measure of assimilation on the one hand and in an illustrative measure of acculturation on the other hand.

Some Issues in the Analysis of Ethnics and Social Class in the U. S.

In the past, few sociologists writing on stratification have paid much attention to ethnicity except as another ascriptive kink in the system. However, almost no discussion of an ethnic group has been undertaken without reference to its relationship to the social-class system. Regarding the latter, to oversimplify, among those who look at American social class more or less holistically[1] there are two essentially opposing views. On the one hand, there are those who perceive social-class mobility of ethnics as destroying ethnic attachments--and, ultimately destroying the ethnic subsystem. On the other hand, there are those who see social-class mobility of ethnics as occurring without a shift in attachments.

Warner and Srole (1945:283) state the former position most un-equivocally as a conclusion of their study of ethnics in Yankee City:

> Our class system functions for a large proportion of
> ethnics to destroy the ethnic subsystems and to increase
> assimilation.... Generally speaking our class order
> disunites ethnic groups and accelerates their assimila-
> tion.

The process of mobility for ethnics may be more or less stressful in Warner and Srole's view. But the end result is both acculturation and assimilation for those who succeed.

Specifically countering this view, Milton Gordon (1964) has offered an alternative suggestion that occupational mobility requires acculturation, but does not necessarily involve detachment from the ethnic group--either in identity or in social relationships. In this view, what Warner and Srole conceptualized as the social class system of American society becomes just one among many--the WASP's, which coexists with those of the major ethnic and religious groups. In Gordon's view, those ethnics who change their reference groups as well as their values tend to become marginal because of the stresses in-volved. But their marginality does not threaten the continued per-sistence of the ethnic subsystem.

Recently, within this sociological dialogue, an intermediate posi-tion has been taken with regard to the functioning of social class for ethnics. Simirenko (1964), in a study of mobility of Russian Ameri-cans, distinguished between two types of upwardly mobile second gen-eration individuals. The first are the "colonists," the conservatives who retain primary loyalty to the ethnic community. The second are the "frontiersmen," the radicals who leave the community both spa-tially and emotionally in the process of occupational mobility. The frontiersmen are, in short, either assimilated members of a higher social class, or well on their way. Colonists approximate the "ethclass" members described by Gordon, acculturated enough to have some occupational success, but remaining in the ethnic subcommunity.

The extent to which there is an option for the ethnic individual between the alternative of seeking identity and support in the "eth-class" and the alternative of seeking them in the larger social class system--varies with many circumstances and differs from one ethnic group to the next. It is clear that the American social class system is far from fully crystallized and far from fully constraining on the behavior of mobile individuals. For ethnic mobiles, the colonist can continue to perceive the social class system in a highly specific fashion, in the light of a prototype provided in school experience, as a relatively specific reward system for relatively specific performances. In such a view, the institutionalized aspects of the class system may represent a barrier or difficulties to be overcome. The frontiersman probably views the social class system far more diffusely, with far more anxiety.

This formulation emphasizing alternative adaptations to occupational mobility permits us to view the mobile ethnic as in a status dilemma. He straddles the ethnic subsystem and the social-class system of the dominant society. He has a foot in each. He can, consciously or not, weigh alternative social sources and kinds of reward. We shall suggest that those in the top stratum <u>within</u> the ethnic subsystem receive comparatively more prestige reward from fellow ethnics for comparatively less accomplishment than those who venture out of the colony. But this top stratum in the colony is essentially unstable for two reasons: first, because its members' status dilemmas are constantly renewed by discrepancies between in-group and out-group rewards for the same performances; second, they are also unstable because their prestige is based more on particularistic than on universalistic criteria and requires more continued interpersonal interaction.

Of course, it must be recognized that we are talking about comparatively large cities in this discussion. Studies of Mexican Americans in smaller communities show considerable variation over time and from community to community in the functioning of the social class system. Thus, several studies of the lower Rio Grande Valley communities show clear evidence of a caste system. But implicit in these, and more explicit in recent studies of similar situations in California, is the hint that such systems are maintained only by "leakage" of the potentially mobile individuals--presumably to the larger cities. The Mexican-American population in any large city is thus constantly enlarged by in-migration from smaller communities. In addition, many cities are enlarged by substantial numbers of immigrants from Mexico itself. Thus the class situation of urban Mexican Americans, we suggest, can be conceptualized as involving options and complexities not present in the smaller towns.

With this brief overview of some alternative conceptualizations of ethnic mobiles in the social class system, we shall move to the next topic--the Los Angeles and San Antonio situations and our samples.

Los Angeles and San Antonio

The two cities differ sharply in most important respects for
Mexican Americans--or any other minority, for that matter. Los
Angeles is a national metropolitan center, with job opportunities
at all skill levels in a wide variety of industries. San Antonio
is a regional center, with job opportunities concentrated primarily
in service industries, (i.e., trade and tourism) and most particularly in military-base employment.

Los Angeles has an extremely heterogeneous population. In addition to a very large number of Mexican Americans, there is an almost
equally large Negro population; it is the second largest Jewish city
in the nation--and the world, for that matter--and the "capital city"
for Japanese Americans. In addition, there is a large influx of both
foreign immigrants and in-migrants from the rest of the nation. San
Antonio has comparatively few Negroes and few sources of U. S. immigrants apart from the military personnel who choose to settle there
permanently. These two facts--greater and more diverse job opportunities and more heterogeneous population in Los Angeles--should
mean greater mobility in Los Angeles than San Antonio. Certainly
this is true in income terms: the median income of our respondents
was about $4800 in Los Angeles and about $2760 in San Antonio.

Data presented in this paper are derived from probability samples of the Mexican-American populations (heads and spouses) of the
two cities--which between them contained one-quarter of the total
ethnic population in 1960. In addition, data from a small Albuquerque
sample are available on one item. In Los Angeles the sample was
divided into thirds by the head's income. In San Antonio only two
income divisions were used, since the median was so low. Income
categories were defined as follows:

	Los Angeles	San Antonio
High income	$6000 +	⌠ . .
Medium income	$3600-$5999	⌡ $2760 +
Low income	- $3599	-$2759

In the following comparisons, we shall designate ethnic "frontiers" and "colonies" in terms of the proportion of Spanish-surnamed
individuals living in the census tract. By these definitions, we can
again divide the Los Angeles population in thirds, the San Antonio
population into only two:

	Los Angeles	San Antonio
Frontier--predominantly Anglo	0-15.0% WPSS	⌠
Intermediate--	15.1-43.8% "	⌡ 0-54.0% WPSS
Colony--predominantly WPSS	43.9-100% "	54.1-100% "

The differences in the divisions reflect differences in the manner of
life in the two cities. For example, only about 10 percent of the
Mexican Americans in Los Angeles lived in census tracts that were
more than three-quarters Mexican, as compared with over half in San
Antonio. The difference also reflects the greater proportion of the

total population that Mexican Americans represent in San Antonio--
41 percent as compared with Los Angeles' 9 percent (1960).

Mentioning only the economic differences and the differences in
population composition and segregation between the two cities indicates their differences as opportunity structures for Mexican Americans. But it glosses over the cultural differences between the two
cities--much as an economic and demographic comparison of Birmingham
and Cleveland would gloss over cultural differences in the two
milieus as residences for Negroes. Maybe such a glossing is somewhat justified, since despite a greater expenditure on schools, welfare and other amenities in California than in Texas, the schools in
both cities show a very high dropout rate for Mexican-American pupils
in ghetto schools, a remarkably low attendance rate in the public
universities, and so on. Overt anti-Mexican prejudice is probably
lower in Los Angeles than in San Antonio, but in important respects
Mexican Americans have been "outsiders" to Los Angeles' social and
political life just as they have been to San Antonio though the
mechanisms may differ. In San Antonio, for example, overt prejudice
has not precluded the development of political representation, while
ecological dispersal in Los Angeles has.

Economic and demographic differences between the cities, in
short, would appear to favor greater individual occupational mobility
in Los Angeles than in San Antonio, since at least the job opportunities are present. On that basis alone, then, there is likelihood of
greater internal diversity in Los Angeles than in San Antonio--and
indeed this is the case.

Colonists and Frontiersmen--Management of Status Discrepancies

Let us turn to a description of the class-related characteristics
of Mexican Americans in the two cities.

Tables 1-3 show the educational and occupational characteristics
of frontiersmen and colonists in the two cities at several income
levels. Let us focus here on the higher levels of achievement, that
is, on high school or over, white collar jobs, and occupational
prestige scores of over 20.[2] The distribution of all three measures,
of course, indicates the generally low status of the population.
With regard to occupational prestige, for example, the 1950 mean
score calculated for the U. S. male population was roughly 30. Fifteen years later only 28 percent of the Los Angeles and 16 percent
of the San Antonio Mexican-American household heads had occupational
prestige scores over 30. Much the same can be said for occupational
title and educational attainment.

The point of interest for this paper, however, is that with all
three status spheres--education, job title, and job prestige score--
the higher levels of attainment are found less frequently among the
colonists than among the frontiersmen, holding income constant. This
is true of even the poverty-level respondents with regard to education,

23

but only of education. But it holds for what roughly might be called the "middle class" (high and medium incomes) with regard to all three measures. This internal difference in what might crudely be called the "middle class" suggests a real difference between those who remain in areas of high ethnic concentration as compared with those who venture out into Anglolandia. Quite simply, in the aggregate the frontiersmen appear to be better equipped to cope with life outside the ethnic ghetto than the colonists by these measures.

In addition to this intra-city diversity, the differences be-tween the two cities show up in the generally lower proportion of high-achievers in San Antonio at all income levels.

Colonists and Frontiersmen--Assimilation

Table 4 shows the extent of ethnic integration in the associational patterns of frontiersmen and colonists in the two cities.

There are three points of interest to the argument here:

First, the table represents three generations in effect. There is (1) the respondent's own childhood--a generation ago; (2) his present associates--the present generation; and (3) his children's associates--the future, if you like. Of course, these are all verbal reports of the respondents, and not actual observations of associates, but nonetheless the generational differences are present at every income level, for frontiersmen and colonists alike, and in both cities. They are dramatic in some cases, such as the middle-income respondents in San Antonio, whose associates have become sharply "Anglocized" over the generational stretch.

Second, there is a striking difference between frontiersmen and colonists in that, irrespective of income attainment, the frontiersmen have far more Anglo associates than the colonists.

Finally, the inter-city comparisons: San Antonio respondents are far more "Mexican" in their associates, and Angelenos far more involved with Anglo associates.

Colonists and Frontiersmen--Acculturation

Let me offer a final illustration of the complexity of social class and ethnicity for Mexican Americans. Table 5 shows responses to a set of questions which are related to the instrument used by Kluckhohn, in her classic study of "Atrisco," New Mexico. The three items shown here relate specifically to the respondent's dependence on relatives. In addition to our Los Angeles and San Antonio samples, the questions were used in a study of Spanish Americans in Albuquerque, New Mexico and in a study of Mexico City. Thus we have four, rather than two urban samples.

As can be seen, in each sample where we have an income breakdown (that is, in all but Mexico City), the higher the income the greater the "acculturation," if acculturation is measured by disagreement with these statements. And the lower the income the greater the traditional reliance on relatives.

However, for the Los Angeles and San Antonio samples, where we can distinguish between the colonists and frontiersmen, respondents living in predominantly Anglo areas tend to be more acculturated than respondents at the same income level who remain in the ethnic colonies. The data are complex, and I will not attempt a fuller interpretation here. The purpose of presenting them is to illustrate the interaction of class factors with ethnic factors.

Finally, we have the notable inter-city differences. As expected, Angelenos are more acculturated than San Antonians by this measure. However, somewhat to our surprise, so are Albuquerquians more acculturated and so are Mexico City residents more acculturated on two of the three items. Thus where we have been able to extend our sample of cities beyond Los Angeles and San Antonio, using the same admittedly limited instruments, we uncover patterns that are certainly not uninterpretable, but which are contrary to common-sense expectations.

Conclusions

There are a number of conclusions suggested by these data.

There are, first, conclusions about Mexican Americans and their persistence as a culturally distinctive group and as a visible part of the urban social systems in which they now cluster.

There are, second, conclusions about how social-class mobility works in such persistence.

And there are, third, conclusions about the uniformity with which the processes are occurring.

First, with regard to the Mexican Americans and their persistence: the data suggest that both assimilation and acculturation are occurring. This is also supported by data on intermarriage of Mexicans and Anglos, which show a fairly high rate for third-generation Angelenos. They suggest that both assimilation and acculturation occur within a social-class context. However, at least up till the present, there is not just one, but two social-class contexts. And the frontier is far more destructive of both ethnic exclusiveness and of ethnic traditionalism than the colony.

Thus upward mobility--the second of our three concluding topics-- is far from monolithic in its destructive potential. It works differently for those who venture forth to the frontiers of the ethnic ghettoes than for those who stay behind. And there seems to be little doubt that the Mexican-American colonies as such will persist for generations to come. They are sustained not only by the ethnic exclusiveness of those city-born Mexican Americans who choose to remain in them, but by their continued functions as receiving areas for newcomers to the city. In the Southwest there seems little chance that they will shrink to the attenuated ethnic "downtowns" that have characterized Eastern and Middlewestern cities--a few ethnic groceries, candle shops, and so on.

Finally, the diversity within the population must again be emphasized. Intra-city diversity complicates the processes. But even more important, inter-city differences--in prejudice, opportunity, cultural retentiveness of the Spanish-surnamed population--preclude easy generalizations about Mexican Americans.

For more general issues in the social sciences, there seems little doubt that a middle ground between the "assimilationists" (as Warner and Srole can crudely be classified) and the "pluralists" (as Gordon can crudely be classified) is possible. Further, this middle ground is a realistic approach to the analysis of stratification and ethnic and racial minorities. Mexican Americans have a long and complex history. "Pluralistic" models have frequently been applied to them, though few social scientists have analyzed Mexicans in an assimilationist framework. Indeed their history has made them a very special group among American ethnic groups, but they are not unique, and analysis of their present situation in a comparative context also bears fruit. This poverty-stricken population is not quite "white" socially (although they are legally white and so listed in the U. S. Census). Neither are they quite "nonwhite" although in many areas they are subject to substantial discrimination and are almost universally considered a "special" population. By virtue of their very ambiguousness and ambiguities, their study helps shed light on stratification processes in general.

NOTES

1. As compared with those who see it more atomistically, as involving sets of discrete statuses, which seems to be the assumption underlying much status-consistency approach. See Lenski (1966).

2. See Reiss (1961) for a discussion of the occupational prestige measure. On occupation and education, greater detail on the 1960 attainments of Mexican Americans is presented in Fogel (1967), in which the population is compared with other populations.

REFERENCES

Fogel, Walter
  1967   Mexican Americans in Southwest Labor Markets. Mexican American Study Project. Los Angeles, University of California.
Gordon, Milton M.
  1964   Assimilation in American Life. New York, Oxford University Press.
Lenski, Gerhard
  1966   Power and Privilege. New York, McGraw-Hill Book Co.

Kahl, Joseph A.
    1965   Some Measures of Achievement Orientation. American
            Journal of Sociology LXX:680-81.
Kluckhohn, Florence Rockwood and Fred L. Strodtbeck
    1961   Variations in Value Orientations. Evanston, Illinois
            and Elmsford, New York, Row, Peterson and Co.
Reiss, Albert J., Jr.
    1961   Occupations and Social Status. New York, The Free Press
            of Glencoe, Inc.
Simirenko, Alex
    1964   Pilgrims, Colonists, and Frontiersmen. New York and
            London, The Free Press of Glencoe and Collier-Macmillan
            Limited.
Warner, W. Lloyd and Leo Srole
    1945   The Social Systems of American Ethnic Groups. New
            Haven, Yale University Press. P. 283.

TABLE 1

HOUSEHOLD HEAD'S EDUCATION
LOS ANGELES AND SAN ANTONIO SURVEY RESPONDENTS
BY INCOME AND NEIGHBORHOOD ETHNICITY, 1965-1966

| | Years of school Completed | | | | | Number |
	0-4	5-8	9-11	12	12+	(= 100%)
Los Angeles[a]						
High Income						
Frontier	7%	21%	21%	29%	22%	191
Intermediate	11	23	34	21	11	104
Colony	13	18	37	23	9	78
Medium Income						
Frontier	15	32	19	26	8	74
Intermediate	15	32	26	21	5	98
Colony	26	35	26	12	2	121
Low Income						
Frontier	18	34	25	13	10	79
Intermediate	56	22	14	5	3	77
Colony	39	29	25	4	3	125
San Antonio[b]						
Medium Income						
Frontier	6	22	31	28	14	133
Colony	24	32	21	18	5	185
Low Income						
Frontier	46	37	8	7	2	45
Colony	54	33	10	3	1	205

[a]Los Angeles: High Income $6000+   Frontier   0-15.0% WPSS
                 Medium Income $3600-$5999   Intermediate   15.1-43.8% WPSS
                 Low Income   -$3599   Colony   43.9-100%

[b]San Antonio: Medium Income $2760+   Frontier   0-54.0% WPSS
                 Low Income   -$2759   Colony   54.1-100% WPSS

TABLE 2

HOUSEHOLD HEAD'S JOB PRESTIGE
LOS ANGELES AND SAN ANTONIO SURVEY RESPONDENTS
BY INCOME AND NEIGHBORHOOD ETHNICITY, 1965-1966

| | Prestige Scores[a] | | | Number (= 100%) |
	0-9	10-19	20+	
Los Angeles				
High Income				
Frontier	10%	32%	58%	195
Intermediate	13	39	48	106
Colony	19	33	48	79
Medium Income				
Frontier	9	47	43	76
Intermediate	15	48	37	98
Colony	22	38	40	124
Low Income				
Frontier	70	24	6	79
Intermediate	64	26	10	77
Colony	70	17	13	126
San Antonio				
Medium Income				
Frontier	17	16	67	135
Colony	33	21	46	191
Low Income				
Frontier	65	28	9	47
Colony	60	20	20	229

[a]Derived from Reiss (1961:263-275).

TABLE 3

HOUSEHOLD HEAD'S OCCUPATION FOR
LOS ANGELES AND SAN ANTONIO SURVEY RESPONDENTS
BY INCOME AND NEIGHBORHOOD ETHNICITY, 1965-1966[a]

	White Collar	Skilled	Semi-Skilled	Unskilled	Number (= 100%)
Los Angeles					
High Income					
Frontier	31%	37%	17%	15%	182
Intermediate	19	32	25	24	106
Colony	13	42	27	18	78
Medium Income					
Frontier	24	19	35	22	74
Intermediate	13	28	33	26	95
Colony	13	26	38	22	121
Low Income					
Frontier	8	19	50	25	24
Intermediate	9	9	29	53	34
Colony	15	17	30	37	46
San Antonio					
Medium Income					
Frontier	27	36	16	21	135
Colony	20	24	22	34	189
Low Income					
Frontier	6	6	21	67	27
Colony	8	12	18	62	156

[a]Housewives, retired and unemployed heads are omitted from this table.

30

TABLE 4

ASSOCIATES OF SURVEY RESPONDENTS AND THEIR CHILDREN:
PERCENT PREDOMINANTLY ANGLO
BY INCOME AND NEIGHBORHOOD ETHNICITY,
LOS ANGELES AND SAN ANTONIO, 1965-66

	Percent Predominantly Anglo Associates					
	Childhood		Respond-ents' Friends	Fellow Workers	Child-ren's Friends	School-mates
	Friends	School-mates				
Los Angeles						
High Income						
Frontier	26%	34%	31%	68%	69%	75%
Intermediate	12	17	13	52	38	47
Colony	13	18	9	50	12	19
Medium Income						
Frontier	21	30	18	74	50	68
Intermediate	10	10	11	39	36	28
Colony	6	6	7	36	11	11
Low Income						
Frontier	13	17	35	89	63	61
Intermediate	8	6	9	52	26	26
Colony	11	13	7	25	13	18
San Antonio						
Medium Income						
Frontier	12	17	13	45	40	38
Colony	6	10	2	19	10	9
Low Income						
Frontier	11	17	8	23	18	22
Colony	4	11	0	25	4	6

31

TABLE 5

RESPONSES TO "INTEGRATION WITH RELATIVES" SCALE ITEMS
(Percent Disagreeing with Statement)

Statement Number[a]

Sample	1	2	3
Los Angeles			
High Income	<u>93.0%</u>	<u>79.6%</u>	<u>78.5%</u>
Frontier	93.8	80.4	77.5
Intermediate	93.3	80.0	79.3
Colony	90.9	77.1	80.3
Medium Income	<u>84.6%</u>	<u>65.8%</u>	<u>64.2%</u>
Frontier	93.2	73.7	67.2
Intermediate	85.1	68.8	68.8
Colony	79.0	59.4	62.2
Low Income	<u>74.0%</u>	<u>52.2%</u>	<u>59.4%</u>
Frontier	83.6	59.8	67.7
Intermediate	68.5	52.1	53.6
Colony	71.7	51.6	58.0
San Antonio			
Medium Income	<u>84.6%</u>	<u>76.3%</u>	<u>71.1%</u>
Frontier	90.1	77.7	79.2
Colony	83.0	75.9	68.5
Low Income	<u>65.1%</u>	<u>50.7%</u>	<u>42.5%</u>
Frontier	78.4	64.5	61.5
Colony	63.8	49.4	40.6
Albuquerque[b]			
High Income	95.5%	86.4%	95.5%
Medium Income	98.0	74.0	94.0
Low Income	71.8	59.0	71.8
Mexico City (Males)[c]	74.5%	72.5%	40.2%

[a]Items: 1. "When looking for a job, a person ought to find a position in a place located near his parents, even if that means losing a good opportunity elsewhere."
      2. "When you are in trouble, only a relative can be depended on to help you out."
      3. "When you have the chance to hire an assistant in your work, it is always better to hire a relative than a stranger."
Source for items: Kahl (1965:680-81).
[b]Data provided by Nicandro Juarez, Operation Ser, Santa Monica,

TABLE 5 (continued)

California.
^cData provided by Joseph A. Kahl, Washington University.

THE STUDY OF MIGRANTS AS MEMBERS OF SOCIAL SYSTEMS

Lyle W. Shannon
University of Iowa

Introduction

A continuing study [1958 to the present] among Mexican Americans, Negroes, and Anglos in Racine, Wisconsin, has shown that measures of economic absorption and cultural integration--occupational level, occupational mobility, income, level of living, level of educational and occupational aspirations for children, acceptance in the community, language usage and world view--have, in the three groups, quite different patterns of intercorrelation with such antecedent and intervening variables as years of formal education, place of education, first job, place of origin, extent of prior urbanization, occupational level of parents, and level of aspiration for self.[1]

These findings emphasize the gulf between widely held notions of how society works or what "should" occur in our society and what actually happens. To be explicit, members of the larger Anglo society more often than not assume that if education, work experience and high levels of aspiration lead to economic success among Anglos they should lead to the same kind of success among Mexican Americans, Negroes, or any other ethnic or racial group. Appropriately motivated [from the Anglo viewpoint] members of these groups may find that demands from within their own group as well as constraints imposed by the larger society make it difficult to take full advantage of the educational and economic opportunities known to them. Furthermore, if they have successfully taken advantage of the limited opportunities allowed them in the urban-industrial community, they may choose to enjoy their income and leisure in ways unlike that of the so-called working class or blue-collar Anglos.

Economic absorption and cultural integration are gradual processes. The process of economic absorption is more narrowly defined than cultural integration. It involves not just securing work but becoming a part of the regularly employed labor force at a level consistent with one's capabilities and the capabilities of others at various positions in the economic institution. Cultural integration refers to integration into the whole gamut of institutional life. It involves the transformation of values, the acquisition of new behavioral patterns, and social participation beyond one's own primary group, although not necessarily in this order. Both processes have been operationally defined by the measures selected for use in this research.

If the consequences of interaction of members of subgroups with each other and with the larger society are represented by a correlation diagram in which economic absorption and cultural integration [assuming that absorption and integration are goals and measured as indicated above] increase with education, work experience, association with appropriate role models, and level of aspiration [some of the assumed determinants of success], we would expect most persons in the society to fall along either a fairly straight line or a slightly curved line. Although the Racine data may be arranged to show this sort of pattern, oversimplification in analysis and failure to introduce appropriate controls could result in misleading conclusions about the determinants of successful absorption and integration.

Almost any measure of either the hypothesized determinants of successful absorption and integration or of economic absorption and cultural integration resulted in high Anglo scores, usually intermediate Negro scores, and low Mexican-American scores. As a consequence of this almost invariable rank-ordering of Anglos, Negroes, and Mexican Americans on each measure, the kinds of correlations that would be expected for the larger society were produced in the combined samples for Racine. However, when race and ethnicity were controlled, these statistically significant relationships tended to either decrease, disappear, or change in direction (Shannon and Morgan 1966; Krass, Peterson and Shannon 1966).[2] What this means is that a description of the manner in which measures of success [selected by the researchers and their Mexican-American associates] are related to success-generating variables in the larger society, i.e., in Racine as a whole, does not apply to Mexican Americans and Negroes.

But the rank-ordering of Anglos, Negroes, and Mexican Americans on a number of social and economic variables does not lead to a model of society organized and operating as a stratified social class system. The evidence indicates that a more useful model of the organization of society commences with the assumption that it is composed of numerous unranked and to some extent overlapping sub-societies, within which individuals may be ranked. The individual may have positions and achieve status in more than one group and may thus participate in more than one subculture. A description of the parameters of the sub-societies or subcultural groups within the larger society is not a simple task. Some of the dimensions that have been assumed to be characteristics of race and ethnic subcultural groups may be even more appropriately associated with societal segments that have been generated out of or developed from occupational, educational, and income differences.

This paper has two kinds of concerns, methodological and substantive. Methodologically, we ask what happens when a category of respondents defined as "uncomprehending" are removed from the sample.

The substantive concerns of this paper are: (1) whether "world view" and "level of aspiration," as measured by responses to a series of questions, are more closely related to race and ethnicity or to sociologically meaningful categories of people in the urban-industrial society, and (2) how world view and level of aspiration relate to each other, to the organization of society and its subgroups, and more speculatively, some of the probable consequences thereof.

A Methodological Concern

Analysis of the data from the Racine sample has made it possible to present a series of detailed statistical descriptions of the relationship of locale of socialization, education, first work experience, work careers, and other variables to measures of economic absorption and cultural integration. These analyses have involved zero-order correlations and very little partialling or systematic control of anything but the simplest demographic variables such as age and length of residence in the community. But quite apart from that, the author has been concerned about the validity of several of the more complex measures and indexes utilized in the study. These methodological concerns have culminated in further evaluation and analysis of the world view data. The results are presented here as a preface to more extensive treatment of the relationship of world view to other variables and these to the organization of the larger society and its components. The open-ended world view questions did not work out very well in the 1959 survey. When it was decided to attempt to measure world view in 1960 with closed questions we first thought that the questions should be constructed so as to elicit an individualistic, work-oriented view, on one hand and a fatalistic, group-oriented view on the other. As we tried out various questions with the Mexican Americans who were assisting us in pretests it became apparent that three facets of world view were represented--group values, temporal orientation and manipulative power. Thus, world view as defined for this research consists of a person's perception of his own manipulative power versus the organization of the society or some other more powerful determinant, his time perspective as oriented toward the present versus the future, and his hierarchy of values that places individual achievement against ties to the group. A seven-item Guttman scale was developed from the following questions:
1. Not many things in life are worth the sacrifice of moving away from your family.
2. The secret of happiness is not expecting too much and being content with what comes your way.
3. The best job to have is one where you are part of a group all working together, even if you don't get much individual credit.
4. Planning only makes a person unhappy, since your

36

plans hardly ever work out anyway.
5. Nowadays, with world conditions the way they are, the wise person lives for today and lets tomorrow take care of itself.
6. Not many things in life are worth the sacrifice of moving away from your friends.
7. When a man is born, the success he is going to have is not already in the cards; each makes his own fate.

Respondents with the most individualistic orientation, also referred to as active respondents, did not agree with the first six statements on the scale but did agree with the last statement. Respondents with the next most individualistic orientation agreed with the first statement but did not agree with the statements below it except for the last statement, and so on with each type of respondent down to the most fatalistic and group-oriented, also referred to as passive respondents, who agreed with every statement except the last, and with that they disagreed.[3] To be acceptable a scale must have a Coefficient of Reproducibility of .9000. This scale had a Coefficient of Reproducibility of .9011 and a Minimum Coefficient of Reproducibility of .7125. The lower the Minimum Coefficient of Reproducibility, the greater the improvement of the scale over marginal reproducibility.

At this juncture, we are concerned, not with how well this sample of world view questions represent the universe of questions that could have been asked or whether they were the "best" questions to ask at this point in the life cycle of respondents, but with whether or not the questions were as meaningful to respondents in the Racine samples as they were to persons on whom they were initially pretested in another community of more acculturated Mexican Americans. If the world view questions were not meaningful to a portion of the respondents, should that portion be removed from the sample prior to analysis of the world view responses? If the views of a substantial portion of the Negro and Mexican-American respondents were not properly represented by their replies to the world view questions, might not elimination of those who were not properly represented by their responses decrease or eliminate differences between Mexican Americans, Negroes, and Anglos? If only those who found the questions meaningful were included in the analysis, would the relationship between world view and other variables be changed?

But to include in the analysis only persons who appear to find the questions meaningful might present a different set of findings for still another reason—those who were judged not to have comprehended the questions might be persons who were absorbed into the economic system at a lower level and less integrated into the larger society. Persons remaining in the sample would be those who had been integrated into the larger society to the extent that they responded to the world view questions on the interview schedule in essentially the same way as their integrated counterparts [Mexican-American and

Negro interviewers who were second and third generation residents in
an urban-industrial community in northern Illinois] would expect them
to respond. Since less integrated Mexican Americans and Negroes would
be most likely to be eliminated, respondents who were left would be
theoretically more homogeneous than those making up the larger sample.
Such a biased sample would preclude the possibility of describing the
relationship of antecedent and intervening explanatory variables to
the full range of absorption and integration. The process of spoon-
ing out unintegrated respondents who least understood the world view
questions might have eliminated differences in patterns of intercorrelation between race and ethnic groups. On the other hand, if
difficulty with the world view questions was more or less random,
then the concerns that have just been expressed would not be operative; essentially the same world views and relationships would be
found in the smaller sample as were found in the larger sample.

    With all of the foregoing in mind, 265 respondents were elim-
inated from the larger sample--respondents who did not appear to
comprehend the world view questions.[4] The criterion for omission
was not an evaluation by those who were conducting the analysis but
an evaluation by the interviewers. Mexican Americans and Negroes
were eliminated disproportionately to Anglos, but it should be remembered that Mexican-American and Negro interviewers were judging
the reaction of Mexican-American and Negro respondents. Those who
were confused or who failed to answer the questions were eliminated.[5]

    Before proceeding further we must decide whether or not essen-
tially the same differences between groups remained after the 265
respondents who did not appear to comprehend the world view questions
were eliminated, i.e., were those who were eliminated randomly distributed or were they the least absorbed and least integrated of
each group?

A Comparison of the Original Sample
and the World View Sample

    The original 1960 sample consisted of 236 Mexican Americans,
284 Anglos, and 280 Negroes; it will be referred to as S^1 in tables
and references throughout this paper. The subsample, for which
those who failed to comprehend the world view questions were eliminated, includes 164 Mexican Americans, 163 Negroes, and 218 Anglos;
it will be referred to as S^2. The distribution of scores for both
samples is shown in Table 1.
    There was little difference between the sample of 800 and the
reduced sample of 545. In both cases Anglos had significantly more
active world view scores than did Negroes, but Negroes, although more
active in world view than Mexican Americans, were not significantly
so.[6] Removing confused respondents and those who failed to answer
the questions did not result in significant change in the pattern of
world view scores by race and ethnicity, although differences between

38

TABLE 1

WORLD VIEW SCALE, 1960

Scale Type	Scale Scores	Percentages					
		Mexican		Negro		Anglo	
		S^1	S^2	S^1	S^2	S^1	S^2
Individualistic, Active	0-3	37	39	44	48	77	81
Group-oriented, Passive	4-7	63	61	56	52	23	19
Total		100	100	100	100	100	100

			Mexican	Negro	Anglo
S^1	N =	800	236	280	284
S^2	N =	545	164	163	218

samples were in the direction expected. Fatalistic and group-oriented or passive respondents were disproportionately eliminated, but the smaller samples were only three or four percent more individualistic or active than the original samples.

A Level of Aspiration for Children scale was constructed based on stated educational and occupational aspirations for children. The distribution of scores for both samples is presented in Table 2. The person whose responses indicated the highest level of aspiration is the person who wants college for children, would only be satisfied if children went through college, thinks it will be financially possible to send children through college and wants children to be professionals.[7] The sample of 545 did not differ significantly from the sample of 800. And every test of the significance of differences between the three subgroups in both the larger and smaller samples showed each race and ethnic group to rank significantly higher than the one below it. Anglos had significantly higher aspirations for their children than did Negroes, and Negroes had significantly higher aspirations than did Mexican Americans.

The question on vocational aspirations for children, although not separately analyzed and related to other variables in this paper, presented a rather sharp contrast between response patterns for Mexican Americans and Negroes on one hand and Anglos on the other.[8] Anglos had significantly higher aspirations for their children than did Negroes, but only when "leaving it up to children," a response given by almost half of the Anglos, was classified as a high response and included in the test of significance.[9] On the other hand, Negroes, and Anglos had significantly higher aspirations for their children than did Mexican Americans including or excluding "leave it up to the

TABLE 2

LEVEL OF ASPIRATION FOR CHILDREN

| Scale Type | Scale Scores | Percentages | | | | | |
| | | Mexican | | Negro | | Anglo | |
		S^1	S^2	S^1	S^2	S^1	S^2
Lowest Aspirations	0	63	67	32	35	22	21
	1	13	12	22	24	19	10
	2	9	8	20	18	15	15
	3	3	3	11	10	28	28
Highest Aspirations	4	12	11	15	13	16	15
Total		100	101	100	100	100	98

Coefficient of Reproducibility = .8984; Minimum Coefficient of Reproducibility = .6675.

S^1 N = 800
S^2 N = 545

children." Overall, the original sample of 800 and the sample of 545 were similar.

Length of residence was dichotomized with long residence defined as ten or more years in Racine and short residence defined as less than ten years in Racine.[10] Anglos had lived in the community significantly longer than Mexican Americans in both samples. In the sample of 545, Mexican Americans had lived in the community significantly longer than Negroes, but overall the sample of 545 did not significantly differ from the sample of 800.

Education was dichotomized with better educated respondents defined as those with nine or more years of education and less educated respondents those with less than nine years of education, a meaningful cutting point for urban-industrial persons with backgrounds similar to those of our respondents. Although the two Mexican-American samples were almost identical, the sample of 545 had fewer less educated Negroes and fewer less educated Anglos, the difference being statistically significant for the Anglo sample.[11] While it might seem surprising that less educated Mexican Americans were not eliminated from the sample of 545, it is apparent that years of formal education had nothing to do with determining whether or not a question was meaningful to a Mexican-American respondent. Some Mexican Americans laughed at some of the questions and stated that the world view questions were "silly." Fewer years of education was not the crucial component in failure to respond--being Mexican-American was. By contrast, those who were eliminated from the Negro and Anglo samples were persons with less education--presumably the questions were more meaningful or at least could be responded to more readily by better educated Negroes and Anglos than by the less educated.

Total family income was utilized in this study as a measure of absorption into the economy and divided into three categories: up to $4499, $4500 to $5499, and $5500 or more. As in any research, how such a variable is conceptualized depends on the process being investigated and the point at which one ties into a time sequence or experiential chain. Income can equally well be conceived as an antecedent of world view, taking world view as an indicator of cultural integration. In essence, changing world view may be the antecedent of increasing income [an indicator of economic absorption] and increasing income may be the antecedent of changing world view [an indicator of cultural integration]. And both may simultaneously follow other antecedent variables or chains of events. Anglos had significantly higher incomes than Negroes and Negroes had significantly higher incomes than Mexican Americans. There were no significant differences between the larger and smaller samples.[12]

At this point it can be concluded that with the exception of less educated Anglos, those who were eliminated from the larger sample on a basis of their confusion or inability to respond to the world view questions were eliminated on a more or less random basis. Less absorbed and less integrated Mexican Americans and Negroes were not systematically excluded by the process. It should also be noted that if the Coefficient of Contingency is utilized as a measure of the association of the aforementioned six variables with race and ethnicity, years of education is more closely associated with race and ethnicity than is any other variable, both in the original sample and in the smaller sample that will now be utilized in further analyses.

The Pattern of Relationships

The Relation of World View to Time, Education, and Income

At this point we shall turn to a discussion of world view and its relationship to three control variables: time in the community, education, and income. We hypothesize that an active world view is associated with long residence, high education, and high income, and that a passive world view is associated with the opposite. The rank ordering of Mexican Americans, Negroes, and Anglos on world view, education, and income and, to some extent, length of residence is such that all are related to world view in a systematic fashion.

Table 3 may be used to generate two different series of statistics. One series deals with the relationship of time in the

TABLE 3

THE RELATION OF WORLD VIEW TO EDUCATION AND LENGTH OF RESIDENCE

Percentages

| | Mexican | | | | Negro | | | | Anglo | | | | | |
| | Low Education | | High Education | | Low Education | | High Education | | Low Education | | | High Education | | |
	SR	LR	SR	LR	SR	LR	SR	LR	SR	LR	All	SR	LR	All
Individualistic, Active	34	32	80	50	38	41	50	57	0	62	69	85	87	83
Group-oriented, Passive	66	68	20	50	62	59	50	43	100	39	31	15	13	18
Total	100	100	100	100	100	100	100	100	100	101	100	100	100	101
	N = 113		N = 32		N = 62		N = 95		N = 29			N = 185		

Short residence (SR) = less than ten years.
Long residence (LR) = ten years or more.
Always lived in Racine (All).

Low education = less than nine years.
High education = nine years or more.

42

community or length of residence to world view and the other series deals with the relationship of education to world view. In each case the influence of one variable on world view may be observed with the other controlled. With race and ethnicity controlled, in no case is there a significant relationship between world view and length of residence in the community.[13] And with controls introduced for race and ethnicity and years of education, world view and length of residence produced no statistically significant relationships. The largest correlation, a modest correlation in the opposite direction of the general hypothesis that persons longest in the community would have the most active world views, was .28 for Mexican Americans in the nine years or more of education category but not statistically significant. On the other hand, this correlation made sense, considering the characteristics of the Mexican-American sample retrospectively. Younger, better educated, new arrivals were actively seeking economic opportunities. Although age of respondent does have some influence on answers to questions, this varies from one area of concern to another. For example, with age of male controlled, occupational level varied significantly with race and ethnicity in the larger sample. Similarly, with age of male controlled, income varied significantly by race and ethnicity. Age of respondent and age of male had scattered correlations with other variables, but there were neither uniformities nor patterns that would lead to the conclusion that age should be controlled in the analysis at hand.

When world view scale scores and years of education are correlated for the combined Mexican-American, Negro and Anglo samples without length of residence controlled, there is a statistically significant but modest correlation of .34 between education and world view; high education is associated with an active world view and low education with a passive world view. With time in the community controlled, education continues to have a significant relationship to world view. When controls are introduced for race and ethnicity, years of education and world view are significantly related among the Mexican Americans and Anglos but not among the Negroes. When race and ethnicity and length of residence were controlled, seven tables could be produced. The relationship between world view scale scores and education remained in every table but was statistically significant in only two cases, among those Anglos and Mexican Americans who had lived in Racine less than ten years. On a strictly statistical basis one must conclude that respondents with a better education are neither more individualistic or active than those with less education--but, considering the general pattern of correlations and the two significant correlations among short term residents, education is more closely related to world view than is time in the community. As in the single case where length of residence appeared to be related to world view [.28 for Mexican Americans with nine or more years of education], short-residence, better educated Mexican Americans had more active world views than did their short-residence, less educated Mexican-American counterparts. The same relationship also existed for short-residence Anglos and, although not statistically significant, was apparent to a lesser degree among the Negroes. But one only need examine the place of origin of most Negro versus most Mexican-American and Anglo respondents in order to gain some idea of how the influence of years of formal education on world view could well have been washed out by other variables in their environment prior to recent arrival in Racine.

The hypothesis that length of residence in the community and education are closely related to world view must be rejected. It is, however, apparent that both, in concert with race and ethnicity, do have some relationship to world view, length of residence playing the more minor part in it. The statistically significant relationship between world view and education disappears in most cases when controls are introduced. The uncontrolled correlations were generated by the fact that Anglos tended to have active world view scores, be well educated, and be long-time residents of the community, while the Negroes and Mexican Americans had the least education, the shortest period of residence, and the most passive world views. In sum, the greatest contrast in world view was between passive, long-residence, less educated Mexican Americans and active, long-residence, better educated Anglos.

Considering the distribution of income and world view by race and ethnicity as presented in Table 4, it is not surprising that when the samples were combined before controlling for ethnicity, over twice as many high income persons had active scores as had passive scores while twice as many low income persons had passive as had active scores. When low, medium, and high income persons were compared, holding ethnicity constant, world view varied significantly with income within the Mexican-American and Anglo samples but not within the Negro sample.[14] In each case, low income persons are more likely to be passive and high income persons are more likely to be active. But when the three income categories within each race or ethnic group are compared two at a time, only the high and low income categories are significantly different in world view in the Mexican-American group, the low and high income categories do not reach the .05 level among the Negroes, and only two pairs are significantly different in the Anglo group.

Now, it is just this sort of finding that was so disconcerting when analyses were made of the larger sample. However evident it was that the world view scale differentiated between Mexican Americans, Negroes, and Anglos, the distribution of scores was so skewed toward the lower end of the scale for Mexican Americans in particular, that subcategories of Mexican Americans could scarcely be differentiated by their world view scores.

In addition to the world view questions that were asked of all respondents, it is quite apparent that a separate series of questions should have been provided for Mexican Americans, Negroes, and Anglos,

TABLE 4

THE RELATION OF WORLD VIEW TO INCOME

	Percentages								
	Mexican			Negro			Anglo		
	Low	Medium	High	Low	Medium	High	Low	Medium	High
Individu-alistic, Active	31	40	57	40	45	59	59	71	87
Group-Oriented, Passive	69	60	44	61	55	41	41	29	13
Total	100	100	101	101	100	100	100	100	100
N =	81	30	46	43	29	75	22	31	143

Low = less than $4499; medium = $4500-$5499; high = $5500 or more.

a series that would have permitted each group to be distributed over a broader range of scores on questions that would have been particularly meaningful to persons with their background. These questions could have been generated by members of each racial and ethnic group independently of the overall scale or developed by members of each racial and ethnic group as more explicit sub-categories of the kinds of questions that were most differentiating between and within each group. Had this been done, it might well have been found that there were significant differences, however fine, in world view that do develop within each racial and ethnic group with time in the city, with increasing increments of education, and that are more closely associated with income. But with the data that have been collected, statistically significant differences tend to show up mainly on a basis of race and ethnicity.

When income is controlled, the world view of Mexican Americans, Negroes, and Anglos continues to differ significantly, with world view having its closest relationship to ethnicity within the high income category. When race and ethnic groups are compared two at a time with income controlled, the Mexican-American and Anglo groups differ significantly on world view within each income category. The Mexican-American and Negro groups never differ significantly. And, as stated in the previous paragraph wherein the nature and short-comings of the world view scale were discussed, differences in world view between ethnic groups of the same income category, are somewhat greater than the differences in world view between income categories within each ethnic group. Although high income persons tend to be active and low income persons tend to be passive, variation based on

45

ethnicity within income categories is more marked than variation based on income within race and ethnic groups.

The Relation of Level of Aspiration for Children to World View

The second dependent variable with which we are concerned in this paper is level of aspiration for children. A detailed analysis of how level of aspiration for children relates to length of residence in Racine, education, and so on, will not be presented inasmuch as the picture is essentially the same as that for world view. Table 5 is similar to Table 4, except that level of aspiration for children has been substituted for income and world view.[15]

Before controls were introduced, income and level of aspiration for children varied significantly with each other, high income persons having the highest aspirations for their children. As soon as race and ethnicity were controlled significant variation disappeared except among the Anglos. When income categories within each race and ethnic group are taken two at a time, most of the variation in level of aspiration with income disappears. But by contrast, and as in the case of income and world view, when variation in level of aspiration between race and ethnic groups is observed within income categories, there is significant variation in aspiration within each income category, particularly the high income category. Even when race and ethnic groups are taken two at a time, significant differences in level of aspiration remain between all pairs except the Negro and Anglo pairs. Mexican Americans and Negroes did not differ significantly on world view within income categories, but it must be remembered that the difference between Mexican Americans and Negroes was not significant on world view. Similarly, Negroes and Anglos differed less than did Mexican Americans and Negroes on level of aspiration for children. Essentially what we are finding is that race and ethnicity make for greater differentiation in the dependent variable, level of aspiration for children, than does income.

The relationship of level of aspiration scale scores for children to dichotomized world view scores is presented in Table 6. When level of aspiration scores are compared with world view scores, passive persons tend to have lower aspirations for their children and active persons tend to have higher aspirations for their children.[16] These scales would be expected to correlate with each other since world view, as measured by at least some of the questions on the world view scale, can be considered as part of a broad universe of attitudes and views of which aspirations for children are also a part. While both active and passive Mexican-American and Negro respondents are skewed toward the low aspiration end of the scale, passive persons are more skewed toward the low aspiration end of the scale than are actives. When race and ethnicity are controlled, active and passive respondents within each racial and ethnic group have significantly different distributions of level of aspiration

TABLE 5

TOTAL ANNUAL FAMILY INCOME AND LEVEL OF
ASPIRATION FOR CHILDREN

Percentages

Scale Scores	Low Income			Medium Income			High Income		
	Mexican	Negro	Anglo	Mexican	Negro	Anglo	Mexican	Negro	Anglo
Low Aspirations									
0	67	37	36	67	31	36	50	25	17
1	11	28	36	17	24	16	15	16	18
2	9	19	9	13	17	16	7	24	17
3	3	7	18	- -	14	23	7	13	30
4 High Aspirations	11	9	- -	3	14	10	22	21	19
Total	101	100	99	100	100	101	101	99	101
N =	81	43	22	30	29	31	46	75	143

47

TABLE 6

THE RELATION OF WORLD VIEW TO LEVEL OF
ASPIRATION FOR CHILDREN

	Percentages					
Scale Scores	Mexican		Negro		Anglo	
	Active	Passive	Active	Passive	Active	Passive
Low Aspirations						
0	45	75	22	42	18	41
1	19	9	22	21	20	17
2	14	5	27	14	16	10
3	3	3	15	7	32	14
4	19	8	15	16	15	19
High Aspirations Total	100	100	101	100	101	101
	N = 164		N = 163		N = 218	

scale scores, passive respondents having lower educational aspiration scores for their children than active respondents. Level of aspiration for children has significant variation with race and ethnicity within each world view category, as well. But world view has even greater significant variation with race and ethnicity within the two halves of the level of aspiration scale. When race and ethnic groups are taken, two at a time, with world view controlled, level of aspiration differences between groups continue to be statistically significant, particularly within the active category, except for the Negro-Anglo pairs. Anglo actives are skewed towards higher aspirations while among the passives all groups are skewed toward low aspirations, the Mexican Americans being skewed the most and the Anglos the least. In assessing the relationships found in Table 6, relationships that are consistent with others described in this paper, three things must be remembered: (1) Negro-Anglo differences were not significant in other tables where level of aspiration for children was involved; (2) there was less difference between Negroes and Anglos in level of aspiration for children than between other groups; and (3) Mexican-Negro patterns were similar when world view was considered. The major contribution of this table is to show that the relationship of world view to race and ethnicity not only stands up but is even more significant with level of aspiration controlled, except in the Mexican-Negro pairs.

There are really two questions here. One is whether level of aspiration for children is more closely related to world view or to race and ethnicity; the other is whether world view or level of aspiration for children is more closely related to race and ethnicity. The answer to the first question is that level of aspiration for children is a bit more closely related to world view than to race and ethnicity. The answer to the second is that world view is more closely related to race and ethnicity than is level of aspiration for children.

But perhaps most interesting of all is Table 7, presenting the relationship between world view and level of aspiration for children, controlling for race, ethnicity, and income. These data enable us to determine the extent to which high levels of aspiration for children and active world views, and low aspirations and passive world views, are associated within income categories and race and ethnic groups. This relationship is present to a greater or lesser degree in every case except among medium income Negroes. Among medium income Negroes, actives are skewed towards low aspirations but passives are about evenly divided. In every other income category of every racial and ethnic group, persons with active world views have either high level of aspiration scores for children or scores skewed toward low aspirations to a lesser extent than persons with passive world views.[17] To put it differently, respondents with passive views had aspiration scores skewed toward the low end of the scale in every case except among medium income Negroes and high income Anglos, while respondents with active world views were either less skewed toward the low end of the aspiration scale or were skewed toward the high end, as in the case of high income Anglos. Unfortunately, the number of cases in the cells of some tables were rather small and the distribution of cases on the level of aspiration continuum was such that only two statistically significant differences were found--they were in the high income Negro and high income Mexican-American categories. If cutting points within each segment of the table had been selected with the strategy of maximizing chances for significant differences, other statistically significant differences could have been found, but this would not have been consistent with the cutting point procedures utilized in this paper.

High income Mexican Americans and Negroes with active world views have high aspirations for their children to a significantly greater extent than do high income but passive Mexican Americans and Negroes. High income active and passive Anglos have high aspirations, but the actives do not have significantly higher aspirations for their children. With world view controlled and income dichotomized, there are no statistically significant relationships between income and level of aspiration for children within race and ethnic groups and world view categories. Only one significant difference is found if the Chi Square test is utilized with two degrees of freedom, and that is among active world view Negroes.

TABLE 7

THE RELATION OF WORLD VIEW AND LEVEL OF ASPIRATIONS FOR CHILDREN WITH INCOME AND RACE AND ETHNICITY CONTROLLED

MEXICAN-AMERICAN

Scale Scores	Low Income		Medium Income		High Income	
	Active	Passive	Active	Passive	Active	Passive
Low Aspirations						
0	52	73	50	78	35	70
1	12	11	25	11	23	5
2	16	5	17	11	12	--
3	4	2	--	--	4	10
4	16	9	8	--	27	15
High Aspirations Total	100	100	100	100	101	100

NEGRO

Scale Scores	Low Income		Medium Income		High Income	
	Active	Passive	Active	Passive	Active	Passive
Low Aspirations						
0	18	50	46	19	14	42
1	41	19	23	25	11	23
2	29	12	15	19	30	16
3	6	8	15	13	20	3
4	6	12	--	25	25	16
High Aspirations Total	100	101	99	101	100	100

50

TABLE 7 (continued)

Scale Scores	ANGLO					
	Low Income		Medium Income		High Income	
	Active	Passive	Active	Passive	Active	Passive
Low Aspirations						
0	23	56	32	44	14	33
1	39	33	23	--	18	11
2	8	11	14	22	18	6
3	31	--	23	22	32	17
4	--	--	9	11	17	33
High Aspirations Total	101	100	101	99	99	100

Conclusion

In _Immigrants on the Threshold_, Judith T. Shuval (1963) employs an "active-passive" continuum to measure the value orientations of various class and ethnic groups in Israel and relates these orientations to such variables as occupational aspirations, levels of education, and length of residence in Israel. Her examples were selected in 1949 and 1950 from transit camps in Israel following the War of Liberation. Dr. Shuval realized, however, that her data had more general significance in relation to other migrants whose spatial mobility might be related to other kinds of mobility aspirations.

Shuval's comparison of European and non-European immigrants to Israel led to the conclusion that value orientation as "active" or "passive" was an important determinant of educational and occupational aspirations, and that the value distinction was maintained even when ethnic and class controls were introduced. Furthermore, the "active" orientation of immigrants increased with time spent in Israel.

The data described in this paper provide further evidence in general support of Shuval's position. Those Negroes and Mexican Americans in Racine who have had less exposure to traditions which favor an active, change-it-yourself attitude toward the world reflect a more passive attitude toward change than do Racine Anglos. But differences based on length of residence in the community are not of uniform or great significance in Racine, as we have described in detail in this paper. Secondly, in both cases there is direct relationship between active or passive value orientations and the aspirations of respondents for their children.

It is apparent that upper-class Mexican Americans and Negroes who are "active" seek education for their children as a way of implementing their general aspirations. This is not a surprising finding, but it has important implications when we remember that an earlier analysis of the same data revealed that education provided only limited access to higher level occupations for Mexican Americans and Negroes (Shannon and Krass 1963). An occupational ceiling did exist for Mexican Americans and Negroes, so that regardless of their education few Mexican Americans were employed above a level for which an eighth grade education would suffice and few Negroes above a level for which high school was sufficient qualification.

In other words, education, although sought for their children by persons with an active world view and with high levels of aspiration for their children, may not be as useful to their children as they expect. Unless success-making variables have the same pattern of relationships to measures of economic absorption among Mexican Americans and Negroes as they do among Anglos, higher education will be of relatively less value to Mexican Americans and Negroes than it has been to Anglos.

As further evidence of how the system works for Mexican Americans, Negroes, and Anglos, a five-point scale of occupational mobility [based on occupation of male's father, and first, next to present, and present occupation of male] was constructed with data from the larger sample. Fifty-one percent of the Mexican Americans in Racine were in the constant low occupational status category, as against only 13 percent of the Negroes and seven percent of the Anglos. At the opposite end of the scale were those whose occupational status had always been high--55 percent of the Anglos, 13 percent of the Mexican Americans, and 10 percent of the Negroes. In between were late mobility, intermediate and early mobility types, with fewer Mexican Americans than Negroes in these categories.

At the beginning of this paper it was pointed out that patterns of intercorrelations between numerous antecedent and intervening variables (such as education, first work experience and prior urbanization) and measures of economic absorption and cultural integration (such as occupational level, income, level of living and world view) differ markedly with race and ethnicity. It was particularly emphasized that the interrelationship of measures of success such as occupational level and income and assumed success-generating variables such as education and work experience is not the same for Mexican Americans and Negroes as it is for Anglos. Not all Mexican Americans and Negroes have the same definitions of success as do Anglos. Those who do find that the larger society is not organized in such a manner that the payoff comes to them in the same way that it comes to Anglos.

NOTES

1. This study of value assimilation among inmigrant workers was initiated in 1958; 1500 interviews were conducted during the summers of 1959, 1960, and 1961, with the support of the research committee of the University of Wisconsin Graduate School, a grant from the National Institutes of Health (Project RG-5342, RG-9980, GM 10919, and CH 00042), and the Ford Foundation Urban Grant. Support for analysis of the data continued from NIH until 1965. Since that time, the project has been supported by the College of Liberal Arts and the Division of Extension Services at the University of Iowa.

2. The basic findings in this study have been described in a series of lengthy mimeographed reports to the National Institutes of Health and in professional journals, selected items may be found in the References.

3. The Spanish version of the World View scale is as follows:
1. Pocas cosas en la vida valen el sacrificio de estar lejos de su familia.
2. El secreto de la felicidad es no esperar mucho y estar contento con lo que le venga.
3. El mejor trabajo es uno en que se trabaja en grupo todas las personas juntas, aunque la persona no reciba crédito por sí misma.
4. El hacer planes para el futuro sólo entristece a la persona, ya que las cosas casi nunca salen como una las quiere.
5. Hoy en día con las condiciones en el mundo lo que son, la persona inteligente vive para hoy y deja que mañana traiga lo que sea.
6. Pocas cosas en la vida valen el sacrificio de mudarse de donde están sus amigos.
7. Cuando un hombre nace, el éxito que va a tener no está determinado; cada cual es responsable por su futuro, el mismo.

4. Certainty of responses was measured on a four-point scale: (1) understood questions--response well formulated; (2) understood questions--response not well formulated; (3) predominately acquiescive response pattern; (4) confused, failed to answer questions.

5. Claire Peterson (Vanderbilt) selected the subsample and constructed a set of tables that served as a starting point for the present analysis. Elaine Krass (Stanford) assisted in the writing of an earlier version of this paper.

6. A series of tests of the significance of differences between samples and subgroups within samples is presented with each table. An overall or total test of the differences between the two samples is presented, followed by tests for each of the subgroups. These in turn are followed by tests of the significance of differences between subgroups within the same sample, all taken at once. Since three separate samples were independently selected, it is also appropriate to test for the significance of differences between samples, two at

a time. Generally speaking, unless a difference is significant at the .05 level the difference is not considered significant, although χ^2 values indicating a lower level of confidence to .10 are reported. Two measures of association are utilized. When the data may be grouped in 2 x 2 tables, r_4 is presented; when comparisons involve other than two dichotomies, $\overline{C}$, the coefficient of contingency corrected for grouping is presented.

Tests of Significance of Differences Between World View in S^1 and S^2 and Subgroups of S^1 and S^2

S^1-S^2 χ^2 = 2.81, 1 d.f., p < .10

Mexican S^1-S^2 χ^2 = .11, 1 d.f., not significant
Negro S^1-S^2 χ^2 = .68, 1 d.f., not significant
Anglo S^1-S^2 χ^2 = .60, 1 d.f., not significant

Mexican-Negro-Anglo S^1 χ^2 = 102.18, 2 d.f., p < .001; $\overline{C}$ = .50
Mexican-Negro-Anglo S^2 χ^2 = 76.78, 2 d.f., p < .001; $\overline{C}$ = .51

Mexican-Anglo S^1 χ^2 = 91.74, 1 d.f., p < .001
Mexican-Anglo S^2 χ^2 = 67.94, 1 d.f., p < .001

Negro-Anglo S^1 χ^2 = 65.14, 1 d.f., p < .001
Negro-Anglo S^2 χ^2 = 42.42, 1 d.f., p < .001

Mexican-Negro S^1 χ^2 = 2.38, 1 d.f., not significant
Mexican-Negro S^2 χ^2 = 2.59, 1 d.f., not significant

7. The Level of Aspiration for Children scale was based on the following questions:

(1) About how much schooling would you (have) like(d) your child(ren) to have?

(2) It's sometimes hard to tell how things will actually work out. If things (had) turned out that your children completed junior high school (9th grade), and then went to work, would you (have been) be satisfied, or dissatisfied? high school? 2 yrs. college? college degree?

(3) You can't always tell about the way things will work out. Here are some statements. Tell me, as far as you can see, which statement would come the closest to the one that you would agree with.

    1. For a person in my financial position, it will be practically impossible to keep my children in school past the 9th grade.
    2. 12th grade.
    3. to put my children through college.

(4) Is there any special line of work that you would like any of your children to go into? (If children are no longer in school read: Was there any line of work that you would have liked your children to go into?)

<u>Tests</u> <u>of</u> <u>Significance</u> <u>of</u> <u>Differences</u> <u>Between</u> <u>Level</u> <u>of</u> <u>Aspiration</u> <u>for</u>
<u>Children</u> <u>in</u> <u>S^1</u> <u>and</u> <u>S^2</u> <u>and</u> <u>Subgroups</u> <u>of</u> <u>S^1</u> <u>and</u> <u>S^2</u>

S^1-S^2 χ^2 = 1.31, 4 d.f., not significant

Mexican S^1-S^2 χ^2 = .52, 4 d.f., not significant
Negro S^1-S^2 χ^2 = 1.31, 4 d.f., not significant
Anglo S^1-S^2 χ^2 = .07, 4 d.f., not significant

Mexican-Negro-Anglo S^1 χ^2 = 64.83*, 2 d.f., p < .001; $\overline{C}$ = .39
Mexican-Negro-Anglo S^2 χ^2 = 38.40*, 2 d.f., p < .001; $\overline{C}$ = .38

Mexican-Negro-Anglo S^1 χ^2 = 113.09**, 2 d.f., p < .001; $\overline{C}$ = .51
Mexican-Negro-Anglo S^2 χ^2 = 71.51**, 2 d.f., p < .001; $\overline{C}$ = .50

Mexican-Anglo S^1 χ^2 = 55.95*, 1 d.f., p < .001
Mexican-Anglo S^2 χ^2 = 34.53*, 1 d.f., p < .001

Mexican-Anglo S^1 χ^2 = 105.58**, 1 d.f., p < .001
Mexican-Anglo S^2 χ^2 = 65.22**, 1 d.f., p < .001

Negro-Anglo S^1 χ^2 = 26.53*, 1 d.f., p < .001
Negro-Anglo S^2 χ^2 = 96.92*, 1 d.f., p < .001

Negro-Anglo S^1 χ^2 = 12.07**, 1 d.f., p < .001
Negro-Anglo S^2 χ^2 = 4.20**, 1 d.f., p < .05

Mexican-Negro S^1 χ^2 = 7.42*, 1 d.f., p < .001
Mexican-Negro S^2 χ^2 = 4.56*, 1 d.f., p < .05

Mexican-Negro S^1 χ^2 = 49.66**, 1 d.f., p < .001
Mexican-Negro S^2 χ^2 = 31.29**, 1 d.f., p < .001

*[cutting point 0-2, 3-4]; **[cutting point 0, 1-4].

    8. <u>Vocational aspirations</u> for children were divided into three
levels: those with high aspirations wished their children to become
doctors, nurses, priests, ministers, nuns, teachers, engineers, or
enter other professions or to become managers, proprietors, or techni-
cians; those with medium aspirations wished their children to become
entertainers (sports, music or acting), white-collar workers, unspeci-
fied clerical workers, or to attain any "easy" job; those who were
classified as having low aspirations desired to have their children
become skilled laborers, mechanics, carpenters, etc.

Vocational Aspirations for Children

	Percentages					
	Mexican		Negro		Anglo	
	S^1	S^2	S^1	S^2	S^1	S^2
Low Aspirations	6	7	2	1	3	2
Medium Aspirations	22	19	10	10	6	6
High Aspirations	24	26	26	25	22	20
Leave it up to children	26	29	22	20	47	48
Not ascertained or inapplicable	22	20	42	44	24	24
Total	100	101	102	100	102	100

S^1 N = 800; S^2 N = 545

Tests of Significance of Differences Between Vocational Aspirations for Children in S^1 and S^2 and Subgroups of S^1 and S^2

S^1-S^2 χ^2 = 1.11, 4 d.f., not significant

Mexican S^1-S^2 χ^2 = 1.39, 4 d.f., not significant
Negro S^1-S^2 χ^2 = .75, 4 d.f., not significant
Anglo S^1-S^2 χ^2 = .68, 4 d.f., not significant

Mexican-Negro-Anglo S^1 χ^2 = 88.26, 8 d.f., p < .001; $\overline{C}$ = .38
Mexican-Negro-Anglo S^2 χ^2 = 67.83, 8 d.f., p < .001; $\overline{C}$ = .41

Mexican-Anglo S^1 χ^2 = 13.62, 2 d.f., p < .01
χ^2 = 43.38, 3 d.f., p < .001
Mexican-Anglo S^2 χ^2 = 7.21, 2 d.f., p < .05
χ^2 = 28.40, 3 d.f., p < .001

Negro-Anglo S^1 χ^2 = 2.36, 2 d.f., not significant
χ^2 = 23.44, 3 d.f., p < .001
Negro-Anglo S^2 χ^2 = 1.09, 2 d.f., not significant
χ^2 = 18.41, 3 d.f., p < .001

Mexican-Negro S^1 χ^2 = 11.31, 2 d.f., p < .01
χ^2 = 12.11, 3 d.f., p < .01
Mexican-Negro S^2 χ^2 = 6.52, 2 d.f., p < .05
χ^2 = 6.52, 3 d.f., p < .10

[Not ascertained, inapplicable and leave it up to children excluded when computing χ^2 with 2 d.f. Not ascertained and inapplicable excluded when computing χ^2 with 3 d.f.]

9. Rodman (1963) has pointed out that "middle class" Anglos respond that they would leave it up to their children but they mean

leave it up to their children to pick a high level occupation. Also
see Aberle and Naegele (1952).

10. Length of residence was determined by the following questions:

(1) Have you always lived here in Racine or did you move here
from somewhere else?

(2) How long have you lived here in Racine?

Length of Residence in Racine

| | Percentages | | | | | |
| | Mexican | | Negro | | Anglo | |
	s^1	s^2	s^1	s^2	s^1	s^2
Less than 10 years	44	37	51	52	13	18
10 years or more	56	63	49	48	87	82
Total	100	100	100	100	100	100

Tests of Significance of Differences Between Length of Residence
in Racine in S^1 and S^2 and Subgroups of S^1 and S^2

s^1-s^2 χ^2 = .21, 1 d.f., not significant

Mexican s^1-s^2 χ^2 = 1.45, 1 d.f., not significant
Negro s^1-s^2 χ^2 = .02, 1 d.f., not significant
Anglo s^1-s^2 χ^2 = 2.37, 1 d.f., not significant

Mexican-Negro-Anglo s^1 χ^2 = 99.85, 2 d.f., p < .001; $\overline{C}$ = .48
Mexican-Negro-Anglo s^2 χ^2 = 46.49, 2 d.f., p < .001; $\overline{C}$ = .42

Mexican-Anglo s^1_2 χ^2 = 61.27, 1 d.f., p < .001
Mexican-Anglo s^2 χ^2 = 14.71, 1 d.f., p < .001

Negro-Anglo s^1 χ^2 = 92.16, 1 d.f., p < .001
Negro-Anglo s^2 χ^2 = 44.93, 1 d.f., p < .001

Mexican-Negro s^1 χ^2 = 2.24, 1 d.f., not significant
Mexican-Negro s^2 χ^2 = 6.25, 1 d.f., p < .02

11. The following question was asked in order to determine years
of formal schooling: "How many years of school have you had?"

Years of Education for Respondents

	Percentages					
	Mexican		Negro		Anglo	
	S^1	S^2	S^1	S^2	S^1	S^2
Less than 9	76	78	46	39	22	14
9 or more	24	22	54	61	78	86
Total	100	100	100	100	100	100

Tests of Significance of Differences Between Years of Education in S^1 and S^2 and Subgroups of S^1 and S^2

S^1-S^2 χ^2 = 5.35, 1 d.f., p < .05

Mexican S^1-S^2 χ^2 = .12, 1 d.f., not significant
Negro S^1-S^2 χ^2 = 1.51, 1 d.f., not significant
Anglo S^1-S^2 χ^2 = 4.96, 1 d.f., p < .05

Mexican-Negro-Anglo S^1 χ^2 = 151.29, 2 d.f., p < .001; $\overline{C}$ = .58
Mexican-Negro-Anglo S^2 χ^2 = 149.18, 2 d.f., p < .001; $\overline{C}$ = .69

Mexican-Anglo S^1 χ^2 = 149.07, 1 d.f., p < .001
Mexican-Anglo S^2 χ^2 = 146.44, 1 d.f., p < .001

Negro-Anglo S^1 χ^2 = 35.92, 1 d.f., p < .001
Negro-Anglo S^2 χ^2 = 31.25, 1 d.f., p < .001

Mexican-Negro S^1 χ^2 = 45.96, 1 d.f., p < .001
Mexican-Negro S^2 χ^2 = 44.14, 1 d.f., p < .001

12. Total family income was based on responses to the following question but it should be noted that respondents were also asked a variety of other questions on income, such as hourly wages, hours worked per week, weeks worked per year, and so on. These were checked against response to the single question and it was decided that this was sufficiently accurate for analysis by category. "Approximately what was your total family income last year (1959)?"

Total Annual Family Income

| | Percentages | | | | | |
| | Mexican | | Negro | | Anglo | |
	S^1	S^2	S^1	S^2	S^1	S^2
$5500 or more	27	28	41	46	64	66
$4500-5499	17	18	21	18	15	14
Less than $4499	50	49	28	26	13	10
Not ascertained	6	4	10	10	8	10
Total	100	99	100	100	100	100

Tests of Significance of Differences Between Total Annual Family Income in S^1 and S^2 and Subgroups of S^1 and S^2

S^1-S^2 χ^2 = 1.87, 2 d.f., not significant

Mexican S^1-S^2 χ^2 = .11, 2 d.f., not significant
Negro S^1-S^2 χ^2 = 1.49, 2 d.f., not significant
Anglo S^1-S^2 χ^2 = .95, 2 d.f., not significant

Mexican-Negro-Anglo S^1 χ^2 = 103.13, 4 d.f., p < .001; $\overline{C}$ = .47
Mexican-Negro-Anglo S^2 χ^2 = 81.00, 4 d.f., p < .001; $\overline{C}$ = .50

Mexican-Anglo S^1 χ^2 = 96.39, 2 d.f., p < .001
Mexican-Anglo S^2 χ^2 = 80.26, 2 d.f., p < .001

Negro-Anglo S^1 χ^2 = 33.48, 2 d.f., p < .001
Negro-Anglo S^2 χ^2 = 21.50, 2 d.f., p < .001

Mexican-Negro S^1 χ^2 = 23.43, 2 d.f., p < .001
Mexican-Negro S^2 χ^2 = 18.30, 2 d.f., p < .001

[Not ascertained omitted in computing χ^2]

13. World View and Length of Residence

Short residence-long residence and always lived in Racine
χ^2 = 7.96, 1 d.f., p < .01; r_4 = .13
Short residence-long residence-always lived in Racine
χ^2 = 29.84, 2 d.f., p < .001; $\overline{C}$ = .34

World View and Length of Residence with Education Controlled

Low Education: residence cutting point as above
χ^2 = .53, 1 d.f., not significant; r_4 = .06
High Education: residence cutting point as above
χ^2 = 3.28, 1 d.f., p < .10; r_4 = .11

Low Education: residence cutting points as above
$\chi^2 = 5.79$, 2 d.f., $p < .10$; $\overline{C} = .25$
High Education: residence cutting points as above
$\chi^2 = 8.30$, 2 d.f., $p < .02$; $\overline{C} = .23$

<u>World View and Length of Residence with Race and Ethnicity Controlled</u>

Mexican $\chi^2 = .34$, 1 d.f., not significant; $r_4 = .06$
Negro $\chi^2 = .28$, 1 d.f., not significant; $r_4 = .05$
Anglo $\chi^2 = .00$, 1 d.f., not significant; $r_4 = .00$

<u>World View and Length of Residence with Race, Ethnicity and Education Controlled</u>

	Mexican	$\chi^2 = .00$, 1 d.f., not significant; $r_4 = .02$
Low Education	Negro	$\chi^2 = .03$, 1 d.f., not significant; $r_4 = .01$
	Anglo	$\chi^2 = .44$, 1 d.f., not significant; $r_4 = .19$
	Mexican	$\chi^2 = 1.47$, 1 d.f., not significant; $r_4 = .28$
High Education	Negro	$\chi^2 = .27$, 1 d.f., not significant; $r_4 = .07$
	Anglo	$\chi^2 = .21$, 1 d.f., not significant; $r_4 = .05$

<u>World View and Education</u>

Low education-high education $\chi^2 = 58.20$, 1 d.f., $p < .001$; $r_4 = .34$

<u>World View and Education with Time in the Community Controlled</u>

Short residence $\chi^2 = 13.40$, 1 d.f., $p < .001$; $r_4 = .29$
Long residence $\chi^2 = 42.85$, 1 d.f., $p < .001$; $r_4 = .35$

<u>World View and Education with Race and Ethnicity Controlled</u>

Mexican $\chi^2 = 6.38$, 1 d.f., $p < .02$; $r_4 = .22$
Negro $\chi^2 = 2.79$, 1 d.f., $p < .10$; $r_4 = .14$
Anglo $\chi^2 = 9.09$, 1 d.f., $p < .01$; $r_4 = .22$

<u>World View and Education with Race, Ethnicity and Time in the Community Controlled</u>

	Mexican	$\chi^2 = 5.27$, 1 d.f., $p < .05$; $r_4 = .36$
Short residence	Negro	$\chi^2 = .69$, 1 d.f., not significant; $r_4 = .11$
	Anglo	$\chi^2 = 9.12$, 1 d.f., $p < .01$; $r_4 = .33$
	Mexican	$\chi^2 = 1.65$, 1 d.f., not significant; $r_4 = .16$
Long residence	Negro	$\chi^2 = 1.64$, 1 d.f., not significant; $r_4 = .17$
	Anglo	$\chi^2 = .61$, 1 d.f., not significant; $r_4 = .11$

14. <u>World View and Income</u>

Low-Medium-High $\chi^2 = 53.40$, 2 d.f., $p < .001$; $\overline{C} = .45$

<u>World View and Income with Race and Ethnicity Controlled</u>

Mexican $\chi^2 = 8.04$, 2 d.f., $p < .02$; $\overline{C} = .45$

Low-Medium $\chi^2 = .46$, 1 d.f., not significant; $r_4 = .08$

Medium-High $\chi^2 = 1.37$, 1 d.f., not significant; $r_4 = .16$
Low-High $\chi^2 = 7.00$, 1 d.f., $p < .01$; $r_4 = .25$

Negro $\chi^2 = 4.44$, 2 d.f., not significant; $\overline{C} = .25$

    Low-Medium $\chi^2 = .04$, 1 d.f., not significant; $r_4 = .05$
    Medium-High $\chi^2 = 1.10$, 1 d.f., not significant; $r_4 = .12$
    Low-High $\chi^2 = 3.27$, 1 d.f., $p < .10$; $r_4 = .18$

Anglo $\chi^2 = 12.99$, 2 d.f., $p < .01$; $\overline{C} = .36$

    Low-Medium $\chi^2 = .36$, 1 d.f., not significant; $r_4 = .12$
    Medium-High $\chi^2 = 4.07$, 1 d.f., $p < .05$; $r_4 = .17$
    Low-High $\chi^2 = 9.20$, 1 d.f., $p < .01$; $r_4 = .26$

<u>World View and Race and Ethnicity with Income Controlled</u>

Low Income $\chi^2 = 5.96$, 2 d.f., not significant; $\overline{C} = .29$

    Mexican-Anglo $\chi^2 = 4.77$, 1 d.f., $p < .05$; $r_4 = .24$
    Negro-Anglo $\chi^2 = 1.52$, 1 d.f., not significant; $r_4 = .18$
    Mexican-Negro $\chi^2 = .60$, 1 d.f., not significant; $r_4 = .09$

Medium Income $\chi^2 = 6.79$, 2 d.f., $p < .05$; $\overline{C} = .38$

    Mexican-Anglo $\chi^2 = 4.74$, 1 d.f., $p < .05$; $r_4 = .31$
    Negro-Anglo $\chi^2 = 3.21$, 1 d.f., $p < .10$; $r_4 = .26$
    Mexican-Negro $\chi^2 = .01$, 1 d.f., not significant; $r_4 = .05$

High Income $\chi^2 = 29.73$, 2 d.f., $p < .001$; $\overline{C} = .47$

    Mexican-Anglo $\chi^2 = 18.80$, 1 d.f., $p < .001$; $r_4 = .33$
    Negro-Anglo $\chi^2 = 21.71$, 1 d.f., $p < .001$; $r_4 = .33$
    Mexican-Negro $\chi^2 = .00$, 1 d.f., not significant; $r_4 = .02$

    15. <u>Income and Level of Aspiration for Children</u>

Low, Medium and High Income $\chi^2 = 49.80$, 8 d.f., $p < .001$; $\overline{C} = .37$
Low, Medium and High Income $\chi^2 = 35.41$, 2 d.f., $p < .001$*; $\overline{C} = .38$
    *[cutting point 0, 1-4]

<u>Income and Level of Aspiration with Race and Ethnicity Controlled</u>

Mexican $\chi^2 = 10.91$, 8 d.f., not significant
       $\chi^2 = 3.83$, 2 d.f., not significant; $\overline{C} = .22$

    Low-Medium Income $\chi^2 = .05$, 1 d.f., not significant; $r_4 = .00$
    Medium-High Income $\chi^2 = 1.43$, 1 d.f., not significant; $r_4 = .16$
    Low-High Income $\chi^2 = 2.75$, 1 d.f., $p < .10$; $r_4 = .16$

Negro $\chi^2 = 7.55$, 8 d.f., not significant
     $\chi^2 = 1.86$, 2 d.f., not significant; $\overline{C} = .16$

    Low-Medium Income $\chi^2 = .08$, 1 d.f., not significant; $r_4 = .06$
    Medium-High Income $\chi^2 = .11$, 1 d.f., not significant; $r_4 = .06$
    Low-High Income $\chi^2 = 1.32$, 1 d.f., not significant; $r_4 = .12$

Anglo $\chi^2 = 17.28$, 8 d.f., p < .05
$\chi^2 = 8.21$, 2 d.f., p < .02; $\overline{C} = .29$

Low-Medium Income $\chi^2 = .05$, 1 d.f., not significant; $r_4 = .01$
Medium-High Income $\chi^2 = 2.22$, 1 d.f., not significant; $r_4 = .20$
Low-High Income $\chi^2 = 3.51$, 1 d.f., p < .10; $r_4 = .17$

Level of Aspiration and Race and Ethnicity with Income Controlled

Low Income $\chi^2 = 12.82$, 2 d.f., p < .01; $\overline{C} = .41$

Mexican-Anglo $\chi^2 = 5.43$, 1 d.f., p < .02; $r_4 = .25$
Negro-Anglo $\chi^2 = .04$, 1 d.f., not significant; $r_4 = .01$
Mexican-Negro $\chi^2 = 8.75$, 1 d.f., p < .01; $r_4 = .28$

Medium Income $\chi^2 = 9.12$, 2 d.f., p < .02; $\overline{C} = .44$

Mexican-Anglo $\chi^2 = 4.75$, 1 d.f., p < .05; $r_4 = .31$
Negro-Anglo $\chi^2 = .01$, 1 d.f., not significant; $r_4 = .05$
Mexican-Negro $\chi^2 = 6.13$, 1 d.f., p < .02; $r_4 = .35$

High Income $\chi^2 = 20.48$, 2 d.f., p < .001; $\overline{C} = .39$

Mexican-Anglo $\chi^2 = 18.81$, 1 d.f., p < .001; $r_4 = .33$
Negro-Anglo $\chi^2 = 1.76$, 1 d.f., not significant; $r_4 = .10$
Mexican-Negro $\chi^2 = 6.61$, 1 d.f., p < .02; $r_4 = .25$

16. World View and Level of Aspiration

Individualistic, Active-Group Oriented, Passive vs. Aspiration Scale
$\chi^2 = 65.98$, 4 d.f., p < .001; $\chi^2 = 54.95$, 1 d.f., p < .001; $\overline{C} = .32$

World View and Level of Aspiration with Race and Ethnicity Controlled

Mexican $\chi^2 = 10.09$, 1 d.f., p < .01; $r_4 = .26$
Negro $\chi^2 = 6.71$, 1 d.f., p < .01; $r_4 = .21$
Anglo $\chi^2 = 9.03$, 1 d.f., p < .01; $r_4 = .22$

Level of Aspiration and Race and Ethnicity with World View Controlled

Individualistic, Active $\chi^2 = 13.48$, 2 d.f., p < .01; $\overline{C} = .29$

Mexican-Anglo $\chi^2 = 12.35$, 1 d.f., p < .001; $r_4 = .23$
Negro-Anglo $\chi^2 = .48$, 1 d.f., not significant; $r_4 = .05$
Mexican-Negro $\chi^2 = 5.45$, 1 d.f., p < .02; $r_4 = .21$

Group Oriented, Passive $\chi^2 = 14.74$, 2 d.f., p < .001; $\overline{C} = .36$

Mexican-Anglo $\chi^2 = 10.29$, 1 d.f., p < .01; $r_4 = .29$
Negro-Anglo $\chi^2 = .20$, 1 d.f., not significant; $r_4 = .06$
Mexican-Negro $\chi^2 = 9.42$, 1 d.f., p < .01; $r_4 = .24$

World View and Race and Ethnicity with Level of Aspiration Controlled

Low Level of Aspiration $\chi^2 = 19.58$, 2 d.f., p < .001; $\overline{C} = .42$

Mexican-Anglo $\chi^2 = 17.00$, 1 d.f., p < .001; $r_4 = .35$
Negro-Anglo $\chi^2 = 8.93$, 1 d.f., p < .01; $r_4 = .32$

Mexican-Negro χ^2 = .19, 1 d.f., not significant; r_4 = .05

High Level of Aspiration χ^2 = 33.88, 2 d.f., p < .001; $\overline{C}$ = .44

    Mexican-Anglo χ^2 = 17.39, 1 d.f., p < .001; r_4 = .29
    Negro-Anglo χ^2 = 45.07, 1 d.f., p < .001; r_4 = .41
    Mexican-Negro χ^2 = .02, 1 d.f., not significant; r_4 = .02

17. <u>World View and Level of Aspiration for Children with Income and Race and Ethnicity Controlled</u>

	Low Income	χ^2 = 2.61, 1 d.f., not significant; r_4 = .21
Mexican	Medium Income	χ^2 = 1.41, 1 d.f., not significant; r_4 = .29
	High Income	χ^2 = 4.34, 1 d.f., p < .05; r_4 = .35
	Low Income	χ^2 = 3.32, 1 d.f., p < .10; r_4 = .33
Negro	Medium Income	χ^2 = 1.40, 1 d.f., not significant; r_4 = .29
	High Income	χ^2 = 6.28, 1 d.f., p < .02; r_4 = .32
	Low Income	χ^2 = 1.22, 1 d.f., not significant; r_4 = .33
Anglo	Medium Income	χ^2 = .06, 1 d.f., not significant; r_4 = .12
	High Income	χ^2 = 2.80, 1 d.f., p < .10; r_4 = .17

<u>Income and Level of Aspiration for Children with Race and Ethnicity and World View Controlled</u>

Mexican

Individualistic, Active χ^2 = .52, 1 d.f., not significant; r_4 = .12
Group Oriented, Passive χ^2 = .03, 1 d.f., not significant; r_4 = .00

Negro

Individualistic, Active χ^2 = .00, 1 d.f., not significant; r_4 = .03
Group Oriented, Passive χ^2 = 1.17, 1 d.f., not significant; r_4 = .15

Anglo

Individualistic, Active χ^2 = 2.88, 1 d.f., p < .10; r_4 = .15
Group Oriented, Passive χ^2 = .45, 1 d.f., not significant; r_4 = .17

REFERENCES

Aberle, David F. and Kaspar D. Naegele
    1952   Middle-Class Fathers' Occupational Role and Attitudes Toward Children. American Journal of Orthopsychiatry 22:371.
Krass, Elaine M., Claire Peterson and Lyle W. Shannon
    1966   Differential Association, Cultural Integration, and Economic Absorption among Mexican-Americans and Negroes in a Northern Industrial Community. The Southwestern Social Science Quarterly 47:239-252.
Rodman, Hyman
    1963   The Lower Class Value Stretch. Social Forces 42:205-215.

Shannon, Lyle W. and Elaine M. Krass
    1963   The Urban Adjustment of Inmigrants: The Relationship
            of Education to Occupation and Total Family Income.
            The Pacific Sociological Review 6:37-42.
Shannon, Lyle and Patricia Morgan
    1966   The Prediction of Economic Absorption and Cultural Inte-
            gration among Mexican-Americans, Negroes, and Anglos in
            a Northern Industrial Community. Human Organization 25:
            154-162.
Shuval, Judith T.
    1963   Immigrants on the Threshold. New York, Atherton Press.
            P. 216.

QUANTITATIVE ANALYSES OF THE URBAN EXPERIENCES
OF SPANISH-AMERICAN MIGRANTS

Robert C. Hanson, Ozzie G. Simmons, and William N. McPhee
University of Colorado, Boulder

The ultimate objective of our research[1] is the generation of a theory of urbanization processes, but we will not discuss theoretical ideas or present substantive results in this paper. Rather, we will describe our attempts to cope with the methodological problems of arriving at generalizations based on complex and dynamic life history data, and of discovering and describing social processes implicit in these data.[2]

The context for the discussion has been well stated by Kenneth Bock in his The Acceptance of Histories (1956:129): "Sooner or later the richly varied world of concrete experiences must be accepted and struggled with and conceptually subdued." We are indeed struggling with the world of concrete experiences in our research. Our strategy for managing the mass of detail available in case histories is spelled out in this paper.

If our objective is the construction of dynamic theory from the concrete details of individual life histories, we are confronted from the outset with almost overwhelming complexity. This kind of complexity has been vividly presented by Samuel Stouffer in his "Notes on the Case Study and the Unique Case" (1962:255):

> Finally, let us consider Smith's ratings on all three traits [each with four possible values] in both time periods as constituting a single complex dynamic configuration.... Such a configuration might be illustrated by the fragment of a case history. Before Smith was married, he got into fast company (a_2) and drank heavily (b_1) and, perhaps because of drink, had great difficulty holding a job (c_4). Since marriage he has given up the fast company (a_3') although he still drinks too much (b_1'), and, consequently perhaps, has been having some, though less, difficulty in holding his job (b_3'). The number of possible complex dynamic configurations of this type $(4^3)^2 = 64^2 = 4,096$. If there were ten traits, the number of possible complex dynamic configurations would be $(4^{10})^2 = (1,048,576)^2 = 1,099,511,627,776$.

It can be easily seen that by extending either the number of trait values or categories or the number of time periods, the number of different complex dynamic configurations becomes astronomical. Yet the researcher must cope with this kind of complexity in attempting to generalize from case history materials. Moreover, the social processes implicit in the case histories must somehow be identified. Traditional arrangements of data for correlation or other kinds of "static" analyses simply do not begin to meet the challenge.

In the first part of this paper we deal with the problem: how can the particulars available in individual case histories be raised to a level of generalizability such that the resultant theory retains the capacity to predict the behavior of the individual case? Detailed case histories, such as The Children of Sanchez by Oscar Lewis (1961), or the poignant vignettes collected by Edward Rose and his colleagues from the persons who live on Skid Row (Leuthold 1965), convey a feeling for the total situation from the perspective of the participants in the situation that gives the reader the impression he understands what is happening. These kinds of descriptions, presented from the point of view of the participant, meet the objections of Herbert Blumer and others to the emphasis in contemporary sociology on "variable analysis" (1954, 1956). Yet the emphasis on description and on the perspective of the participant in the situation means necessarily that no generalizations are explicit, that a theoretical framework is either lacking or implicit, and, finally, that an objective of explicit predictability is precluded.

The approach described below is a compromise. We gain explicit theoretical prediction of individual behavior while losing the impressionistic understanding of the total situation emphasized in the single case study. For purposes of illustration, four equations predicting individual behavior are presented in the first part of the paper.

In the second part of this paper, we deal with another problem: how can we organize case history data so that the dynamic aspects, the implicit social processes, will be made explicit? We will describe a time series program which employs a comparison group strategy to identify social processes. In this case, we give up the aim of predicting the behavior of the individual case, but gain the ability to make explicit the dynamic aspects of the behavior of a defined group of migrants.

The Data Base and Model Variables

In our research we have collected data on the urban experiences of 66 rural migrants to Denver. Open-ended interviews, guided by the concept of a "role path" (Hanson and Simmons 1968), provided us with retrospective accounts of significant changes in status and living situations of the migrants for up to seven years of experience. The detailed case histories were read, summarized, and discussed until a conceptualization of the interaction of the migrant with opportunities provided by the city became the basis for the construction of a simulation model. The variables required for model operation then governed the specification of details to be coded from the case history manuscripts, month by month, for each case. A code book with complete instructions for coding each variable was prepared. Using the manuscripts of the case histories plus the role path chart available for each case, coders were able to specify the changes of status and associated attributes and life situation variables month by month for each migrant. For example, in a particular month, a man may change from unemployed to employed status and from no earned income per week to $50 per week; "family size" increases when a child is born, etc. These data were then punched on IBM cards and a series of factor analyses were undertaken for the purpose of reducing the large number of concrete details of each case to a smaller number of indexes and concepts. These variables, coded month by month, characterize the life situation of the migrant and are necessary for the implementation of our simulation model of urbanization processes.

The model and principal concepts have been described elsewhere.[3] Briefly, the model simulates how migrants from rural settings interact with the city environment. A miniature city is created with opportunities such as jobs, housing, and consumer goods represented by set structures. The migrant searches, confronts, and accepts or rejects the opportunities communicated through the opportunity structures, the persistence, range, and acceptance criteria of his search depending on his attributes at a particular time. Thus, his current set of attributes (e.g., health, family size, rent cost, earned income, organization membership, drinking behavior, etc.) become possible variables for predicting the variables governing search behavior next month. There are various ways of searching; our examples below will deal with searching by means of the network of social contacts which can supply information on vacant houses, job openings, etc. Acceptance of an encountered opportunity while searching next month implies a change in attributes (e.g., a new job changes the amount of monthly earned income) which, in turn, will change the character of search behavior the following month, and so on. Each month 84 predictor and criterion variables were coded for the empirical analysis which would yield the equations necessary for operation of the model.

The Arrangement of Case History Data for Predictive Analysis

First, all 84 predictor and criterion variables used in the analysis were standardized to a range of values from .00 to .99. For dichotomous variables (for example, Catholic vs. non-Catholic), this was accomplished by assigning the alternative values of either .00 or .99. For quantitative variables the value of a particular variable was divided by the mean plus three standard deviations of that variable, yielding values that fall within the range from .00 to .99 (with an occasional exception at the upper limit which was then confined to the .99 extreme).[4]

Second, the data were arranged on IBM cards so that a regression analysis could be used to provide prediction of "next month's" behavior from "this month's" complex of variables. The arrangement of data for the regression analysis is illustrated in Figure 1. Note that, for each case, t provides the values of "this month's" series of variables, and t+1 provides "next month's" values on these same variables. Thus, any group of variables at time t can become the independent or "predictor variables" for any particular criterion at time t+1 (i.e., the dependent or predicted) variable. The result of this arrangement of case history data is a new definition of the unit of analysis, the "man-month." From the 66 case histories we have now obtained 3,415 man-months of data on 84 predictor and criterion variables. With regression analysis, we can produce equations which predict the next month's behavior of any particular man from his current set of attributes and life situation variables.

Regression analysis results give estimates of the coefficients in linear difference equations. Four examples are shown below. Each such equation represents a "small theory" where the relative importance of the variables in the theory can be approximately estimated by the size of the regression coefficients (since the variables have all been standardized to the same range).[5]

Note that "next month's" behavior on the criterion variables of each individual can now be predicted. We merely substitute the values of his current attributes and states, which make up the predictor variables in the equation, and compute the value which becomes the predicted value for that criterion variable next month. For purposes of illustration, we will present four equations of the kind we are using in our simulation model.

Equations 1 and 2 concern the search behavior that a man will exhibit next month in looking for housing or jobs. The variable being predicted is the degree of "quiescence" in the use of friends and relatives in search activity for either job or housing next month. Quiescence is the complement of a variable called "persistence" in search activity; since they are complements, any equation predicting one implicitly predicts the other. In the present case, high values of quiescence indicate little or no searching through friends and relatives; low values indicate intensive use of friends and relatives in search activity. Equation 1 states a small theory that (in addition to a personal constant) a man who did not use friends and relatives (his social net) in search for a job this month, who is satisfied with his job this month, and who has a small sized social net, will be quiescent in his use of the social net for job searching next month.

Equation (1)

$$X_{t+1} = .762X_t + .055Y_t + .033Z_t + \text{personal constant}$$

68

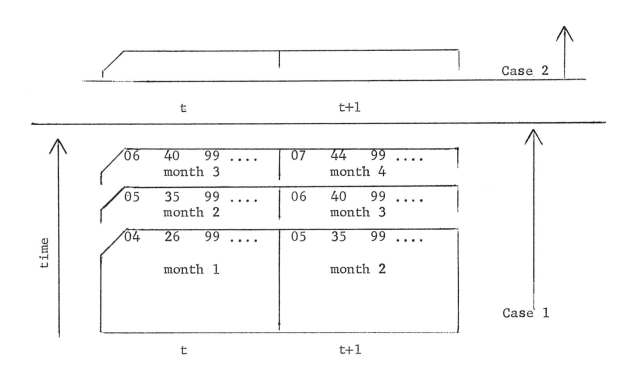

Figure 1. Arrangement of Data for Predictive
Multiple Regression Analysis

where: X_{t+1} = quiescence in use of social net for job searching next month
$\qquad$ X_t = quiescence in use of social net for job searching this month
$\qquad$ Y_t = job satisfaction this month
$\qquad$ Z_t = net size this month, complemented (higher values indicate smaller nets)

Similarly, as can be seen in Equation 2 predicting the use of the social net in looking for a residence next month, the quiescence of the search will depend on (1) quiescent use of the social net in the housing search this month, plus (2) how satisfied the man is with his housing this month, plus (3) a family cycle variable, plus (4) his propensity to purchase durable consumer goods including furniture and appliances this month, and (5) his personal constant relevant to housing search using the social net.

Equation (2)

$$Q_{t+1} = .687Q_t + .080P_t + .052R_t + .070S_t + \text{personal constant}$$

where: Q_{t+1} = quiescence in use of social net for residence searching next month
$\qquad$ Q_t = quiescence in use of social net for residence searching this month
$\qquad$ P_t = housing satisfaction this month
$\qquad$ R_t = family cycle index, taking into account current marital status, family size, and number of teenagers
$\qquad$ S_t = propensity to purchase durable consumer goods this month

We have discussed elsewhere, in describing the model (see footnote 3), how the search activity of the man interacts with opportunities coming from the structures of the city with the consequence that a change in status and attributes of the man may alter the search behavior of the man for the next month.

Equation 3 illustrates the prediction of a satisfaction variable needed for model operation. Predicted satisfaction with leisure activity next month is dependent on (1) the migrant's degree of satisfaction with leisure activity this month, plus (2) quiescence in his use of the social net in searching for leisure activities this month, plus (3) the number of non-deviant associates in his social net, plus (4) his personal constant relevant to leisure satisfaction.

Equation (3)

$$Y_{t+1} = .741Y_t + .134X_t + .024Z_t + \text{personal constant}$$

where: Y_{t+1} = leisure activity satisfaction next month

70

Y_t = leisure activity satisfaction this month
X_t = quiescence in use of the social net in searching for leisure activities this month
Z_t = number of non-deviant associates

Equation 4 illustrates the estimation of another dependent variable needed for model operation, namely, food and general household expenses. Other types of expenses, such as rent, durable goods payments, leisure expenses, legal costs and illness expenses, are carried by each individual, each month, as attributes of the opportunities he has accepted (e.g., acceptance of a housing opportunity carries with it a certain cost for rent each month) or incidents he has experienced (e.g., getting fined for a traffic violation or paying a doctor bill for an illness in the family). But general household expenses must be estimated so that the expense can be added to the other types of expenses in arriving at "total expenses" for the month.

The equation with which we estimate food costs and general household expenses next month includes as predictor variables: (1) the migrant's earned income this month, (2) the amount of supplementary income this month, (3) his job pay demand this month, (4) total expenses this month, (5) a family cycle index taking into account current marital status, family size, and number of teenagers, and (6) the personal constant of the man relevant to the general household expense variable.

Equation (4)

$$Z_{t+1} = .232Y_t + .511X_t + .169W_t + .417V_t + .150U_t + \text{personal constant}$$

where:
Z_{t+1} = food and other household expenses next month
Y_t = earned income this month
X_t = supplementary income this month
W_t = job pay demand this month
V_t = total expenses this month
U_t = family cycle index, taking into account current marital status, family size, and number of teenagers

Each month 55 equations are used to estimate the values of the variables which govern a man's search behavior in each of four sectors (that is, work, housing, purchasing, and leisure activity) for the next month; for the estimation of other dependent variables such as supplementary income and household expenses; for the assignment of probabilities for the occurrence of incidents such as illness, legal trouble, the arrival and departure of relatives, births in the family, changes in the social net; and for the estimation of satisfaction variables in each of the four sectors. With the exception of equations for incident occurrences the multiple correlations are at .70

71

or above so that in most of our equations the small theories account for more than 50 percent of the variance in the data.[6]

The Generation of Time Series Data

In addition to the task of constructing theory which would enable us to predict the behavior of individual cases we also faced the problem of how to elicit and describe the social processes implicit in the case history data. Moreover, we had to find a means of comparing model output with the actual empirical data in our 66 cases. This problem has been resolved by building a computer program which demonstrates what happens over time to variously composed and defined groups of migrants.[7] In essence, the time trend program allows the researcher to follow the behavior of up to four arbitrarily defined groups over time, that is, over a 48 month period.[8] The 66 subjects are initially dichotomized by a defined binary variable (for example, Catholic vs. non-Catholic; those above the mean on IQ vs. those at the mean or below; and so on). Additionally, a minor dichotomization may be specified. These two or four groups of subjects are then held fixed and their behavior on one to four subsequently defined variables is computed each month over the four-year period. For each month and each group and each subsequent variable the program computes the mean (for a continuous variable) or a percentage (for a binary variable).

For either the original variables which define the groups to be held constant over time, or for the subsequent variables which trace the behavior of groups over time, the groups or subsequent variables may be constructed by using any logical or arithmetic operation or relation, that is, plus, minus, times, divide, equals, not equals, and, or, not, greater than, equal to or greater than, less than, and finally, equal to or less than. As many as 34 steps may be used to construct a single original or subsequent variable, for example, a complicated "adjustment" index.[9]

For the purpose of this program the data are reorganized as shown in Figure 2. The variables are ordered by months, from month 1 up to month 48, and the cases are ordered within each month from 1 to 66. This allows the observer to discover what happened on some defined variable for some defined group in month 1, then what happened in month 2, and so on, for 48 months.[10]

Illustration of the Output of the Time Series Program

To illustrate the output of the program let us look at some of the data which show the effect of an important variable, such as socioeconomic status at the time of arrival in Denver, on some later indicator of adjustment, in this case, "financial independence" which is the complement of the degree of welfare help received. Table 1 shows what happens when the migrants have been divided in the first

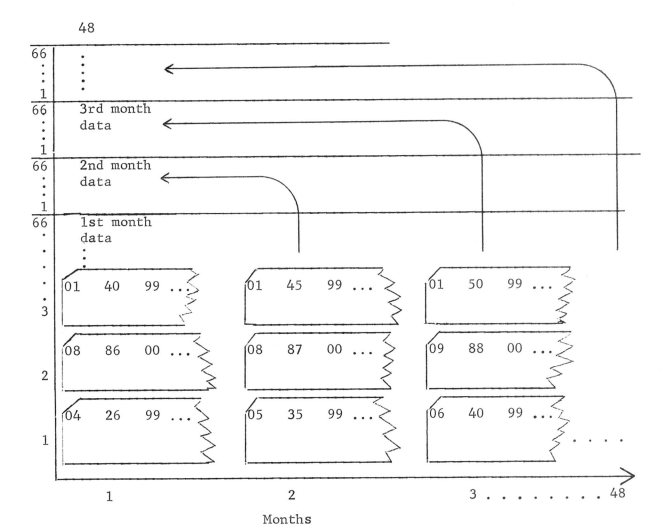

Figure 2. Arrangement of Data for
Time Trend Analysis

73

TABLE 1

FINANCIAL INDEPENDENCE (COMPLEMENT OF THE AMOUNT OF WELFARE
HELP RECEIVED) AMONG MIGRANTS CLASSIFIED BY SOCIOECONOMIC
STATUS ON ARRIVAL IN THE CITY

Month	High SES N=35	Low SES N=31
1	.906	.955
2	.886	.959
3	.945	.931
4	.945	.957
5	.958	.922
6	.939 (N=35)	.911 (N=31)
.	.	.
.	.	.
.	.	.
24	.915 (N=33)	.828 (N=31)
.	.	.
.	.	.
.	.	.
42	.980 (N=24)	.749 (N=22)
.	.	.
.	.	.
.	.	.

74

month into those equal to or above the mean on socioeconomic status--a group of 35--versus those who were lower than the mean on socioeconomic status in the first month--a total of 31 cases. Then for each month the means for the variable, financial independence (or, degree of welfare help, complemented[11]) were computed. The table shows the first six months of data; the graph in Figure 3 shows what happened to these two groups for the total 48 months. Figure 4 shows these same data after the curves have been smoothed by means of an averaging procedure.[12]

The graph clearly shows that while the migrants with high socioeconomic status started out at approximately the same level of receiving welfare help as those with low socioeconomic status, they soon (after approximately ten months) gained the position of receiving little or no welfare help and retained that high level of financial independence throughout the 48 months. On the other hand, by the tenth month, the migrants with lower socioeconomic statuses were beginning to receive welfare help more than those with high socioeconomic status and continued in a trend toward receiving more and more welfare help throughout the 48 months. When the curves have been smoothed through some common procedure, it is not difficult to define the trend as a mathematical function, for example, a straight line, an exponential curve, and so on. Forecasts or predictions about the behavior of a group can then be made by extrapolating or projecting the curve into the future. Note, however, that in moving to the group prediction level, we give up the attempt to predict the behavior of the individual case--we are dealing with comparison groups which are "populations as wholes" in the search for social processes.

Table 2 shows the first few months of data for a more complicated definition of comparison groups, which is as follows. Group 1 consists of those migrants who in the first month were equal to or above the mean in their demand for job security.[13] In addition Group 1 consists of those migrants who were also equal to or above the mean in their demand for a job with high pay. Group 2 migrants are also equal to or above the mean in demand for job security, but are less than the mean in their demand for high pay. Group 3 consists of a small group of migrants who in the first month did not demand high job security, but who did demand high pay, and finally, Group 4 consists of those migrants who in the first month were below the mean on both demand for job security and demand for high pay. The month by month data show the average for each of these groups in the amount of earned income the groups received, graphed over the 48 months.

Figure 5 shows clearly that all groups climb in average earned income during the first six to eight months. But then the differences begin to become apparent. Those who originally demanded both high pay and high job security keep increasing their income slightly throughout most of the 48 months. Secondly, although it is risky to

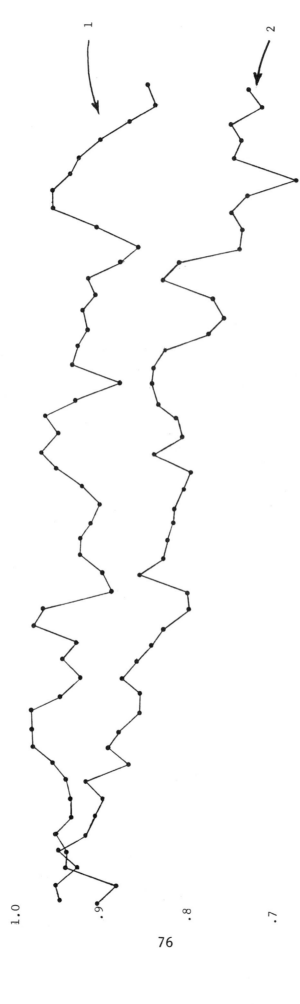

(1) High SES, $\geq$ 0.46   1st month N = 35

(2) Low SES, < 0.46   N = 31

Figure 3. Financial Independence (complement of the amount of welfare help received) among Migrants Classified by Socioeconomic Status on Arrival in the City.

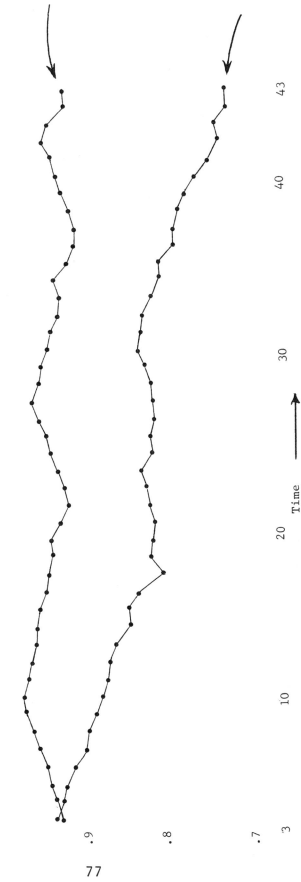

(1) High SES, ≥ 0.46   1st month N = 35

(2) Low SES, < 0.46   N = 31

Figure 4. Financial Independence (complement of the amount of welfare help received)
among Migrants Classified by Socioeconomic Status on Arrival in the City
Smoothed by a Moving Average of Order Six.

TABLE 2

AMOUNT OF EARNED INCOME FOR MIGRANTS CLASSIFIED BY JOB SECURITY AND JOB PAY DEMANDS ON ARRIVAL IN THE CITY

| | Demand High Security | | Demand Low Security | |
| | Demand High Pay | Demand Low Pay | Demand High Pay | Demand Low Pay |
Month	(1) N=25	(2) N=22	(3) N=4	(4) N=15
1	.298	.146	.140	.045
2	.383	.203	.242	.056
3	.446	.247	.215	.073
4	.462	.253	.220	.073
5	.452	.293	.228	.080
6	.471 (N=25)	.287 (N=22)	.242 (N=4)	.077 (N=15)
.	.	.	.	.
.	.	.	.	.
.	.	.	.	.
24	.452 (N=24)	.280 (N=21)	.240 (N=4)	.123 (N=15)
.	.	.	.	.
.	.	.	.	.
.	.	.	.	.
42	.537 (N=15)	.354 (N=18)	.277 (N=3)	.091 (N=10)
.	.	.	.	.
.	.	.	.	.
.	.	.	.	.

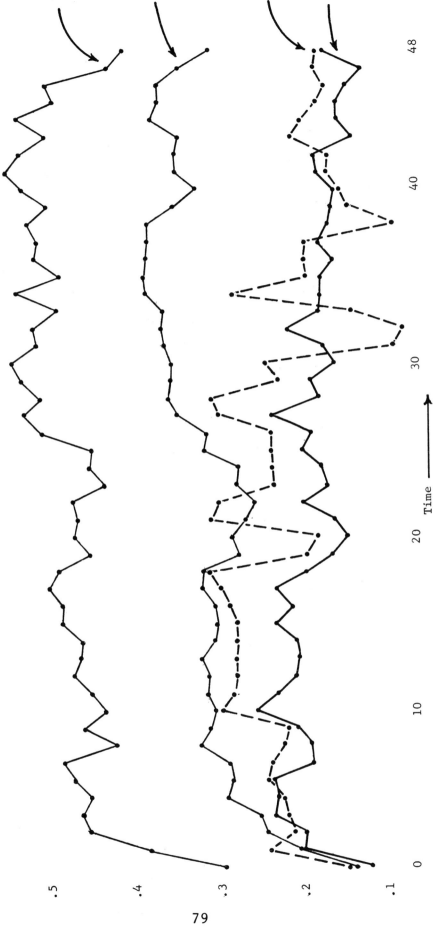

(1) Demand High Job Security ($\geq$.32) and High Pay ($\geq$.35) on Arrival
(2) Demand High Job Security ($\geq$.32) but Accept Low Pay ($<$.35) on Arrival
(3) Accept Low Job Security ($<$.32) but Demand High Pay ($\geq$.35) on Arrival
(4) Accept Low Job Security ($<$.32) and Low Pay ($<$.32) on Arrival

Figure 5. Amount of Earned Income for Migrants Classified by Job Security and Job Pay Demands on Arrival in the City

79

generalize on the basis of such small samples, the data suggest that initial job security demands prove to be more important for later earned income than job pay demands. Group 2, which had high original job security demands, but less initial demand for high pay, continued to increase their income over time in much the same manner as Group 1 which had demands for both high security and high pay. The few men in Group 3, on the other hand, who had original demands for high pay but low demands for security, display a great variation in earned monthly income and end up at a low level. Finally, Group 4, which had initial demands for neither high job pay nor good security, continued at a fairly steady low rate of income throughout the 48 months.

Some Apparent Advantages of the Time Series Program

An obvious advantage of this kind of program, which allows the investigator to define comparison groups in almost any way he wishes, is that the probability of discovering significant social processes is increased. It is obvious that many interesting questions can be formulated and the behavior of variously defined groups observed. Hopefully, this strategy will lead to the discovery of processes not yet formally or explicitly presented in the literature on urbanization.

As our understanding of the data increases through analysis of the outputs of the program, we will be able to decide which kinds of groups and variables will be most useful for testing and judging the adequacy of our model designed to simulate urbanization processes. We will require the output from the model to fit, with reasonable adequacy, the output that we have observed empirically in the 66 cases, using this kind of a program.

NOTES

1. The project, "Urbanization of the Migrant: Processes and Outcomes," is supported by the National Institute of Mental Health, Grant No. MH 09208. Ozzie G. Simmons and Robert C. Hanson are co-principal investigators; Robert J. Potter, William N. McPhee, and Jules J. Wanderer are associate project directors. We wish to thank Fu-Chin Shih and Geraldine Macdonald for assistance in the analysis and preparation of data presented here. This research is being conducted in the Program of Research on Social Processes, Institute of Behavioral Science, University of Colorado. This is Publication 110 of the Institute.

2. While differing in particular respects, our general approach to the generation of theory resembles the strategy recently advocated by Glaser and Strauss in their book, The Discovery of Grounded Theory (1967).

3. A description of the model was presented in a paper at the annual meetings of the American Sociological Association, San Francisco,

1967. A revision of the paper, "A Simulation Model of Urbanization Processes," will be submitted for publication in the near future. For an illustration of the model concepts by analysis of two case histories, see Simmons, Hanson, and Potter (forthcoming).

4. For example, the mean age of the migrants was 29.41 with a standard deviation of 6.96. The mean plus three standard deviations equals 50.3. A man of 20 would have a standardized scale value of .40; a man of 40, .80; and a man of 60, .99 (although we had no respondents that old).

5. The variables in the equation do not always or necessarily consist of the top predictors obtained on a purely empirical basis. Rather, we have selected what seemed to us to be the theoretically relevant variables among the ten top empirically best predictor variables. We also avoided negative signs in equations when possible, either by complementing the variable (when plausible considering its role in other equations) or by suppressing the variable in later runs.

6. Actually, in addition, since we use an empirically determined constant term unique for each man for each prediction, rather than the "group data" constant term provided by the regression analysis, the variance accounted for is higher than reported here.

7. The program was written by Richard Jones of the Institute of Behavioral Science; the full details are available from the Institute.

8. The selection of 48 months as the time period is arbitrary but based on two considerations. We wanted to retain as many data points as possible for time series analysis but, also, to avoid excessive loss of cases due to shorter lengths of time in the city.

9. A simple illustration of how a new variable may be constructed follows. Suppose we want to construct a new index, "relative per capita income," from the variables earned income (V032), supplementary income (V033), welfare income (V042), and family size (V046), and to keep the new variable in the range from .00 to .99. The construction could proceed in the following five steps:

(1) New variable (V087) = V032PLV033   PL for +
(2) New variable (V088) = VO87PLV042
(3) New variable (V089) = V088DV3.0   DV for ÷
(4) New variable (V090) = V046PL1.0
(5) New variable (V091) = V089DVV090

The new variable V091 represents the desired index of per capita income, a continuous variable whose mean will be computed month by month for each comparison group when it is defined as a subsequent variable. The new variable could also be used to split the migrants into two comparison groups--high vs. low per capita income groups--and behavior on other subsequent variables could be observed over time. In addition the program provides an option for designating a particular time period for data to be used in constructing a new variable, for example, first month only, first 12 months (01-12), months 13-24, last 6 months, and so on.

   10. Since not all respondents had lived up to four years in the city, the size of the comparison groups decreases over time, creating some instability in trends in the later months due to smaller sample size.

   11. A man who received no welfare help this month would have a value of .99; a man who received $116 this month from welfare would have a value of about .50; the more the help, the lower the value.

   12. In this illustration we have used a moving average of order 6 (i.e., the mean of six months of data for each point) to smooth the series. Other methods, for example, the method of least squares, could also have been used. See Spiegel (1961:Chapters 13 and 16).

   13. The operational definition of job security demand, based on the coder's knowledge of the case, is: .0, ignores security; .1, no evidence of consideration of security; .3 = might consider security; .6 = would seriously consider security; .9 = insists upon job permanence. The operational definition of job pay demand is the coder's estimate of the minimum monthly pay acceptable in dollars. The mean is $271.90 with a standard deviation of $115.19.

REFERENCES

Blumer, Herbert
   1954   What is Wrong with Social Theory? American Sociological Review 19:3-10.
   1956   Sociological Analysis and the "Variable." American Sociological Review 21:683-690.
Bock, Kenneth E.
   1956   The Acceptance of Histories: Toward a Perspective for Social Science. University of California Publications in Sociology and Social Institutions 3:1-132.
Glaser, Barney G. and Anselm L. Strauss
   1967   The Discovery of Grounded Theory: Strategies for Qualitative Research. Chicago, Aldine Publishing Co.
Hanson, Robert C. and Ozzie G. Simmons
   1968   The Role Path: A Concept and Procedure for Studying Migration to Urban Communities. Human Organization (in press).
Leuthold, Frank, ed.
   1965   Larimer Vignettes: Collected from Conversations Between the Men on the Street and Gary Barnett, Frank Leuthold, Edward Rose, and I. J. Singer. Bureau of Sociological Research Report No. 28. Institute of Behavioral Science, University of Colorado.
Lewis, Oscar
   1961   The Children of Sanchez. New York, Random House.
Simmons, Ozzie G., Robert C. Hanson and Robert J. Potter
   1968   The Rural Migrant in the Urban World of Work. In

Proceedings of the XI Interamerican Congress of Psychology.
Mexico City, University of Mexico (forthcoming).

Spiegel, Murray R.
1961   Theory and Problems of Statistics. New York, Schaum
Publishing Company.

CHILD'S-EYE-VIEWS OF LIFE IN AN URBAN BARRIO

Mary Ellen Goodman and Alma Beman
Rice University

Introduction

In this paper we summarize what we have learned, from the children themselves, about the life styles and values of school-age children in a Mexican-American "pocket of poverty."

The data presented here are a small part of the findings from a three-year study of Houstonians of Mexican ancestry.[1] A report on the full study--an urban ethnography--is now in preparation.

In metropolitan Houston some 7.5 percent of the population--more than 100,000 people--are Mexican Americans. These people are widely dispersed through the city and greatly varied with respect to acculturation, education, and economic status. There are, however, sections of the city in which the residents are solidly Mexican-American, largely of very low income and education, and minimally to moderately acculturated.

We selected one such enclave for intensive study. "El Barrio," as we call it, is a kind of "urban village" (Gans 1962) encircled by highways, railroad tracks, and a string of warehouse and industrial structures. It lies about a mile from downtown Houston, but it is socially much further removed. Some forty families, plus partial families and detached individuals, make up the Barrio population.

Barrio household heads and their spouses are mainly (c. 70%) Texas-born. A relatively small proportion (23%) are Mexican-born, and only a few persons were born in states other than Texas. Nearly all the Barrio adults are Spanish speaking, but they use a patois nearly unintelligible to people who speak standard Spanish. In their vernacular, English words are liberally intermixed with local slang, with grammatically distorted and with poorly enunciated Spanish.

From the viewpoint of the middle-class Houstonian El Barrio is a slum. Its turn-of-the-century buildings are unkempt, its streets narrow and rutted, its sidewalks broken and discontinuous. Home ownership is rare, and some of the larger old homes are now rooming houses. The heart of the Barrio is an intersection around which are clustered a small grocery, four modest cafes, and a taxi dance lounge. On one edge of the "village" there is a small Roman Catholic church with an adjacent playing field for softball and basketball.[2]

Barrio life styles are more varied than an outsider might suppose. There are "routine-seekers" as well as "action-seekers" (Gans 1962), stable families as well as street-corner boys and men, winos, taxi dancers, and others whose life-ways are out of key with family routines and responsibilities. Outside the Barrio its best known features are its more lurid ones.

> The _____ Lounge attracts men and women from outside the neighborhood, although some taxi dancers and Lounge customers have lived in El Barrio. People now resident in the neighborhood often refer to the _____ Lounge as a place of trouble from which a person would be wise to stay away. ...Violence at the Lounge...is not rare. Fights, stabbings, shootings, and murders have occurred....
>
> Mexican-American men from [other]...parts of the city seek out Barrio friends at night. These men and their friends usually drink at one of the several bars or cafes. They, like their friends, are laboring men... (de la Isla 1968:11-12).

Child's-Eye-View

We studied the Barrio in three different ways: (1) participant observation (including a five-month residence maintained by José de la Isla); (2) neighborhood census through a lengthy systematic interview with the head of each independent living unit; and (3) lengthy interviews with each Barrio child in grades one through six. In this paper we review only the child interview data.

Before we proceed to those data, however, we must emphasize a methodological point of major importance.

Our point is that children are an excellent and under-utilized source of ethnographic information, that

> what we can learn from child informants is unique and indeed indispensable to a comprehensive view of [a] society and culture...That part of culture which is known to the child [must]...have a peculiar significance, since what is learned early is likely to be fundamental, pervasive, and persistent in the culture (Goodman 1960).

In studies utilizing children as informants (e.g., Leighton and Kluckhohn 1947; Nadel 1937; Dennis 1940; Goodman 1957, 1962, 1964) the focus is not on the mechanics of enculturation or upon how grownups view and deal with children. Rather, the focus is such that the investigator in effect stands beside the child and looks out with him upon the social scene. The child's-eye-views we report here are to be understood in these terms.

For this study we designed and pre-tested a rather lengthy interview schedule. It contains 123 questions, largely open-ended. The interviews required a minimum of half an hour, often as much as an hour. However we found the child informants highly cooperative.

Nearly always the children seemed surprised and even proud that their opinions were sought. It was a novel experience, and they enjoyed talking.

We have interviewed lower-class Negro and Anglo children as well as the Barrio children. A full and comparative report will be made in a later paper. Here we focus on the Mexican-American children.

The Barrio interviewers are undergraduate and graduate men students who are equally at ease in Texan Spanish and in English.[3] They found ample use for both languages. Two of the children used Spanish throughout the interview, and all of them used at least a sprinkling of Spanish terms. Spanish was used especially in references to kin and to food.

The interview content ranges through factual items such as a list of family members and accounts of the child's everyday home and school routines. We also asked for judgements about good and bad people, good and bad "things to do," "best" and "worst" memories, and plans for the future. We included a few questions designed to sample the child's knowledge about the larger society (e.g., "What town do you live in?" "What state?" "Who is President of the United States?"). These questions were placed near the end of the interview lest the stigma of "test" inhibit communication (see the appended interview schedule).

An interviewer who worked with the children, and later with the Barrio adults as well, commented on the lack of stereotype in the children's responses. Their spontaneity and candor was indeed remarkable. The protocols contain a wealth of detail which we have preserved to a large extent in the process of coding the responses. We do not burden this report with an account of our coding, tabulating, and analytical procedures. It should be understood, however, that what we report in qualitative terms is not impressionistic; it is based on careful coding and tabulation of the responses to each question, and on subsequent analysis and grouping of responses in significant categories (e.g., child's-eye-views of the physical world, of the social world, and of the values realm).[4]

Background for the Child's-Eye-View

In the Barrio we interviewed 34 school-age children living in sixteen households. There are seventeen boys and seventeen girls, well distributed across the age range seven to thirteen.[5] The modal household has in it six children. There are a few families of eight or nine children, and a few of two or three.

The households to which the informants belong are simple nuclear families in only seven of the sixteen cases. In nine households there are grandparents or other relatives in addition to or (in two cases) in place of parents.

The parents of our children are poorly educated and their earning power is low. Formal schooling ranges from none to eleven years, with four to six years the level most frequently attained. Fathers are unskilled laborers in construction work, or employed as janitors, service station attendants, and the like. The most skilled and best paid is a "plastic molder" who earns $89.00 a week. This father supports a wife and eight children ages three to twelve years. Two other fathers, each having eight children of approximately the same age range, support their families on $75.00 and $55.00 a week, respectively. Four mothers and one grandmother are reported (by the children) to work outside the home.

Most of the families claim membership in the Barrio's small Catholic church. When asked "What do you do on Sunday?," two-thirds of the children tell us they go to church. A nine-year-old and a twelve-year-old serve as altar boys.

Given names provide a small clue to family levels of acculturation. Of our child informants two-thirds bear "Anglo" names or at least use Anglicized names (e.g., Juan Enrique is known as "Henry").

However, the prevalence of compadre/comadre relationships is but one of many evidences of the retention of Mexican traditions. Nearly all the parental generation claims one, two, three or four such relationships with people in the neighborhood or in other sections of the city.

There are no schools inside the Barrio. Our interviewees, between them, attend three different elementary schools located six to nine blocks from their homes. All the children, except two who travel by bus to quite distant special schools, walk to and from these three elementary schools. Their routes take them across railroad tracks and streets bearing heavy traffic. Most of them "carry" their lunches and do not return home until mid- to late afternoon.

Home Relationships and Routines

In the child's-eye-view the central feature is home, and the people at home. Around this focus there are the wider worlds of neighborhood and school. What lies beyond is likely to be fuzzy and vague even to the older children. The Barrio does not figure as a unit in the views of the children, although their elders regard it as a neighborhood and recognize its physical boundaries.

In the child's world of people there are household members, friends, and close neighbors, all ranged in an orderly classification, and clearly differentiated. These "significant others" the child places in his personal world--his social space. We infer that the placing depends mainly on his assessments in three dimensions: respect, authority, and affectionate warmth.

The respect dimension is closely linked with age. In general, the older the person, the more respect is due him. Grandparents are in no way deprecated by any of the children, and there are numerous comments suggesting deference. One must not "talk bad" to grandmother. In one household "Abuelita" (little Grandmother) has her own bedroom, even though the rest of the family must sleep together in one other room. Many children say they love their grandparents, and they make such comments before they even mention resident parents.

Grandparents appear to be highly influential, as distinguished from being powerful. The children express appreciation; e.g., because grandparents teach "what is right and not right," because "they are good with me and drag me out of bed," and because they are "fun." Many grandmothers and grandfathers work; this too is admirable. A solicitous attitude is sometimes expressed; e.g., it is a good thing "to save [pick] up my toys so Grandmother does not trip over them."

On the authority dimension the father takes precedence. He is seen as a somewhat distant authority, but not easily forgotten. Nevertheless, the boys seem rather to slight him. Few say they go to him with questions, either for information or for permission to do something. Only four boys want to be like father when they grow up. Two think father is great, but none plans on having a job like father's in later life. That there is a certain remoteness between boy and father may be due mainly to father's frequent absences because of work or for other reasons. He usually leaves home before the children are up and around. Yet our informants were sure to tell us whether he had supper with them, and they report that his home-coming usually determines suppertime.

The girls' attitudes toward parents are quite different. They speak much more often of "Mother and Father" as an entity. They feel that their parents are equally available to answer questions. Four girls say they ask only father, if they need answers. None interpreted this as seeking permission to do something. Girls can describe father's work better than the boys can.

Boys and girls agree on two roles for the male head of household. A man goes out to work to earn money for the family, and he is the high court of discipline. The men of the family, either father or grandfather, handle crises and major indiscretions--putting a stop to rock fights, for example.

Mothers and grandmothers fill many domestic roles in the child's world. They prepare the breakfast, the "carried" lunch, after-school snacks, and the supper--likely to be beans, tortillas, and rice. They do the dishes, sweeping and mopping, bedmaking and "making everything clean for us," with help from the girls, and occasionally from boys. Mother sets hours to get up, to come in from play, and to go to bed. She scolds, she sometimes slaps or spanks for diso-beying small rules, and she stops sibling squabbles. Even in the few families where mother goes out to work, the children feel that her prime activity is at home.

In spite of the continuous and repetitive nature of mother's tasks she is not thought of as a drudge. "She's good and looks pretty," "She is always helping us and is a lot of fun." Toward

their mothers and mother surrogates the children express a feeling
of warmth and closeness, a strong bond of affection.

The strength of intra-family affection declared by Barrio children is conspicuous by contrast with responses of the Negro and Anglo
children we interviewed. We asked of all the children, "Who do you
love?" No Barrio child included any but relatives in his roster of
persons loved, not even a non-related peer or a close neighbor.
Friends figure importantly for Anglo children and for Negro boys.[6]
We might dismiss these findings as indicating mainly a distinctive
Barrio definition of the word "love," except that they are wholly
congruent with the overall pattern of home-centeredness so evident
in the Barrio protocols.

The older brothers, sisters, cousins, uncles and aunts who are
out of school are regarded in a variety of ways. They are accorded
mixtures of respect and affection, and they have some authority.
The jobs they hold can be described explicitly, often more so than
father's: "he [big brother] works in a furniture factory," "she
[older cousin] baby-sits for a secretary," "she [young aunt] types,
copies whatever they tell her." Several girls hope to be like these
slightly older relatives. The not-quite-adult members of the family
are looked upon as legitimate disciplinarians, particularly in settling quarrels between children.

Brothers and sisters in their own age range the children praise
and censure in about equal proportions. They play together, and
they fight together. Sisters have a way of calling names, and being
hated for it. One Barrio child calls her brother "stupid Negro,"
a label intended and understood as particularly insulting. The
children tend to be highly critical of their age mates, but not of
young people significantly older than themselves.

The youngest members of the family are mother's responsibility,
though many of the girls feel they have an active share in caring
for pre-schoolers. They give the little ones wagon rides, teach
them to play "catch," or just make them laugh. The girls do not seem
to feel that this is a burden. They think that even two-year-olds
should know how to play, talk, walk, write, "color," and "be good."
Only two children mentioned unpleasant things two-year-olds may do:
they know how "to bite" and "to fight."

Since most job-holding family members leave home before the
children's breakfast, and the school children are gone until afternoon, it is not until evening that the family has a chance to be
together. Supper is a family affair; father's return from work sets
its time, even though many children are indoors earlier, particularly
in winter. The norm is that everybody eats together. The houses of
El Barrio are small, the families large, yet we heard one, and only
one, comment about lack of space: "It gets kinda crowded sometimes."

Weekend routines, like the rest of life, are home-centered.
They differ from school-week routines mainly in allowing more time
for play, television, and household chores. In three families the

children are sometimes taken to visit relatives in other parts of the city. Most of them go to church on Sunday mornings.

Television viewing is a favorite pastime at almost any hour day or evening. Barrio people are most likely to watch in the evening, around suppertime and after, when custom dictates "resting and letting the food go down." For children the popular viewing times are, in order: early evening of any weekday, Saturday morning when cartoons come one after the other, afternoons after school, and anytime on Sunday. Only one family does without a set, a deprivation sorely felt by the girls of the household. More than half the children stay up beyond nine o'clock to watch late TV shows. In the close quarters of the house, one might surmise that the set is a dominant feature. It may be impracticable to restrict viewing hours. In fact, bedtime often seems to be set in terms of programs to be seen. A few boys and girls spoke of doing homework or chores before watching, but they were rare. One young lady says she watches all the time, except, perhaps, when she is mopping in the kitchen and cannot see the set.

The boys prefer programs of high adventure and fighting. Girls have no taste for this sort of thing; they prefer comedies, especially those dealing with family situations. We have some evidence that the children learn from TV about certain social types and are inspired to emulate them. Models and ballerinas offer a glittering occupational goal to some of the girls. The boys admire the policemen, firemen, astronauts and "Green Berets."

A few succinct statements taken from our protocols will suggest salient features of relationships within the El Barrio home:
   (1) My aunt protects me from my brother and sister, mother takes me shopping, and father gives money (girl, age 10).
   (2) Q. When you do something bad, who yells at you?
       A. Almost everybody, because I am the littlest one (boy, age 10).
   (3) When I ask my grandmother a question, she says to ask my father and my father tells my big sister to go help me (boy, age 9).
The boundary between the inner core of home and the periphery of neighborhood is blurred. In part this is because many of the neighbors are also relatives. Eddie lives with his grandparents, uncles and aunts, just a block away from his mother, stepfather, and their children. Some neighbors of long standing have won the kind of respect and appreciation ordinarily felt for relatives. There is Mrs. Guzman, who is regarded as a great person because she has helped other families in times of trouble. There is a "storekeeper lady" who has given fruit to the children. Small incidents cumulate, the children discuss them among themselves, and form their own consensus about El Barrio society.

The story of Eddie's escapade, pieced together from interviews with several children, serves as a prototype of how the children share in neighborhood gossip. Eddie had saved up enough money to go to the movies. He persuaded his friend to go with him, at night, without telling any adult about it. He later told us it was a very bad thing to do--to worry his grandparents, aunts and uncles. His partner in crime was punished, and Eddie "got in big trouble." Eddie's stepbrother heard all about the "big trouble" and felt that Eddie was a very bad person to stay out so late. The stepsister says it is a bad thing when someone stays out late and worries everybody. Going to the movies at night became a cause cèlebre.

The boys are impressed by certain rules, and they explained their importance to us. Rock fights are forbidden; about this Barrio adults present to the children a united front. They were united too when they called a halt to playing in the ditch where men were building a road. Inter-sibling quarrels are strongly but not severely discouraged in Barrio homes. We asked: "When you fight with your brother(s) or sister(s) what does your mother do?" The Mexican children, boys especially, report mainly that they are spanked or "hit," but not whipped. Anglo children claim they are likely to be whipped or scolded. The reports of the Negro children of both sexes emphasize whipping ("whuppin'"). Of the three groups it is the Negroes who are most likely to be encouraged to "fight back."

The Barrio

Other gossip, current at the time of interviewing, involved the arrival of a few Negroes in the Barrio. Attitudes were mixed. Members of a Negro family had been seen fighting in the street. This the children found shocking. Fights should be contained within one's own house. If children fight, "We tell their parents, and they take them in and spank them."

The Barrio is a rather closed society and difficult for any newcomer, even Mexican Americans, to penetrate. Two sisters, ages 8 and 10, recently had moved from their parent's hometown some seventy miles away. The girls are keenly aware of being outsiders. They constantly hark back fondly to life in their small native town. Jo Ann sighed, "I don't know where anyone lives here."

Although there are in the Barrio many transients and unattached inhabitants, the children made no comments about them to us. The small grocery store, a favorite stopping place in the morning, was often mentioned but there was no mention of the Barrio's taxi dance hall, or of the bars. The boys play soccer or baseball in the park sometimes. A pair of older girls, close chums, may walk around the park. However, most of the children who play in the afternoons jump rope, play tag or "catch" around their own houses. "Indoors by dark, or when Father comes home from work," is the rule.

In their movements through the neighborhood the children must certainly observe outsiders and people they have been warned against, e.g., winos, prostitutes, and action-seekers of other sorts. But the action-seekers seem to be remote to the young, whose focus of attention is on children's pursuits. The firm demarcation between El Barrio "insiders" and "outsiders" no doubt also works to put the latter on the periphery of attention. The fact that transients are for the most part men may be significant, because the young of the more stable families live mainly in a world of women. It seems likely that the boys we interviewed, the older ones particularly, are well aware of street corner men and other action-seekers. It is reasonable to suppose that some of the boys admire these types. Their complete silence in the matter suggests a careful avoidance. It may be that they have learned already a male code of silence about men's pursuits outside the home.

There are "buffers" between the stable families and the action-seekers, but they cannot be depended upon fully to isolate children from the action-seeker society and mores. As the children of the less cohesive family units grow older, and are less subject to family rules, some will probably join the action-seekers. Two cases are illustrative of the many variables at work.

Eddie, who sneaked off to the movies, is in a difficult position. He is like the children in one other household in that he is cared for solely by his grandparents, but he is unique in having younger step-siblings living nearby. The tightly knit inner circle of El Barrio, with its shared fund of gossip, tends to accentuate the peculiarities of Eddie's position. Even if he is never the instigator of another cause celèbre, the "villagers" are not likely to forget that or any later indiscretions. On the other hand, Eddie has much "going for him." He is responsive and intelligent. He feels a great deal of respect, affection, and appreciation for his grandparents. He is twelve years old now, an altar boy at church. He wants to be like an astronaut, but he expects only to finish high school and then work as a fireman. If he were without notable personal resources we would be uncertain whether he might in three or four years identify with the action-seekers and take up their life style. In view of his assets that seems unlikely.

The Coulombo girls are not as fortunate as Eddie. Aged 8 and 9 years, they have two younger sisters and three younger brothers, bearing two other last names. Theirs is probably the poorest home in the neighborhood, and the only one lacking a recognized male household head. Mother works in a laundry during the day. The interviewer notes that one of the girls "was shy and reserved and sometimes barely audible," the other "loud and inattentive. ...sometimes her answers didn't make sense. Giggled a lot for no reason at all." Both girls are still in first grade. Having neither cohesive family nor strong personal attributes it is quite likely that as they grow up these girls will gravitate toward the action-seekers and perpetuate their mother's life style.

El Barrio action-seekers are for the most part detached individuals men and women who have no children, or none of school age living in the Barrio. Among action-seekers there are a few young toughs, street-corner boys, whose wives live in the households maintained by the man's parents. Some have very young children. But the seamy side of Barrio life--the side sustained by resident action-seekers and by action-seeking transients and visitors to El Barrio--is practiced by few of the adults who live in the households of our child informants. At home they are exposed mainly to a routine-seeking life style.

Outside the Barrio

The children's only regularly recurring departure from the neighborhood is their trek to school each day. The detached observer may note the hazards of the trip (e.g., traffic; railroad crossings), but the children find this a time "to play con los muchachitos" (with the boys and girls), to have little adventures, and for such minor entertainments as "throwing mud at ants." In the morning there may be a stop at the store to buy something to add to lunch, and here they may meet their friends. The trucks and cars going by are fun to watch, and if the first graders cannot be trusted to stop and wait for traffic, older brothers and sisters are charged with looking after them. The only danger the children see is the chance of being late if a long train should block the railroad tracks that must be crossed.

From the child's point of view school is divided into two parts, work and play. Very few of our informants are enthusiastic about the work, but if they must rank subjects (as we asked them to do), the boys favor arithmetic, the girls favor spelling and reading. There seems to be no relationship between subject preference and whether a child is up to grade level for his age.

Evaluations of the teacher's efforts are largely in terms of the "work" part of school. "My teacher is good, because she teaches us how to read in arithmetic," or "she lets us talk softly after we have finished our work." One teacher is a favorite because she lets the children stop at her home for help after school. Teachers' disciplinary measures--yelling, spankings and whippings--are reported by more than half our informants.

The play portion of school hours--the recess, lunch hour, and just "fooling with friends"--is not considered part of a learning experience because it is not work. It is the best part of school though. Few denied that.

The schools the children attend are integrated, and in describing their classmates, many spontaneously mention ethnicity. Only two state a preference for Latins, however, and three think the "other kind" (i.e., Negroes) is better.

The children--three-fourths of them--know that their parents and siblings care about their work and progress at school. It is the mother especially who expresses interest, but only a third of the children report comment as specific as "You ought to learn more."

It is likely that few parents are able to give much help with home-work. This we infer from the low average level of their education and from remarks such as "My mother tells me if she knows," "My teacher tells me to look into a book and find the answer," and "If it's not for school, mother will help me."

In the world of school the Barrio children are often at a dis-advantage. Many of them go to summer school in hope of catching up. Some have at school a friend who is not of the Barrio; e.g., "My best friend is John. I never go [to his house]. I just see him at school." The physical distance between school and home--some six to nine blocks--is much less than the social and cultural distance.

Throughout the interviews, the _muchachitos_ show us that from their vantage point what is beyond El Barrio is far indeed. Small excur-sions loom large in their recollections; a class excursion, a fishing trip with grandfather, a trip downtown with mother--these are import-ant and big events. Only one child has been to Mexico, or anywhere else at all remote. In the close-at-hand world of the Barrio the children center their activities, their interests, and find their heroes and models. Members of their own households are most numerous among the people they admire. Only a local garage mechanic, one teacher, and a few television characters figure as admired but non-household people.

Values

The children's views on what is good or bad, their likes and dislikes, the people they admire or dislike, and their hopes and wishes for the future--these provide our major clues to their values. We are of course aware that they no doubt spoke to us largely in terms of ideal patterns, and that ideal patterns may diverge con-siderably from behavioral patterns. But the ideal patterns offered us by the Negro and Anglo children are quite different from those of the Barrio, and it is reasonable to suppose that their behavioral patterns differ too. Ideal pattern statements are prime indicators of the standards to which a people aspire and teach their children to accept as proper standards. Without such standard-setting and such teaching children are unlikely even to pay lip service to values which run counter to ego impulses, immediate gratifications, and the gross acquisitiveness which seems to appear in the cultures of all urban industrial societies. Among Barrio children, though not among Negro and Anglo children, the ideal patterns run strongly counter to these orientations.

The Barrio children value their parents and other kin, of all ages. No one and nothing takes precedence over kin in their values hierarchy. In this the Mexican Americans are unlike the Anglo and Negro children, who are much more oriented toward age-mates and friends.

For Barrio children the "good thing to do" is also the pleasurable

94

thing. In this linkage they are not unlike the Anglo and Negro youngsters. But in the Barrio protocols there appears another value linked with the good and the pleasurable--an "others-orientation" reminiscent of what has been reported for Japanese children (Goodman 1957). This others-orientation is a matter of concern for and sensitivity to the feelings and wishes of people who are important to Ego. It is evident in such comments, from the Mexican children, as these: it is good "to play nice with my sisters and brothers," "to play ball with the boys when they want to," to do well at school [responding to parents' wishes], to be obedient, and to help around the house. In this frame of reference the "bad to do" things are largely the reverse side of the same values coin, but with stress on the badness of disobedience and of "talking back" to elders.

Work is valued. The El Barrio girls, more than the boys, have opportunities to work. More girls have earned money for their work. Both girls and boys accept work as they accept play; it is an expected, a taken-for-granted, part of life. It is good to work, bad if father does not have a job. One should not avoid work. We asked: "At your house, who works and what do they do?" Unlike the Anglo and Negro children, the Mexican children answered including those who help at home, as well as the wage earners; e.g., "My father fixes refrigerators. My sister takes care of the [younger] boys when I'm not here" (girl, 10 years old).

The Mexican children perhaps value work less for itself than as participation and contribution. In an industrial world's definition, work is closely allied with the acquisition of things and status. But for most of these children, whether they are describing careers or tasks at home, the stress is not on the activity itself, nor on the personal achievement. It is, rather, on the contribution made. In the family everybody works in his own way; this is a part of living, like enjoying family meals, watching a television show, or playing with other family members. "Helping," being part of a larger endeavor, fitting into the life at hand, this is the way they have learned to view the chores they perform--the sweeping, mopping, dishwashing, gardening, and taking out of trash.

Power, wealth, high prestige--these are either little valued or little thought about, one way or another. So we judge from the modest aspirations stated by the Mexican children. The future vocations they talk about represent few leaps from the humble roles their parents play. Television has given scope to a certain amount of fancy, but most of the children think of their futures in terms of the roles they have experienced directly--e.g., policeman, fireman, mother, secretary, teacher. It appears that in thinking of the future there is a pervading caution. For girls, however, even planning to go to work represents a certain amount of daring, because it is a departure from the roles of most mothers and most other adult women the girls know.

The same caution, the reaching for goals within easy reach, is reflected in responses when we asked: "If you could make three wishes and get what you wished for, what would you wish?" Only one child wished for money. The greatest number of wishes were for small things--a doll, coloring books, a new pair of shoes, perhaps a guitar. The second largest body of wishes were either abstract-- to be happy, to be smart, not to be afraid, or wishes for someone else--an education for my brother, for mother to be a teacher. In view of the modest circumstances of El Barrio it is perhaps not surprising that the tangible things the children wish for are on a modest scale. But Negro and Anglo children in equally low economic situations tend to reach for the moon. Possession, power and wealth are not wholly disdained by Barrio children; e.g., "I wish for my father to have a Cadillac." But such expressions are rare. Moreover, it should be noted that this wish is for the father, although we invited the child to state his wishes for himself.

Summary and Conclusions

We know now something of the child's-eye-view and of its wealth of detail, unimpaired by retrospection. In conclusion, we shall consider the Barrio children as we know them, and their present situation in relation to the larger context of the city and their prospects in that larger society.

El Barrio is a shrinking "village," physically and socially. There was once a public school in the neighborhood. It has been torn down. The Catholic Church has closed since the completion of our work with the children; services are held now in a new building north of the tracks. Over the last three years a number of Barrio houses have been vacated and demolished to make space for a new highway. The very magnitude of surrounding city growth accentuates neighborhood attrition.

The changes are unwelcome to Barrio people, both adults and children. The appearance of a few Negroes causes particularly lively comment and some expressions of shock, resentment or animosity. As yet, the Barrio children do not speak of leaving the neighborhood. They view the changes as wrong, rather than find fault with the home environment.

In appraising external, non-Mexican influences, we conclude that the children give equal weight to school and television. To be good in school is important, and it takes thought and effort. The goals attainable through schooling are distant and nebulous, whereas those made vivid on television can be tied in to everyday experiences. The Mexican children aspire mainly to simple and locally familiar work roles, and pay little attention to the glamour roles and the riches they see on television.

The remarkable solidarity of the majority of El Barrio homes goes far to explain the happy tranquility which colors the Barrio child's-eye-view. Training in helping, in discipline, and in respect

96

for others all occur early. Most children have numerous relatives who take active interest in them. It is a situation conducive to security, ego satisfaction, and a firm sense of identity.

There are, of course, some breaks in family cohesion. Low economic status has much to do with this; there are under-employed or non-working fathers in all three of our groups of children in low income areas. The Mexican ideal of the powerful male would seem to make economic impotence or severe limitations especially threatening. These fathers can hardly swell with pride in their performance as providers, nor can they command respect from their children on this basis. However, most Barrio fathers do command respect, and most Barrio households in which there are school-age children do have fathers, legally and functionally.

On average the children aspire to jobs somewhat better than those their adult relatives now have, and they seem aware that job holding means responsibilities. They have no soaring expectations, but rather, a quiet hope, and a tendency to observe and evaluate their situation and their life chances rather realistically. That quiet hope of the children has its parallel among the grown-ups. In the larger study, of which this child study is a part, our research group has learned that the mood of the Mexican-American community in Houston tends to be expansive and optimistic. Anglo prejudice is lessening, the Spanish language is more accepted, things Mexican are gaining in popularity. The rapid industrial development of Mexico has no doubt helped to enhance the image of the nation and its customs, and of Mexican Americans as well. Certainly the Mexican Americans now take a considerable pride in their ethnic heritage.

It is our impression that the life styles and values of the Barrio children are on the whole conducive to modest success in the contemporary urban society. It seems likely that their life chances are on average significantly better in this respect than those of the Negro children we interviewed, and perhaps almost as good as those of our Anglo informants. Barrio children in stable families-- and they are a large majority of the children we interviewed--are growing up without great ambition but with self-respect and with "character." A recent editorial in El Sol, the principal newspaper published by and for Mexican Americans in Houston, states clearly a sense of responsibility for self which we find well developed among stable families in the Barrio, and among their children. Referring to the federally-supported anti-poverty programs, El Sol said:

> The government can give us opportunity within certain limits, but in the end it is the individual that will determine if he succeeds or fails. One thing Washington cannot give is character (Guerra and Goodman 1968).

1. This study was begun in September, 1965. It will be continued through Summer, 1968.

The study is under the general direction of Mary Ellen Goodman. José de la Isla has served as Coordinator and as principal field worker.

We join in thanking the Texas Department of Mental Health and Mental Retardation for a grant in support of the early phases of the research, and the Center for Research in Social Change and Economic Development, Rice University, for continuing support. This Center-sponsored research was funded by The Advanced Research Projects Agency under ARPA Order No. 738 and monitored by the Office of Naval Research, Group Psychology Branch, under Contract Number N00014-67-A-0145-0001, NR 177-909.

We express also our deep appreciation to the sixteen persons--graduate students, undergraduates, and secretarial assistants--who have aided in important ways in the work of the project.

2. This statement refers to the "ethnographic present." The church is not in use now.

3. The Barrio interviewers are Ruben Gonzalez and Roberto Guerra. The interviews were conducted during the spring and summer of 1967.

4. Our reference to differences between groups (Barrio, Anglo, and Negro) are based on statistical significances. Where use of Chi might be feasible, a rough approximation of differences required [translated to percentages] was arrived at using Zubin's nomograph, as appears in Oppenheim. Note also that a given difference (say, fifteen percentage points) may be significant at the extremes, where one of the percentages approaches zero or one hundred, but not in the middle ranges (Oppenheim 1966:288). We present sample values in the mid-range, the largest differences required should two groups only be compared.

Significance Level	N_1=34, N_2=43	N_1=17, N_2=17	N_1=20, N_2=23
10%	58% and 42%	64% and 37%	63% and 38%
5%	62% and 40%	67% and 34%	65% and 36%
1%	65% and 35%	72% and 29%	69% and 31%

5. It was our intention to interview all Barrio children of first through sixth grades. We are short of that goal, but we have interviewed 75 percent of the school age children.

6. Question #113: Who do you love? (% of children giving response)

	Barrio		Anglo		Negro	
	M	F	M	F	M	F
Relatives, only	88	88	44	20	53	94
Non-relatives and relatives	--	--	56	80	35	6
No One	6	--	--	--	12	--
No Reply	6	12	--	--	--	--
	100	100	100	100	100	100

In the responses to this and to other questions as well, we have the interesting finding that a certain class of answers given by children of one group was absent in another.

REFERENCES

De La Isla III, José
  1968   Aspects of Social Organization of a Mexican-American
            Urban Barrio. Unpublished paper. Rice University
            Center for the Study of Social Change and Economic
            Development.
Dennis, Wayne
  1940   The Hopi Child. New York, Appleton-Century.
Gans, Herbert J.
  1962   The Urban Villagers. New York, The Free Press of
            Glencoe.
Goodman, Mary Ellen
  1957   Values, Attitudes, and Social Concepts of Japanese
            and American Children. American Anthropologist 59:
            979-999.
  1960   Children as Informants: The Child's-Eye-View of
            Society and Culture. The American Catholic Sociological
            Review 21:136-145.
  1962   Culture and Conceptualization: A Study of Japanese
            and American Children. Ethnology 1:374-386.
  1964   Race Awareness in Young Children. New York, Collier
            Books.
Guerra, Roberto and Mary Ellen Goodman
  1968   A Content Assessment of El Sol, A Community Newspaper.
            Unpublished paper. Rice University Center for the
            Study of Social Change and Economic Development.
Leighton, Dorothea and Clyde Kluckhohn

1947   Children of the People. Cambridge, Massachusetts, Harvard University Press.

Nadel, S. F.
    1937   A Field Experiment in Racial Psychology. British Journal of Psychology 28:195-211.

Oppenheim, A. N.
    1966   Questionnaire Design and Attitude Measurement. New York, Basic Books, Inc.

SCHEDULE

CHILD INTERVIEW

1. Interviewer_____Date_____Where interviewed_____
2. Name_____   4. Sex_____
3. Address_____   5. Age_____
    _____   6. Grade_____

Persons in Household

7. Father_____
8. Mother_____
9. Brothers_____ Age_____
10. Sisters_____ Age_____
11. Others in household, and relationship, if possible.

_____

12. What time do you get up?_____
13. Who gets you up?_____
14. Do you ever get up without anybody waking you up? Yes___ No___
15. Does somebody tell you what clothes to wear to school?
                                     Yes___ No___
16. Do you have breakfast before you go to school? Yes___ No___
17. Who fixes your breakfast?_____
18. What did you have for breakfast this morning?_____
19. Do you eat breakfast with somebody? Yes___ No___
20. If 'yes,' who eats breakfast with you?_____
21. How do you get to school? Walk_____ School Bus_____ Regular Bus_____ Some other way?_____
22. How much time does it take you to go to school in the morning?__
23. Do you stop on the way to school? Yes___ No___
24. If 'yes,' why do you stop?_____
25. What is the name of your school?_____
26. What kind of person is your teacher?_____
27. What kinds of kids are at your school?_____
28. Which kind of kids are best?_____
29. What are some good things your teacher does?_____
30. What are some bad things your teacher does?_____
31. What is your best subject at school?_____
32. Where do you eat lunch?_____
33. If at school, how do you get your lunch?_____

34. What is the most fun at school?_____
35. What is bad about school?_____
36. What time do you get out of school?_____
37. What do you do when you get out?_____
38. Where do you stop when you don't go straight home from school?
39. What do you do when you stop there?_____
40. What time do you usually get home?_____
41. Do you show your school work to anyone at home? Yes___ No___
42. If 'yes,' who do you show it to?_____
43. What does_____ say about it?_____
44. What do you do when you get home in the afternoon?_____
45. When do you have supper?_____
46. Who fixes your supper?_____
47. What did you have for supper last night?_____
48. Do you eat supper with anybody? Yes___ No___
49. If 'yes,' who eats with you?_____
50. What do you do after supper?_____
51. What time do you go to bed?_____
52. Who sleeps with you?_____
53. Who else sleeps in the same room with you?_____
54. Where does your best friend live?_____
    How many blocks is that from your house?_____
55. What do you do on Saturdays?_____
56. What do you do on Sundays?_____
57. What did you get for Christmas?_____
58. What did you give for Christmas?_____
59. What's the best thing that ever happened to you?_____
60. What's the worst thing that ever happened to you?_____
61. Where do you play after school? School yard_____
    Friend's house_____ Open lot_____ Playground_____
    Other place--what kind of place?_____
62. Do you have a friend who lives about 5 blocks away?
    Yes___ No___ 10 blocks away? Yes___ No___ Further away?
    Yes___ No___
63. When do you go over to the friend's house--The friend that
    lives_____ (the furthest distance) away?_____
64. Is there some place around here where you and your friends
    meet? Yes___ No___
65. If 'yes,' where do you get together?_____
66. Who's a great person that you know--somebody that lives around
    here?_____
67. How old is he/she?_____
68. What does he/she do?_____
69. Who else that you know is a great person?_____
70. How late do you stay out at night?_____
71. Who tells you what time to be home?_____
72. What happens if you don't come home at that time?_____
73. What is your favorite thing to play with?_____

74. What games do you play outside the house?_____
75. Which <u>one</u> of these would you rather have?
    Boys: little toy car   Girls: a doll
           building blocks   little playhouse
           toy rocket   coloring books
           comic books   comic books
76. What work do you do around the house?_____
77. What TV show do you like best?_____
78. Why do you like it best?_____
79. When do you watch TV?_____
80. Are there some days when you don't watch TV at all, even after
    dark? Yes___ No___
81. If 'yes,' why not?_____
82. Who do you want to be like when you grow up?_____
83. Tell me about him/her_____
84. Why do you want to be like him/her?_____
85. Where do your relatives live--your grandparents, aunts, uncles,
    and cousins?
    Relative:_____ Town:_____
86. Did you go to school before you went to 1st grade?
    Yes___ No___
87. If 'yes,' what is the name of that school?_____
88. What was good about that school?_____
89. What was bad about that school?_____
90. Who else around here went to a school before first grade?
    Names; first and last_____
91. What school(s) did he/they go to?_____
92. What should little kids about two years old know how to do?___
93. What is the first thing you remember from when you were a
    little kid?_____
94. When you fight with your brother(s) or sister(s) what does your
    mother do?_____
95. Who else does something?_____
96. What does___ (person just named) do?_____
97. What did you know how to do when you were about two years old?
98. When you want to know something--how to do something, or why
    something happens--who do you ask?_____
99. What does___ (person just mentioned) do when you ask?_____
100. What is something that's a good thing to do?_____
101. What else is good to do?_____
102. What is something that's a bad thing to do?_____
103. What else is bad to do?_____
104. What happens to kids who do this/these bad things?_____
105. Have you ever earned any money? Yes___ No___
106. If 'yes,' what have you done to earn money?_____
107. How else do you get money?_____
108. What do you do with your money?_____
109. When you do something bad, who yells at you?_____

102

110. Who else yells at you?_____
111. What else happens?_____
112. What do you think you'll be when you grow up?_____
113. Who do you love?_____
114. Why?_____
115. Who do you hate?_____
116. Why?_____
117. How far do you think you'll go in school?_____
118. At your house, who works and what do they do?_____
     Person; work_____
119. Who is President of the United States?_____
120. What town do you live in?_____
121. What state do you live in?_____
122. The United States is a big country. What are some other big
     countries?_____
123. If you could make three wishes and get what you wished for,
     what would you wish? (1)_____ (2)_____ (3)_____
INTERVIEWER'S REMARKS:_____

FOLK MEDICINE AND THE INTERCULTURAL JEST

Américo Paredes
University of Texas

This paper is a discussion of six jests collected in Spanish at the lower end of the Texas-Mexican border and presented here in English translation. They were part of several hundred texts recorded in 1962 and 1963, during a series of field trips in search of jests and legendary anecdotes that might reveal attitudes of Mexicans and Mexican Americans toward the United States.[1] I will attempt to relate them to Texas-Mexican attitudes toward culture change. They are not peculiar to the group from which they were recorded. Some of them have been collected from other Mexican groups, and their basic motifs are universal. The six were recorded from two informants, one narrator telling five, but I heard the same stories from other people during my collecting. It is the circumstances in which the texts were collected that I believe important, and for this reason I will describe them in some detail.

All six texts were collected on tape during two recording sessions at Brownsville, Texas, a bilingual and bicultural community. Jests of this sort are called tallas in the regional idiom, and they are told during regular talla sessions. Francisco J. Santamaría, the Mexican lexicographer, lists talla as a "Texas-Mexican barbarism" for any narrative, anecdote or jest, saying it is derived from the English "tale." This certainly would emphasize the intercultural character of the talla, were it not for the fact that Santamaría is wrong. Whatever the origins of talla, they certainly are not in "tale," to which it has merely a visual resemblance. Santamaría seems to have known, furthermore, that talla is found as far away from Texas as Costa Rica. The term may derive from the verb tallar, to rub or to chafe and by extension to tease. The talla as it is practiced in South Texas often does have a relationship to the Mexican word play known as the albur. Under these circumstances the jests are told as having happened to one of those present, or to one of their close relatives. The victims answer in kind, of course. Talla sessions are common occurrences along the border among males of all ages and at occasions varying from wakes to beer-drinking parties. Women rarely are present.

In collecting my first consideration was to recreate as closely as possible the circumstances of a talla session in its natural context. In Brownsville the sessions were held at a house just

outside of town, which happened to be vacant at the time. A group
of men would be invited, enough so that a total of ten to fifteen
people were present at one time, including the collector. Sessions
began around nine or ten at night and were held outside on the
darkened patio or the lawn, with the participants sitting in a circle. Outside the circle was a washtub full of beer and ice. Also
outside the circle was the tape recorder, but in a direction opposite to that of the tub with beer and just behind where the collector
sat. An empty beer case was placed in the middle of the circle, on
which the microphone rested on top of a cushion. The machine was a
four-track Revere set at a speed of 3 3/4 inches per second, recording one hour per track on a 7-inch tape. This made it possible to
record four hours on one tape without having to bother with the
machine more than three times during the night. Four hours was the
usual length of a session, from about ten until two in the morning.

The disadvantages to this method of collecting are the relatively poor quality of the recordings and the extreme tediousness
of transcription. A four-hour session might well result in a dozen
usable texts. But it is the best method I know for capturing the
free, unself-conscious idiom in which the jests are told. The informants knew they were being recorded, of course, but a fairly
natural atmosphere could be achieved after the first few minutes.
The beer was partly responsible, as was the fact that the microphone was barely visible in the dark, so that the group forgot about
it once beer and talk flowed freely. Most important, though, was
the presence at each session of one or two assistants planted among
the group, whose business it was to make the _talla_ session as
natural as possible and to elicit the kind of materials I was seeking without having to ask the informants for them. Their first
job was to get everybody in the right mood by passing out the beer
and making the usual small talk. The main purpose of my collecting,
however, was to tape-record jokes and other lore about Anglo Americans. So the "plant" went on to tell some familiar joke on the
subject, usually one of the large cycle of jests I have tentatively
labeled the "Stupid American" joke. Since those invited were chosen
because of their abilities as narrators, they responded with jests
of their own, one story suggesting another. The "plant" had one
other important function. The party sometimes wandered off in other
directions, into small talk or verbal dueling, for example, or into
reminiscing and sentimental songs. The "plant" tried to bring
things back into line by telling another of his stories, usually
texts I had already collected. He could do this as long as he stayed
sober himself, something that did not always happen.

The main purpose of my field trip, as has been said, was to
collect folklore making covert or direct expression of attitudes
toward Anglo Americans and their culture. Materials were recorded
in between a series of digressions that the "plants" attempted to
control and redirect toward our agreed-on objective. On first

examining the transcribable texts I brought back with me, I set aside the six discussed here as belonging with the digressions rather than with the material I was looking for. Americans scarcely appear in them. In No. 6 we do have a character of the "Stupid American" stereotype, but it is the Mexican villagers who appear in a ridiculous light rather than he.

All six of the stories do have in common a general situation: there is a sick person, and a group of people seek a cure for him. It is not the patient himself but his family or the community as a whole that seeks help. A doctor or healer is found, who recommends a cure with varying results. Nos. 1 through 5 all are concerned in one way or another with Mexican folk curing practices. Only in No. 6 is curanderismo absent, but the story is a variant of other curandero jests known to the collector in which it is the folk healer who recommends the wrong purgative to the patient, or the right purgative to the wrong person. That is to say, all six jests are parodies of a folktale type known to Latin American folklorists as the caso and sometimes called the "belief tale" in the United States-- a relatively short narrative about miraculous or extraordinary events supposed to have happened to the narrator or to someone he knows. The particular type of caso parodied here is based on a formula well known to students of curanderismo, a simple pattern pitting the curandero against medical science, with science driven from the field in utter confusion.

Somebody falls ill and is taken to a doctor, but the doctor can do nothing for him. The patient gets worse and worse. There may be a consultation attended by several doctors, "a meeting of the doctors," as the casos put it, but the men of science cannot find the cause of the disease or recommend a cure. Or perhaps they say the patient is beyond hope of recovery. Again, they may recommend a painful and costly operation requiring a long stay at the hospital. Then someone suggests going to Don Pedrito or Don Juanito or some other curandero. The patient's relatives are skeptical at first but they finally agree. The whole group journeys to the curandero, who receives them kindly but chides the doubters about their skepticism, which he has learned about by miraculous means even before they arrived. Then he asks a standard question, seemingly unnecessary for his diagnosis but very important to the structured arrangement of the narrative, "And what do the doctors say?"

He is told what the doctors say, and he smiles indulgently at their childish ignorance. Then he prescribes some deceptively simple remedy: an herb perhaps, drinking three swallows of water under special circumstances three times a day, washing at a certain well or spring, or the like. The patient recovers completely. There may be a sequel in which the former patient goes and confronts the doctors. They are surprised, incredible. They visit the old curandero, seeking to find out the secret of the cure. The old man tells them nothing, or he will answer in words such as, "God cured him, not I." The doctors leave, chastened and still mystified.

A number of these casos have been current in south Texas and northern Tamaulipas for generations, most often in association with the saintly figure of Dan Pedrito Jaramillo, the famed healer of Los Olmos, Texas. Ruth Dodson published a number of stories related to Don Pedrito, first in Spanish and later in English translation (Dodson 1934, 1951). More recently, Octavio Romano has studied Don Pedrito as a charismatic figure (Romano 1965). Not all curandero belief tales follow the strict pattern of this formula, though it is perhaps the most widely retold. Another important narrative pattern deals with the scoffer who comes to the curandero pretending to be ill, merely to ridicule or expose him. The curandero punishes him by causing him to have a debilitating and embarrassing case of diarrhea.

The function of the curandero belief tale among Mexican folk groups is clear enough. It helps bolster belief in folk medicine; it encourages acceptance by the younger generation of the old traditions, especially when the group must live among an increasingly skeptical majority. This may be equally true whether the Mexican folk group is living in the United States or across the border in Mexico, since Mexican physicians are at times even more intolerant of folk medicine than their Anglo-American counterparts. But this type of caso plays an important role among rural and semirural Mexican groups in the United States, who see their folk culture assailed not only by modern science and technology but by the belief patterns of rural Anglo-American neighbors, who may have their own folk beliefs but tend to be contemptuous of those held by foreigners.

It is this type of belief tale that is parodied in jests such as the six we are considering. They quite consciously mock the defenses set up by the curandero belief tales, and they express an equally conscious rejection of the folk culture holding such beliefs. On the surface they represent as violent a rejection of Mexican values as that of William Madsen's Mexican American from Hidalgo county, Paul, who wishes he could get the Mexican blood out of his veins and change it for something else (Madsen 1964:43).

Pertinent is the fact that parodies of curandero belief tales are widespread among Mexican Americans, certainly one of the reasons why these six intruded into a session of "Stupid American" jokes. The earliest printed example I know of appeared in the Journal of American Folklore in 1914 in one of Aurelio M. Espinosa's collections of New Mexican folklore. It is a variant of our No. 6, except that it is a curandero rather than a veterinarian who gives the purgative to the wrong person. It works, though, so the curandero justifies his action, saying, "Haciendo la cosa efecto, no importa que sieso sea." ("As long as the thing works, who cares whose ass it was?") (Espinosa 1914, Text No. 48). In the late 1920's, when the celebrated

107

Niño Fidencio was curing the sick, the halt and the blind in Nuevo León, Mexico, similar stories were circulated along the border about some of his cures. In one he cured a hunchback by breaking his spine. The hunchback screamed, "I'm dying!"

"But you'll die straight," Fidencio replied.

These are, of course, adaptations of other stories ranging much farther in space and time. All six contain universal motifs found in Stith Thompson's Motif-Index of Folk-Literature, either under J2450, "Literal fools" or J2412, "Foolish imitation of healing." Nos. 5 and 6 resemble Spanish folktales about the numskull who is told to bathe his grandmother in hot water and boils her to death instead. Or he is told to clean a child, so he cuts its belly open and takes out the intestines. Nos. 2 and 3, especially No. 2, are based on motifs listed by Thompson under B700, "Fanciful traits of animals." There are several methods by which animals that have introduced themselves into people's stomachs are disposed of. For example, in B784.2.1, reported from Ireland, Italy, and the United States, "The patient is fed salt or heavily salted food and allowed no water for several days. He then stands with mouth open before a supply of fresh water, often a running brook. The thirsty animal emerges to get fresh water." Thompson does not tell us if the animal is then beaten to death. Then there is motif B784.2.1.2, reported from India, about which Thompson tells us, "A husband ties a cock near his wife's feet so that a snake-parasite in her stomach will come out to catch the cock. The snake is then killed by the husband." Thompson does not tell us how the snake comes out of the woman's body, an important omission especially for the psycho-analytically oriented investigator. It might also be worth mentioning that we could find parallels to these jests somewhat nearer at hand; No. 6 is very much like North American sick jokes.

The prevalence of feces and other anal motifs as a source of humor in our jests certainly would interest the psychoanalyst. This characteristic may reflect influence from one type of curandero belief tale discussed above, seriously told and believed but causing mirth instead of wonder, when the listener thinks of the discom-fiture suffered by the skeptic inflicted with diarrhea. At least, this points to a favorite source of humor among groups telling the same tales. But it is the other caso formula--in which the curandero vanquishes medical science--that is alluded to in Texts 1 through 5, all beginning very much in the serious belief tale style but becoming tallas when the ending takes a ludicrous twist, by means of which the curandero and his methods are satirized.

Text No. 1 reproduces the sequel following many of the casos, when the doctors come to the curandero and humbly seek to know the secret of his powers--truly a triumph of folk healing over medical science. But our curandero is not reticent about explaining his methods, nor does he attribute his success to divine power. His answer, in fact, has a logic all its own, based on a folkish kind of empiricism one might say. The hit-or-miss character of many folk remedies, their far-fetched sense of causality, and the actual use of drug in curanderismo all come in for ridicule.

Texts Nos. 2 and 3 are variants of the same tale, based on an old and widely traveled motif, B784.2, "Means of ridding person of animal in stomach." It is significant that they were told by the same informant in the order given, 2 before 3, so that No. 3 is an emphatic restatement of No. 2. This jest includes a good part of the belief tale formula: A man falls gravely ill. He is taken to the hospital, where nothing is done for him. Hospital personnel recommend an operation, something the unsophisticated Mexican American dreads. Madsen, for example, reports that for his Hidalgo county informants the hospital is the most dreaded place next to prison and that hospitalization "can become a nightmarish experience when surgery is involved..." (Madsen 1964:93-94). Frightened by the prospect of an operation, the relatives take the patient to the curandero, who asks the formal question, "And what did they say at the hospital?" The hospital wants to operate, but the curandero is reassuring. No operation is necessary; he will cure the patient without much trouble. Up to this point the joke and the belief tale follow more or less identical lines, and it is at this point that the ridiculous is introduced.

There are some other features about Nos. 2 and 3 that should be noted before passing on to the other jests, even though they do not pertain to our belief tale formula. The action is set in Hidalgo county though the story was recorded in the county of Cameron. The narrator first calls the curandero "Don Pedrito," evidently in reference to the celebrated Don Pedrito Jaramillo, though he forgets later and calls him "Don Juanito." Still later, in No. 3, the curandero becomes "Don Fulanito"--Mr. John Doe or Mr. Such-and-Such, making him just any folk healer. More interesting still is the matter of the hospital. According to the belief tale formula the patient's family refuses to put him in the hospital because of their horror of operations, or the American doctors do get him into the hospital but are unable to find a cure. It is different with our bracero's friends, who do want him treated there. Nor do they question at this point the ability of the American doctors to make the patient well. The hospital attendants refuse to admit the patient, and it is because of this that he is taken to the curandero. If we keep this in mind, the emphatic character of the second variant, Text No. 3, becomes significant. The same pattern is stated, but in stronger terms. The demand for money on the part of the hospital staff is emphasized by putting it into English, "Who's gonna pay?" pronounced in a drawling, decidedly unpleasant tone. The "All right. Get out!" of No. 2 becomes "All right. Get out, cabrones!"[2] Even the gentle old curandero suffers a change with his, "There'll be no fuckin operation!" The narrator has warmed up to his theme, whatever his theme may be. At least we can be sure that he intends to be more than merely funny.

Text No. 4 makes an interesting contrast with Nos. 2 and 3. Again the setting is in Hidalgo county, and again the curandero's name is Don Pedrito. But in this story the American doctor is sympathetic; he offers to take the sick girl to the hospital. It is the girl's family who decide to take her to Don Pedrito because he "never goes around recommending operations." Up to this point the jest closely follows not only the usual pattern of the curandero belief tale but also certain supposedly factual cases reported by nonbelievers in curanderismo, in which Mexican Americans are said to have died of such things as appendicitis rather than go to a hospital. Satire begins when Don Pedrito is shown in anything but a humble or saintly mood; he calls the American doctors a bunch of cabrones. His diagnosis of what the doctor has called appendicitis is a parody of such folk diseases as mollera caída and susto pasado (fallen fontanelle and an advanced case of fright sickness).[3] Also satirized is the belief, often encountered by collectors, that only Mexicans can get "Mexican" diseases like ojo and susto, though it should be mentioned that one encounters just as often belief tales about Anglo Americans who are healed by curanderos. Almost twenty percent of Don Pedrito Jaramillo's cures as related by Ruth Dodson are said to have been done to Anglo Americans (1934:129-146).

At first glance No. 5 seems to be different from the preceding four jests, but it really is based on one small part of the belief tale formula we have been considering: the actual treatment of the patient by the curandero. The rubbing down with alcohol is prescribed by curanderos and by old-fashioned M.D.'s alike for any number of ailments. In the original Spanish the doctor prescribes that an egg (huevo) be put on the patient's forehead, huevo being such a common synonym for "testicle" that many prudish people avoid the word altogether, substituting it with blanquillo. The use of an egg and of ashes, however, will be recognized by those familiar with Mexican folk medicine as part of the treatment for diseases like susto and ojo. Even the doctor's reassurance to the patient's family at the beginning, that "It's not as bad as all that," is part of the curandero belief tale formula. Medical science has made a great deal of fuss over the patient's illness, but it will be an easy thing for the curandero to make the patient well. It is obvious that the M.D. in this story really is a curandero is disguise. The sense of the ridiculous is heightened by having an M.D. playing the part of the curandero, or vice-versa, but we must also keep in mind that the doctor to whom the joke is attributed is a Mexican-American. The jest is not identified with any particular doctor, by the way. Even the same narrator will use different names in retelling the story, but the name of a real Mexican-American doctor always is used, most often one that the narrator's hearers know well. I can attest to having heard this same informant tell the same jest downtown, away from a tape recorder, using the name of a different Mexican-

American doctor.

Text No. 6 does not seem to go with the others at all; as it stands there is no _curanderismo_ involved. But a comparison with No. 5 reveals an identical plot structure: a naive group of Mexicans misinterpret instructions for the treatment of a patient, with fatal results for the patient, the ending in both cases being very much like that of the "cruel" or "sick" joke common in North American urban lore. The characters giving medical instructions in the two stories also bear comparison. The American veterinarian is portrayed as a likable simpleton, along the lines of the "Stupid American" stereotype. But he is working for the Aftosa commission, engaged in slaughtering the Mexican peasant's cattle to control the hoof-and-mouth disease, and thus a much resented figure. The Mexican-American doctor, on the other hand, acts like a _curandero_ and thus is comically seen as "one of our boys," but he is also a representative of American medical science and American culture and therefore must share some of the resentments generated by inter-cultural conflicts.

It is this double nature of our texts that makes them especially interesting. In the satirizing of folk medicine and _curandero_ belief tales they express a mocking rejection of Mexican folk culture; in their expression of resentment toward American culture they show a strong sense of identification with the Mexican folk.

The texts, as has been said, were recorded during two sessions in Brownsville, Cameron county, Texas, a bilingual and bicultural community with an influential Mexican-American middle class including doctors, lawyers, teachers, well-to-do merchants, and individuals in elective and appointive public office. These are for the most part descendants of the old Mexican settlers of the region, people with their roots in a past when Brownsville was a "Mexican" town rather than immigrants or children of immigrants from Mexico. By usual North American standards they would belong to the middle class; according to Madsen's class divisions for Mexican Americans in Hidalgo county, they would be "upper class" (Madsen 1964:41-43). The participants in the _talla_ recording sessions were bilingual males between the ages of twenty-five and fifty-five. They speak good English and have received advanced education in American colleges and universities. They play important roles in community life, not in the life of a "Mexican colony" but in that of the city and the county as a whole. In other words, they would seem to be completely acculturated, having adapted to American culture and functioning in it in a very successful way. At the same time, when they are away from the courtroom, the school, the office, or the clinic and congregated in a group of their own, they think of themselves as _mexicanos_. Not only will they speak Spanish among themselves, but it is quite obvious that they place a high value on many aspects of Mexican culture and are proud of the duality of their background. They do in a sense live double lives, functioning as Americans in the affairs of the community at large and as Mexicans within their own closed circle.

In each of the two sessions groups of about a dozen individuals of the type described told jests of the "Stupid American" type, in which tension and hostility toward the majority culture were expressed in joking situations. The _curandero_ parodies were introduced into this context by two of the informants, one at each session. Text No. 5 was told by a lawyer, a friend of the doctor to whom the story was attributed in this particular variant. The doctor was not present at the session. Had he been present the joke might have been interpreted in another way, as part of a verbal duel, with the doctor replying by telling a joke about lawyers in which his friend would have been the main character. This is one way the _talla_ is performed, as was said in discussing the probable origins of the word. In this case, however, the doctor's name was used because he is well known and representative. The narrator practices criminal law; his work brings him into contact with many Mexican Americans of the poorer class, much less acculturated than himself, who are usually in trouble when they come to him. His knowledge of Spanish gains him their confidence, and his Mexican background leads him to identify with them in many ways, but his profession demands that he comport himself in the role of an American lawyer functioning in an American court rather than assuming a "Mexican" role as he does when he is with a group of intimates. Many things repressed in the courtroom find an outlet in the _talla_ sessions. The lawyer always has amusing anecdotes to tell within his own group, some of them revealing the comic naiveté of his clients, others showing their folk wit and hardheaded common sense.

Texts Nos. 1, 2, 3, 4, and 6 were told by the same person, one of the best narrators I know. Only a sound recording can show his sense of intonation and mimicry, and even then his gestures are lost. He told all five stories in the same session, but not consecutively since he was alternating with other narrators present. It is quite clear, however, that one tale brought another to his mind. These are not his stories any more than No. 5 belongs to the lawyer alone. They are common property, but this informant is recognized as telling them better than most other people do. He works for a school system somewhere in Cameron county, and his job brings him into contact--at times into conflict--with Mexican-American parents of the laboring classes. He also has his anecdotes about his job: the naiveté of some of the parents he deals with, their lack of understanding of American values, their reluctance to keep their children in school. Often he parodies these people when he is among his own group. Just as often he will become exasperated with his job, complaining that his work shows no results, that he is butting his head against a stone wall. He seems sincerely committed in his efforts to raise the educational level of Mexican Americans in the county and is emotionally involved in the situation.

The two informants are typical of their group. They are socially conscious members of the middle class, impatient about the slow

acculturation of the average Mexican American and his low economic
and social status. At the same time, they reveal a strong feeling
of identification with the unacculturated Mexican. They are highly
acculturated Mexican Americans who value their ancestral culture in
spite of such aspects as curanderismo, which they would include
among the things the Mexican American must reject in order to com-
pete successfully in an English-speaking world. But their attitude
toward the curandero is not a hostile one. They will admit that
some of these old men are pretty good psychologists in their own
way, and they also point out with evident pride that many Mexican
herbs have been put to use by modern medical science. Furthermore,
the belief in curanderismo is something in their own recent past.
Such celebrated curanderos as Don Pedrito Jaramillo were patronized
a half-century ago not only by the poor and illiterate but by many
of the land-owning families of the area. Some of those present during the talla session I recorded had been treated by curanderos in
their early childhood. So there is identification on the part of
the group not only with the unacculturated Mexican but with
curanderismo itself. This is most clearly seen in No. 5, in which
the curandero's role is given to a highly acculturated Mexican-American physician, an absent member of the group in which the tale was
told.

Curanderismo for this group is a subject viewed with a good
deal of ambivalence, but the ambivalent attitude is anything but rare
in jokes. The best dirty jokes about priests and nuns are told by
Catholics; to be truly effective, the contemporary "cruel" or "sick"
joke has to be told among people who are highly sensitive to human
suffering. The curandero jests release a complicated set of conflicting emotions ranging from exasperation to affection in respect
to the unacculturated Mexican American, coupled with a half-conscious
resentment toward the Anglo-American culture. Also involved is a
definite element of masochism, often expressed in the proverbial
phrase, "¡Ah, que mexicano!" (Ah, what a Mexican!) used to express
jesting disapproval of some bumbling or foolish act. We must keep
in mind that members of this group are quite explicit in identifying
themselves as mexicanos, and that the above phrase is used only in
Spanish, never in English.

So these jests are not after all intrusions into a session of
stories expressing intercultural conflict; they also are expressions
of the same kind of conflict. Only in No. 4 does the doctor, representative of American culture, appear in a favorable light. In Nos.
2 and 3 the matter is quite explicit. The poor bracero must go to
the folk healer because he is refused treatment at the American
hospital. The curandero asks for so little--a small fee or a gift,
something the poorest laborer can pay. One does not have to be a
rich man to visit Don Fulanito. Many such incidents are seriously
told by Mexican Americans of the poorer classes. We find the same
subject-matter here in jokes, told by people who can afford to be

treated at hospitals, but the stories are not quite in the comic vein. There is a good deal of emotional involvement, which members of the group would readily acknowledge among themselves, and that gives an edge to the humor. They may tell you, with a kind of self-directed exasperation, about Mexican laborers who died of appendicitis because they refused to go to a hospital. But they will also tell you other stories of Mexican laborers who died for lack of attention, and it is obvious that these stories arouse their resentment.

Why the events in Nos. 2, 3, and 4 are placed in Hidalgo rather than in Cameron county I am not prepared to say. It may be that Mexican Americans in Cameron county feel that their people in Hidalgo live under worse conditions than they do. It may be a narrative device, placing the action at some distance from narrator and audience. If such is the case, it is worth noting that the device is not a comic one. The comedian uses the opposite approach, relating his story to familiar events and to people close at hand. The introduction of people in the narrator's audience as characters in his jests has been mentioned as typical of one of the aspects of the talla session, when it becomes a verbal contest. Narrators tend to place events some distance away for reasons other than comedy. If characters and events are very far away, in a distant time and a distant land, the effect is one of wonder and romance. But to achieve a feeling of verisimilitude, required in the legendary anecdote, events are placed not too far off—in the next town, the next hollow, or the next county. This again is evidence that these jests are not intended to be as funny as they appear on the surface.

This is not, then, a relatively simple case of second-generation Americans ridiculing the culture of their ancestors and thereby rejecting it. As parodies of the curandero type of belief tale the jests do express the Mexican American's rejection of his traditional culture. But combined with parody is a good deal of resentment against Anglo-American culture, expressed in a stereotypic view of American physicians and hospital attendants as caring little about Mexican patients of the poorer, less educated class. Since the informants are not poor and badly educated themselves but belong to the middle class, the ambivalence of their attitudes is quite marked. Members of the group telling the jests have not lost the feeling that beneath their Americanized exterior they still are mexicanos. There is an underlying conflict between their Spanish-Mexican heritage and an Anglo-American culture they have embraced intellectually without completely accepting it emotionally, in great part because Anglo-American culture rejects part of themselves. The jests help resolve these conflicts brought about by acculturation, involving not only a change from rural to urban values but from a basically Mexican culture to the generalized, English-speaking culture of the majority.

TEXT I

They tell about an old man who was a _curandero_, that they brought him a patient who was sick in the stomach. And he said, "Give him goat turds."

Said, "But what do you mean, give him goat turds!"

"Yes," he said, "Boiled."

Well, so they did it, and the man got well. And then there was a meeting of physicians. Said, "Listen, man," he said. "We never could find out what was wrong with him. And he got well with goat turds."

So they called the old _curandero_. Said, "Well, why did you give goat turds to this man?"

He said, "It's very simple. Because I knew the ailment he had," he said, "could be cured with some sort of herb. But I didn't know which one," he said. "And since goats eat all kinds of weeds and herbs, I knew the plant that was needed would be there in the shit."

Informant No. 24
Brownsville, Texas
October 20, 1962

TEXT II

They went to see Don Pedrito about a poor _bracero_ who was around there in Hidalgo county, and this poor man got up one night to get a drink of water and he swallowed a spider. Well, he got sicker and sicker, so they took him to the hospital at Edinburg.

And they said, "Who's going to pay?"

"Well, there's no money, I guess."

"All right. Get out!"

"So what can we do?" they said. "Nobody can pay. Let's take him over to Don Pedrito."

Well, so the little old man came and looked him over. "And what happened to him?" he said.

"Well, it's like this." Said, "This boy swallowed a spider."

He said, "And what did they say at the hospital?"

Said, "Oh, no! At the hospital they want money to operate on him."

"No," he said, "don't talk to me about operations. I'll take care of him right now. Let's see, turn him over for me with his ass sticking up, with his butt in the air."

They turned him over.

"Now, pull his pants down." They pulled his pants down.

He said, "But bring him out here in the yard." They laid him down in the yard.

He said, "Do you have some Karo corn syrup?"

"Well, yes. Here's some."

Gave his asshole a good smearing with it. "All right, now,"

he said, "Everybody stand back." And he picked up a stick.
     Said, "But what are you doing, Don Juanito?"
     He said, "I'm waiting for the flies to gather," he said. "When the flies start buzzing the spider will come out, and I'll kill it with this little stick."

Informant No. 24

TEXT III

And then there was this other guy who drank the kerosene, this other poor man living in a tent around there who picked up a glass. And they had a lot of milk bottles there, made of glass, and they had water and kerosene in them. And this poor man picked one of them up and downed half a liter of kerosene. And he was choking, so there they go to the hospital at Edinburg.
     And they took him there. "WHO'S GONNA PAY?" [Part in caps said in English.]
     "Well, there's no money, I guess."
     "All right. Get out, cabrones!"
     Well, there was no money, so out! So they took him back, and the poor man was choking. He had downed half a liter of kerosene. Said, "Call Don Fulanito."
     So the old man came. "What's the matter?" he said.
     "He drank half a liter of kerosene."
     "All right. So what did they say at the hospital?"
     Said, "Well, at the hospital they want money. For the operation."
     "Ah, no. There'll be no fuckin operation," he said. "Let's see. Bring him out here for me. Just put him out here and leave him to me." He said, "Don't you have a lantern there?"
     "Well, yes."
     "Let's see, then. Take the wick out of the lantern." They took out the wick. "Does anybody have a pencil around there?"
     "Well, yes. Here's the pencil."
     "Now get out of the way," he said. "Pull his pants down." He stuffed the wick in his asshole with the pencil and said, "Let's have a match." He lighted the wick. He said, "All right, now. Everybody stand back. When the fire is gone," he said, "when the wick goes out, then all the kerosene will be out of him."

Informant No. 24

TEXT IV

This is something they say happened in Mission or McAllen or somewhere over there, in Hidalgo county, you see? A girl began to feel very sick in the stomach, and they took her to the doctor. And the doctor said, "This girl has appendicitis." He said, "We'll have to take out her appendix, no other way. If she isn't feeling better

116

by tomorrow at ten," he said, "I'll come for her."

So then a woman said, "Look," she said, "Don Pedrito is in town. He's a curandero," she said, "and he's a very wise old man."

Said, "What for?"

"He never goes around recommending operations," she said, "and he never makes a mistake."

Well, so they called him. He said, "Let's see, let's see," he said. "What does the doctor say?"

"Oh, the doctor says it's her appendix."

He said, "Oh, no. Those doctors are a bunch of cabrones; all they know is about diseases in English. But this little girl is sick in the Mexican way; she has a Mexican disease," he said. "And it can be only one of three things: fled flesh, bruised blood, or a blocked fart."

Informant No. 24

TEXT V

Z. P. [narrator names a Mexican-American M.D.] went to call on a patient. He examined him and said, "It's not as bad as all that. I'm going to write you a prescription. But I want you to do exactly what I tell you, and I'll come back tomorrow morning. He'll get well, I assure you. But listen very carefully," he says, "because I want you to do it exactly as I am going to tell you."

"Very well, doctor."

He says, "I want you to give him a sponge bath, all right? Soak the sponge in alcohol and give him a good rubbing all over his body. And before the alcohol can evaporate, cover him with a sheet all the way up here to the neck. Then you take a little bit of ashes and sprinkle them around the bed. Pray one Paternoster and three Hail Marys. Then take a ball and balance it very carefully on his forehead," he says. "I'll come back around six or seven in the morning, and I assure you he'll be perfectly all right by then."

Well, so they did as they were told. Next morning the doctor came. But no, the poor man was already dead. "How's the patient?" he says.

"But he already--he's dead."

"But how could he be dead! It wasn't all--it wasn't a fatal disease. You must have failed to do exactly what I told you."

"Oh, no...We did, señor doctor."

"Well, did you give him the sponge bath with alcohol?"

"Yes, of course. As soon as you left. And we covered him with the sheet so the effect would not be lost."

"And the ashes?"

"Well, see for yourself; there they are. Look there, on the bed; you can still see the ashes there."

"And the ball on his forehead?" he says.

"Well, now there, you see doctor. There's where we had a bit of trouble. We had to call three of the neighbors," he says. "And we tried to do it between us four," he says. "But we couldn't pull it up any farther than his navel."

Informant No. 10
Brownsville, Texas
September 7, 1962

TEXT VI

There was a veterinary out there with the Aftosa, a <u>bolillo</u> from around here.[4] And then this little old man was very sick; he had indigestion or I don't know what. So they went. "Here's a doctor from the other side of the border. What more do you want!" So they went to see him.

He said, "Oh, no! Me doctor by the cow. But not by the man. NO GOTTA PERMIT." [Vet's dialogue is in heavily accented Spanish, except part in caps, which is in English.]

Said, "No matter, doctor. What do you give the cows when they are sick in the stomach?"

"Well, <u>hombre</u>," he says, "me give a little Epsom salts."

Said, "How much Epsom salts do you give the cow?"

He says, "Oh, by one big cow me give her a pound of salts in one gallon of water."

So then they said, "Now we can figure the dose ourselves." They went home and measured half a gallon of water and half a pound of Epsom salts. And they made the old man drink it.

Well, so next morning they came. Said, "Oh, doctor, we came to see you."

"How is sick man doing? Is he better?"

"Oh, no, he's dead."

He said, "But how could he be dead!"

"Yes, we came to invite you to the funeral, this afternoon. But don't feel guilty about it, doctor." Said, "It isn't your fault."

He said, "Why you say not my fault?"

Says, "We gave him the salts and the salts worked. He must have died of something else, because even after he was dead he still moved his bowels three times."

Informant No. 24

NOTES

1. My field work was made possible by a fellowship from the John Simon Guggenheim Foundation and a supplementary grant from the University of Texas, which I acknowledge with thanks.

2. <u>cabrón</u>, <u>cabrones</u> (singular and plural). Literally "he-goat; in formal Spanish usage it is the word for cuckold; in current usage, as in the jests, the term is roughly equivalent to the English

"bastard."

3. In Text No. 4 the <u>curandero's</u> diagnosis in the original Spanish is <u>carne juída</u>, <u>sangre molida o pedo detenido</u>.

4. <u>bolillo</u>. One of the many derogatory names for the Anglo American. It seems to have been used originally for the French (<u>bolillo</u> is a small loaf of French bread), but later it was transferred to the North American.

REFERENCES

Dodson, Ruth
    1934   Don Pedrito Jaramillo: Curandero. San Antonio, Casa Editorial Lozano.
    1951   Don Pedrito Jaramillo: The Curandero of Los Olmos. Publications of the Texas Folklore Society 24:9-70.

Espinosa, Aurelio M.
    1914   New-Mexican Spanish Folk-Lore. The Journal of American Folklore 27:105-147.

Madsen, William
    1964   The Mexican-Americans of South Texas. New York, Holt, Rinehart and Winston.

Romano, Octavio Ignacio
    1965   Charismatic Medicine, Folk-Healing, and Folk-Sainthood. The American Anthropologist 67:1151-1173.

Santamaría, Francisco J.
    1959   Diccionario de mexicanismos. Mexico, Editorial Porrúa.

Thompson, Stith
    1955-58 Motif-Index of Folk-Literature. Copenhagen and Bloomington, Indiana University Press. 6 vols.

THE SPANISH-SPEAKING POPULATION OF FLORIDA

M. Estellie Smith
Florida State University

There has been growing attention focused on the Spanish-speaking groups in the United States but, for the anthropologist, it has been largely trained on Mexican Americans in the Southwest and in California. This paper will attempt to indicate briefly the amount of material available on Spanish-speaking peoples in Florida, choosing four communities representing Puerto Ricans, Old and New Cubans, and Mexican Americans. The data are presented as suggestive and programmatic and no attempt will be made to do more than sketch the outlines of these groups so as to call attention to the gap which must be filled if one is to truly deal with "Spanish-speaking populations of the United states."

Before presenting the data, however, I would like to raise several questions which are germane to any theoretical analysis. First, in view of the sociocultural variability which I encountered, I am prompted to ask if such a generic classification as "Spanish-speaking" has any real cultural validity or provides us with a category of primary heuristic usefulness? To be sure, the groups discussed in this paper have common cultural values which can quite easily be designated as an Iberian Culture Core, but the Tiwa Indians of Isleta Pueblo and their neighbors in the nearby Spanish-American village of Los Lunas, New Mexico, seem to have greater cultural commonality than do the Old Cubans of Ybor City and the migrant Mexican Americans of Florida. There seems to me to be more similarity between Sicilian Americans and Puerto Ricans in Buffalo, New York, than there is between Puerto Ricans and New Cubans in Miami. I am not attempting to vitiate the conceptual entry point; rather I would like to sound a cautionary note that a linguistic category is only one cultural criterion. And for ethnologists limning out a model for the analysis of cultural data it may, in some cases, be a deceptive and misleading one.

The second problem, like the first, is of a classificatory nature. There has been a growing emphasis on peasant societies, urban anthropology, and complex societies. Part of this, some anthropologists claim (cf. Despres 1968:3), results from the fact that primitive cultures are fast disappearing. Anthropology must become something other than what it has been, they say, because we are losing our traditional subject matter. Another reason for the changing emphasis is due, of course, to a growing sophistication in our data-gathering

techniques and our analytical methodology. The relevant question
here, then, is, "What kind of anthropology are we doing when we investigate 'Spanish-speaking peoples'?" I will return to these questions and discuss their implications after presenting the ethnographic data.

- - - - - -

The Spanish-speaking population of Florida represents an extremely intriguing problem in contrastive comparison. We find here
what appears to be at least three distinct Spanish-based communities,
but the sociocultures are as distinct from one another as are, say,
Sicilians from Venetians. The groups are the Puerto Ricans, Mexican
Americans, and Cubans--with the latter possibly sub-divided into two
distinct sub-cultures, Old and New Cubans.

Miami's Puerto Rican population, while localized, has high internal mobility. Work is scarce, particularly since the influx of
Cubans, and Bermuda and Bahamian Negroes. Many of the Puerto Ricans
say they are only waiting until a friend or relative in some other
part of the country lets them know that there is a job possibility
and a welcome waiting elsewhere. The Brokerage system is particularly important to these people since it is usually the most effective
and sometimes the only way of getting employment. The Broker (or
Patron) gets someone a job and when, in turn, that person hears of an
opening, he calls the broker to reciprocate the favor. Mr. Trujillo
is one such broker and takes the paternalistic role most seriously.
He stressed that the recent influx of migrants, some better schooled
and others willing to work for very low wages, has made it necessary
for the Puerto Ricans "to stick together and help each other all they
can." He mentioned as one of his problems the fact that a number of
Puerto Ricans are Negroes and, because they want to differentiate
themselves from Island and Southern Negroes, insist on retaining
the use of Spanish as much as possible.

One important function which he performs is emergency aid to
individuals. As he put it:

> Helping out works two ways. People know who to turn to
> when they're in trouble; and everytime I can get people
> to stick together to help somebody they feel more to-
> gether as a group.

He gave an example which had recently occurred. A young man needed
help to fly home for a family illness. He went to Trujillo's store
(which provides the owner with an income, serves to keep him informed
of local news, and acts as an operational base) and told the broker
his problem. After telling the man to come to the social club that
evening, Trujillo began calling people on the phone, asking for dona-
tions. Anyone who came into the store was asked for a donation to
help the boy--"a penny, a nickle, a dime--anything you got to help
the boy--to show him you care--you may be asking him for help someday...." That night, at the social club, Trujillo had the boy tell
his story to the members and then collected from them. He was

jubilant about the final total of $106.13 since, as he explained, the fare to San Juan was $92.50, which meant the boy had some extra money for anything that he might need. (Part of the jubilancy may have been due to the fact that the generosity also reinforced Trujillo's image as a successful broker.)

Social clubs are very important and everyone I met belonged to at least one. Many people also belong to block associations--mutual aid societies that focus on a limited city area of one or two street blocks. Living conditions are not always satisfactory and one important function of these block associations is to cooperate in repairing defective housing. Members felt that the block associations were as important as the social clubs since people in a small group will cooperate more on the pragmatic necessities of everyday living. One young mother said, "If we decide to tell somebody she's got to take better care of her garbage, she won't argue when it's all her next door neighbors that she's got to live with telling her." The members in the block association also engage in the very important reciprocity exchanges of baby-sitting, clothes lending (for social events or job interviews), food, small emergency loans, temporary housing, and so on. The social clubs, larger and more structured in composition, have two main functions--social and political. The Puerto Rican community is very politically conscious and many explicitly verbalize the need for Puerto Ricans to act together and become politically active so as to improve their lot. A bride of only a few months told me, "I make sure my husband goes to that club so we can try to change things--make them better for our kids and us." The clubs also have dances which give young people a chance to meet, and married couples an evening out and a chance to gossip with friends. These are attended by Puerto Ricans from all over the city, even non-members, and help create a stronger sense of group identity and solidarity.

There is a strong sense of equality in the community. Many informants stressed the fact that they were Americans, not foreigners, and stress was often placed on ideal American values, as in the case of one 34-year old male who told of his life in Puerto Rico.

> Back there my parents were poor and we all worked in the
> sugar cane. I didn't get much of a chance to educate
> myself but the life was OK. It was hard but it was
> honest and nothing to be ashamed of. When I came here
> things were better. I got a plant job and they taught
> me how to do the work. I work just as hard and make a
> better life for my family. I miss Puerto Rico but this
> is a place of opportunity if you work for it.

The sophisticated social scientist may point to the flaws of The American Dream, but for many immigrants it is still a reality and, despite the brokerage system and the patronage hierarchy, most Puerto Ricans expressed a belief that "we are all the same." A broker, for example--no matter where placed in the economic structure--

is apparently not perceived as socially superior; he is considered to occupy the status because he is lucky and/or smart, and knows how to work the system. Trujillo expressed it in this way:

> I helped some people because I had a brother-in-law who did pretty well. He put me in touch with other people and I got to know them. Pretty soon it got to work good on both sides; some people calling for help from me, others calling me because they knew I could tell them a good man for the job. In this world you go up and down very easily. Somebody that you help today will help you tomorrow. Anybody who goes up has to stand on somebody's shoulders to do it. So it's important to help each other when we need it.

The Cubans in Miami do not seem to be so tightly knit. The concept of limited good appears much more prevalent here and there is more antagonism expressed towards other Cuban individuals. The Miami Cubans are predominantly of the New Cuban group--Castro refugees. For many, their stay in America is only temporary and they plan to return home when Castro is deposed. There are still many cars which have bumper stickers proclaiming in Spanish that the driver will return to Cuba. Unlike the Puerto Ricans who justify tradition retention and acculturative innovation as part of the American melting pot tradition, the Cubans emphasize retention of traditional values and behavior. Girls and boys are strictly chaperoned, social events are structured by close observance of etiquette, and constant reference is made to "the way things are done at home." A typical social affair would consist of about 30-40 kin in an extended family unit. The entire family, from grandparents to babes in arms attend. Men and women separate to opposite sides of the room and when it is time to eat the women bring out the food and serve the men first. At the end of the evening men notify their wives to gather up the children and they leave. The gatherings emphasize decorum much more than a comparable Puerto Rican family affair. In the latter there is more of a coarse warmness, more joking and teasing, and far more cross-generational interaction. Men and women mix together more freely, and children are not so suppressed in their actions.

Religious activities are much more important among New Cubans than among Puerto Ricans. Church is regularly attended--even by males who were more lax in Cuba. Class distinctions are emphasized and a certain factionalism with the community is apparently generated by hierarchical placement competition. Conversations often focus on the social position of this or that person "back home." And one important way of counting coup is to have had more servants than the person to whom you are talking. As one Old Cuban wryly commented,

> They were all rich, they all came from good families. They all had large estates. And they all had servants--servants, servants, and more servants! That's the big thing for those people. You wonder who was left to work in the fields!

Except for children and teenagers outside the home, Cubans are loath to give up speaking Spanish. Many of the children escape the ethnocentric boundaries because they attend Roman Catholic parochial schools which bring them into contact with non-Spanish American teenagers. While few Cuban girls date outside the group, many Cuban boys date American girls--especially blonds--and, while the Cuban girls speak slightingly of their "boy crazy" American counterparts, it is suspected that they may envy the freedom (and resent the encroachment) of American females. Thus, especially compared to their parents, there is a relatively rapid acculturation process taking place among the young New Cubans. Although, like their parents, they still talk of returning to Cuba, for them (as one American girl put it), "it's 'someday'; they don't have their suitcases packed, with the ship ready to leave tomorrow the way their folks do!"

New Cubans in Miami are making what seems to be a quick adjustment to the economic system but appear to devaluate other American folkways more than the Puerto Ricans. They make a point of patronizing businesses run by their compatriots. Cubans are more resentful of discrimination and often refer to the unexpected hardships they are facing in adjusting to their new life. Although there is not the easy-going camaraderie within the group that one finds in the Puerto Rican community, in the face of the outsider they cling more tightly to the social construct of "The Cuban Community," with something of the attitude that they must all hang together or, surely, they will all hang separately. The idealization of homeland, not uncommon in the history of migrant groups to the United States, is particularly strong for the New Cubans because their stay here is often perceived as only temporary. Indeed, the attitude is extremely influential in creating a new culture out of idealized memories of traditional Cuban patterns. (I might suggest, at this point, that cultural patterns in the ethnic pockets in this country might well be analyzed in terms of the rewriting of history--the culture-creating process of Ideal Realization which is akin to the self-fulfilling prophecy, as well as the selective process of emigrant typology.)

Tampa, on Florida's west coast, has provided a different cultural milieu for the New Cubans. Whereas in Miami the New Cubans moved into the inner city and became part of the Negro-Puerto Rican community, in Tampa the refugees moved into Ybor City--a portion of present-day Tampa established in 1886 by Cuban cigar manufacturers and workers. Ybor City is a "Cuban enclave in Tampa" and, unlike Miami which "just grew," was a deliberately designed company town (Covington 1966:85).

In 1869 Vincente Martinez Ybor moved his cigar business to Key West to escape the Ten Years War (1868-1878) in Cuba. Old time entrepreneurs in Tampa tell me that Key West was at that time a hotbed of Cuban revolutionaries who were trying to free Cuba from Spanish rule. The Spanish, in an attempt to prevent communication between the home-based rebels and the American-based fomenters, tightened tobacco exports. Tradition has it that Ybor was financially powerful enough to arrange a sub rosa agreement with the Spanish authorities: He would move his factories out of the strategic area if they would agree not to curtail tobacco shipments for his factories.

The arrangement was made and Ybor settled upon Tampa as the new location for his Key West Cigar Factory. The Tampa Board of Trade was eager to bring in the industry and assisted Ybor in financing the purchase of over 1,000 acres of land.

> ...plans were laid for the establishment of Ybor City. The site selected for the town was mostly covered with pine trees, palmettoes, and oak trees and had served as a cattle range.... There were several orange groves, marshes, small lakes and isolated farmhouses scattered throughout the area. The primary job at this time was to cut down the trees, clear the land, plot the town and mark off the streets, factory and home sites.
>
> In planning his development Ybor believed that he could make more of a profit by inviting other cigar factories to locate free of land costs in the area and selling cottages to the workers.... Ybor established the Ybor City Land and Improvement Company and land in blocks of 450' x 650' was offered to any cigar manufacturer who would locate in Tampa. Of course, Ybor made a profit by erecting frame buildings to house the cigar factories at an average price of six thousand dollars.... Frame cottages for the cigar factory workers were sold on a time installment plan at a price that averaged about nine hundred dollars. Monthly or weekly payments ranged from thirty-five to seventy-five dollars a month (Covington 1966:86).

Ybor, according to informants, tried to renege on his arrangement with the Spanish, maintaining part of his factory operation in Key West--supposedly both for economic and political reasons. A saboteur fired the factory and in 1886 Ybor moved his entire operation, including all workers, to Tampa.

From this beginning came the tightly knit Old Cuban community of Ybor City. Non-Cubans in Tampa were proud of the settlement and were pleased to have the colorful but hardworking cigar workers; they referred to the settlement as "our Havana." The entrepreneurs attempted to recreate the parent city and encouraged professional and service personnel--as well as additional factory labor--to come to Florida. Restaurateurs, doctors, teachers, barbers, clerics, musicians--all were urged to come to the "Free Havana." A theater, operating in one of the factories, brought outstanding plays and performers from Cuba and Spain. The famous Columbia Restaurant got its start providing plentiful amounts of good quality but inexpensive food in a congenial spot, and convenient to the factories. Job conditions were brightened by workers themselves each contributing a few pennies a week to procure the services of a unique entertainer-- the factory Reader. This man would stand in a pulpit in the factory room and, mornings, would read the latest news from Havana newspapers, while afternoons were given over to poetry readings or selections from the latest Spanish novels. So highly valued was this service that a good reader could make as much as $125 weekly (Covington 1966:87). Only two years after the beginning of Ybor City a weekly newspaper was established. Social and fraternal clubs were encouraged by the various cigar manufacturers who provided meeting rooms, refreshments-- and an abundant quantity of free cigars!

> In 1902, when the Centro Asturiano Hospital was founded, a delegation from the Central Club in Havana came to Tampa and remained for many months to insure that the principles of the Cuban organization would not be ignored. Privileges of this organization included medical benefits--a group service which was very unusual in the United States at this time (Covington 1966:88).

Thus, the immigrants were to adapt slowly and gradually adjust to a new land where the only apparent changes were those for the better, and where, at first, the more things changed the more they remained the same.

Eventually the Cubans began to acquire foreign ways. Children began to learn English and look beyond the Cuban community. Non-Cuban businessmen began to establish businesses in Ybor City; and other ethnic groups began to move into the area, seeking employment in the factories or in the other thriving businesses of the area which had grown up around the factories. All the new Spanish speakers were not from Cuba; immigrants from Spain continued to come in and the acculturative process was tempered by a retention of the regional distinctions of Spain. Even today, it is maintained, one can tell whence came a person's ancestors, and informants' conversations about other individuals were peppered with such remarks as "He's one of those happy-go-lucky Andalusians." Discussions with Puerto Ricans and Mexican Americans rarely include a reference to Iberian antecedents; with both Old and New Cubans this is a major conversational marker.

The Old Cubans, then, have gradually acculturated to American norms and retain an Iberian-Cuban culture core as a matter of pride (and what seems to be a delight in 'local color'). They were not threatened to any significant degree by the surrounding dominant culture--and they were not particularly pushed to "get rid of their foreign ways." Once settled, the Old Cubans themselves acted as the welcoming community to other immigrants; they were receptive to other ethnic groups. Their attitude can be summed up, I think, by one informant's remark (albeit somewhat condescendingly): "Those Mafiosi (Sicilians) are different--but they're good people." Today, the Puerto Ricans are the only foreign group towards which any prejudice is displayed and it takes the form of disdain rather than hostility. Puerto Ricans are "hicks" or "farmers;" worse, "their women have no style;" they are often called 'banditos' "because they're not of a good class;" and people are glad that "there are only a few in Tampa."

When the New Cubans began arriving in Tampa they received a warm welcome. Remembering the 1880's, this seemed history repeating itself. Soon, however, some of the Old Cubans began to complain to one another that these people were "different." Resentment began to be expressed by such remarks as, "We took them in and they look down their noses at us" or "They expect us to be grateful; we can take care of them." New Cubans, it is claimed, make snide remarks about the way the Old Cubans speak and refer slightingly to what they call "Ybor City Spanish." The original settlers often felt they were being treated as provincials, as second-class Cubans. One college student indignantly told me, "After we helped them make a new life the only thing they can talk about is how good it will be to get back to Cuba!" A short period of contact between the two groups has revealed important differences between them. A new kind of identity has been created for the Old Cubans, one that takes the form of local pride in Ybor City's uniqueness rather than its Cuban roots; for many, the reaction has stimulated a more rapid acceptance of acculturative changes than all the previous years of Tampa living.

In addition to Puerto Ricans and Cubans, there is a third group of Spanish-speaking peoples in Florida; these are the Mexicans, a generic term used by Floridians to refer to any Spanish-speaking migrant worker from west of the Mississippi, whether he be Mexican or Spanish American. The particular group of which I speak is especially interesting since it has maintained relative cohesiveness through three generations--and possibly longer. At present, the group has fifty-three members, with only four males being unattached to a family group. Parents, children, and grandchildren of a single family may be found in the group--though in three cases, the oldest generation has now retired to a village in Mexico or south Texas.

The group has a surprisingly stable membership and also has a stable migratory cycle. It moves along the eastern Gulf states, following the harvesting time for various crops--cotton, lettuce, tomatoes, potatoes, celery, and various fruits. Some migrant groups have a larger cycle, moving from Texas to Alabama to Georgia to Florida to New York to Michigan to Texas again. Although this band averages only about 180 paid working days a year, it maintains a migratory pattern year round and never returns to a permanent home village for a portion of the year as some groups do.

Juan is the leader of the group. He has taken over the decision-making position for the family and the band from his father. He owns a truck, an old bus, and a 1959 Buick car. The transportation, together with his managerial capabilities, constitute the bases for his position as crew leader. He arranges contracts (getting the best terms possible) and then uses the vehicles to transport his crew and their few belongings from camp to camp. There are practically no group or individual possessions other than the vehicles, a couple of radios, clothes, personal jewelry, religious objects, kitchen pots and pans, dishes, flatware and glasses, and a very few linens.

Contractors pay wages directly to individuals but Juan is responsible to the contractor and to local shop owners for debts incurred such as an advance on wages, or a charge account at the local grocery. The crew chief also acts as intermediary in most contacts between the group or individuals in it, and the outside community. Primarily he is concerned with making contracts for jobs; thus the crew leader determines the migratory pattern, and establishes the daily travel schedule. But Juan also arranges work schedules, oversees the field work, arranges for charge accounts at the local grocery and drug store (and all charges must show his name as well as the chargee's), and sees to the making of camp when a new site is reached, directing that

> You three go dig the latrine ditches; Joe, look around
> for cardboard to patch these holes in the walls; you bet-
> ter set the kitchen up in that house; Lucinda, you take
> care of the kids today; Tony, you come with me to go in
> and get the food....

In addition he acts as arbiter, watches over the health and morals of his group, and exercises tight control on group and even, at times, individual economics.

Juan's immediate kin group consists of his wife, two small children, his parents, one younger brother, and a younger brother of his wife. But he repeatedly extended kin terms to other members of the band, possibly because he perceives the group as operating "like a big family." Juan is proud of the fact that his people have stayed together as a crew and maintains that such cohesiveness is the reason they are successful in obtaining contracts and are reasonably well housed and paid.

> People remember us. And they remember us from when my
> father was the boss. They know we're dependable and do
> a good job. And they know they got to treat us right
> because I don't put up with a lot of stuff like some of
> the other crews get. But I'm not a sorehead or a trouble-
> maker and if the crop's not ready when we get there I can
> usually get the people to give us some extra work to pay
> us while we're waiting around.

His father still works in the field crew but not regularly; his mother, like several other elderly people with younger, married off-spring in the group, stays in the camp during the day and performs various housekeeping and maintenance chores. Juan feels that in another few years his parents should retire to a village in Chihuahua where they have kin;

> But [he says] they like being with all the family--the
> kids around and all. Any my dad likes to feel he can

still make his way, and help us out instead of being on a handout from us. It's hard to settle down. I tried it once--when my dad was still crew chief. I got a job in a gas station. But I missed my folks, and being with my friends, and the pay wasn't that hot--not as much as I made sometimes picking. So when this Anglo comes along and talks me out of the job so he could have it--me, I was just as happy to go.

Another worker, listening to Juan, added:

You know, my folks, my wife and me, my two oldest kids, my two sisters, and my kid brother--we all pick. That's nine people working. We can pick with the best and even my two kids pick pretty good. We average about 60 cents an hour a piece. Nine times sixty cents is five dollars and forty cents an hour. Figure it out easy at five bucks an hour times eight hours a day is $40 times six days a week and you got us making a minimum of $250 a week. And we don't even have to pay rent out of that! Not bad, eh? You make that much with as little out of it as we get? We're all together; my folks don't worry about welfare noseys and (grinning) we get plenty of fresh air. My dad can barely read and write, all he knows is farming and picking; what could he do if he didn't do this? Wash dishes in a greasy spoon or scratch out a living on a few acres of land? My kid brother--you know how hard it is to be a Mexican in some places? In the village what would he look forward to? And in the city he'd be hanging around with some other punks, in a gang, no job and lucky if he ended up in reform school instead of with a knife in him after a rumble. Same for my sisters: they'd be trying to make out with some punk on a street corner, stealing from ma's purse to buy a lipstick so they can get in trouble all the sooner. Or living from hand to mouth with a bunch of kids they couldn't feed on some farm. You think my folks could keep them out of that? This isn't the best life but these shacks are better than a lot of the slums I've seen people live in--in the cities or in some of the villages. City life! A building full of rats, no fresh air, and a bunch of slobs ready to push you in the guts when the next riot starts. You think that's a better life for my kind?

Here, we're together, we all share the money we make and we got money for what we want when we want it. Everybody works together and we stay out of trouble and we keep our self-respect. Can you tell me where I can go and do better than that?

One noteworthy point here, of course, is that the family operates

129

as a single subsistence unit. Instead of the informant being one producer and his father another, with the two women in non-productive household positions, and the younger members being burdensome consumers, the entire family (including children from about eight years of age up) is one cooperative unit. More important, however, is that these migrants emphasize the positive values from both agrarian and industrial systems to support the continuity and integrity of the group.

Other members of the group, while showing surprising consensus with the last speaker, did vary considerably on their feelings of permanent involvement. Some claimed they were saving their money to buy a small farm someday; others said they liked the life and eventually planned to buy transportation and become crew heads themselves; and still others philosophically shrugged or, apparently unable to understand the point of such questions, said, "It's a life. Where's the world different?"

Except in the case of economics, kin lines are not emphasized as much as group cohesiveness. Children respond to admonitions from any older member of the group. Out of seven marriages in the past two years, two were endogamous, four were with individuals from other crews, and one was out of the migrant group completely. Residence is virilocal; three women joined the group and two left. Illegitimate children are frowned upon and there are none in this group because Juan makes sure there is no fraternization between his people and non-migrants. He says: "Mixing with other crews is OK because then if a girl gets in trouble we can make sure the kids get married."

The philosophical elements of religion are minimal with the emphasis being on sexual morality and group security derived from everyone "doing things right." The magical aspects are most dominant and health and the weather are the major concerns. A great deal of conversation focuses on curing and preventative medicine with rheumatoid illnesses, rashes (which are frequent due to the spraying of plants picked), pregnancy, and "sun attacks" being the most important. Weather is of concern since a drought or cold snap can cancel a contract; even good weather can alter the picking time or amount to be harvested, thus leading to the loss of a job because of contractual conflict. A rainy period of three or four days means no pay--and short rations. It is not unusual for a crew to spend the initial few days after arriving at a job waiting for the chance to begin work. Juan sheepishly told of how his mother had recently covered her saint's statue with a pillowcase "to punish him for not answering her when she prayed for the rain to stop!" Nominally, the group is Roman Catholic but few attend church except in a crisis or ritual situation such as critical illness or marriage. Religion is primarily an individual matter and most people have their own special patron saint and religious paraphernalia.

I am not suggesting that the description of this migrant band represents a truer picture than that usually given of such groups; but

I am familiar enough with migrant workers to know that it is not an atypical group. Certainly, it is different from the data presented by social welfare groups and, in its broad outline, varies markedly from either of the two groups previously described.

- - - - - -

Aside from the more obvious significance of these data, what other implications do they have? Let us return to the questions which I posed earlier; "Does a generic classification such as 'Spanish-speaking' have any real culturological validity, and does it provide us with a category of primary heuristic usefulness?" Second, "What kind of anthropology are we doing when we investigate such non-primitive peoples?" In the following comments the two questions will be treated together.

I think it is clear that I found it impossible to treat the Florida groups as a single sociocultural type. The migrant workers are not capable of being categorized in the same group with the Ybor City Old Cubans; neither can the Ybor City people be classed as "the same as" the Miami Puerto Ricans. On the other hand, I do think it analytically useful to methodologically differentiate between the 'band organization' of the migrants, the acculturative 'peasantry' of the ex-sugar cane workers of Puerto Rico, and the industrially-focused 'urbanites' of Ybor City.

Let me give a few more examples of the problem. No one has thought to do an ethnography of the northern New Mexico village of Penasco, yet it is as culturally unique, as socioculturally isolable, as the nearby Indian pueblo of Picuris. It is the retention of certain religious folkways and a distinct language which has led us to see Picuris as a "different kind of community" from Penasco. But a close examination of the latter would reveal a religious system quite different from that implied when we designate the group as Roman Catholic. If the Picuris have a Deer Dance, do not the Penitentes have a Lenten procession? Tell me of the Green Corn Dance and I'll tell you of the Summer procession in which, regularly, the people from one village, led by their priest, take the statue of the Virgin and bury it in the fields until sufficient rain has fallen for the crops. And, again, I wonder if the unique language of the Picuris is sufficient to treat them as differently as we do.

At Isleta Pueblo they have an annual opening of the irrigation ditches, performed with an accompanying ritual which includes elements of both the native and the Roman Catholic religions. Both Isletans and Spanish Americans participate in the ceremony. Their fields are contiguous and they must depend on the same water supply. It is not unusual for some of the ditch bosses to be from a nearby Spanish-American village, even though the Ditch Associations are part of the Pueblo social structure.

Recently a group of Indians was found living in poverty in Isleta del Sur, a recently incorporated suburb of El Paso, Texas. At least a half-dozen anthropologists have become interested in studying this group--ethnographically, yet for at least 250 years they have been only one segment of the larger Mexican and Spanish-American community, living as their neighbors. They do not even have the exotic linguistic criterion to distinguish them; except for a few isolated Tiwa phrases, and a few people who can speak English, they are speakers of Spanish.

What are the "sames" and "differences" <u>anthropologically</u>, of the Mexican-American migrant workers <u>and</u> the land-hungry Spanish Americans of northern New Mexico <u>and</u> the land-hungry Indians of northern New Mexico <u>and</u> the urbanized Old Cubans of Ybor City?

John Gulick tells the story of how

An Africanist...told me that by selecting certain of his data from a West African city and generalizing them to the whole, he can make the city sound like a stereotypic folk community. By selecting other data from the same city and generalizing them to the whole, he can make it sound like Wirth's stereotype of the city (Gulick 1963: 447)!

In other words, it's how you choose your data and arrange it. I confess to be in the same position as Gulick's Africanist and it seems to be the crux of the problems presented here. I can make the Sicilian Americans of Buffalo, New York, sound like the citizens of Tepoztlan; I can make Isleta Pueblo sound like Detroit; and I can make a group of migrant Mexican Americans sound like a band of Seris.

My solution will no doubt be considered too simplistic by some. I have defined my techniques of data-gathering and methods of analysis in terms of our traditional concern with

(a) delimiting the field of investigation so as to establish the generalized (i.e., homogeneous), on-going behavior patterns, both real and ideal, of the group I wish to study;

(b) examining a still delimited group in terms of the historically dynamic process of culture change, produced by the pressure of external forces--concentrating now on acculturation rather than enculturation;

(c) placing the delimited group within a larger structure (ultimately, the oikumene), a structure composed of similarly delimited 'cells' and studying the mutually affective units of the composite complex.

I am not suggesting that this is a new model; certainly it is stringent in its use (or abuse) of such constructs as "primitive," "peasant," "ethnographic present," and "the city," but otherwise it is what I believe has always been the traditional anthropological procedure.

If our discipline has any scientific validity we cannot now disown its basic methodological and analytical principles and, Freudian fashion, blame any current confusions or inadequacies on our parents or society. We cannot say that anthropological techniques are exotica limited to esoterica and that we must "change our techniques if we are to survive" (Leví-Strauss 1966:126). Yet many of the current theoretical disputes seem to do just this--and many of the ethnographic studies have given them good reason! Our claim has been that we study simple communities so as to eventually expand our insights of sociocultural processes to more complex networks. But we seem to be losing sight of our abilities and our ultimate goals. Some of us seem to have confused the ends with the means and are either engaging in ritual behavior for the sheer sake of the kinetic feedback or, worse, are ready to disown the very basis of our disciplinary uniqueness. Perhaps this is the time to gather together and discuss the issue. Such a conference or symposium may be crucial if we are to fully utilize the amount of available data rather than engaging in a kind of involuted scholasticism. Perhaps we will again be able to prove our cultural uniqueness by making the event simultaneously productive of a rite of passage as well as a rite of renewal.

REFERENCES

Covington, James W.
    1966   Ybor City: A Cuban Enclave in Tampa. The Florida
            Anthropologist XIX:85-90.
Despres, Leo A.
    1968   Anthropological Theory, Cultural Pluralism, and the
            Study of Complex Societies. Current Anthropology 9:
            3-27.
Gulick, John
    1963   Urban Anthropology: Its Present and Future. Trans-
            actions of the New York Academy of Sciences, Series II,
            25:445-58.
Leví-Strauss, C.
    1966   Anthropology: Its Achievements and Future. Current
            Anthropology 7:124-77.

FROM DISSONANCE TO CONSONANCE AND BACK AGAIN: MEXICAN AMERICANS AND CORRECTIONAL PROCESSES IN A SOUTHWEST CITY

Jack O. Waddell
Purdue University

Prior to completing most of my advanced work in anthropology, I had the opportunity to work as an adult probation officer for a criminal district court in a Southwest city. A considerable portion of my caseload consisted of Mexican Americans who had been convicted of violating certain laws of the state. Because of the encouraging support of my colleagues in that particular situation, I was provided with an exceptional opportunity to investigate the ways certain lower-class Mexican Americans viewed their experiences under probation sentences. This, of course, could only be a subsidiary interest because of the formal requirements of the position. The legal-judicial structure and the supportive norms of the dominant social public of the community made the role-tasks of the court's personnel quite specific. This formal structure required certain things of its officers and in turn granted them the authority to make certain decisions and to assert certain powers that had frightening implications for both the subjects under court supervision and any sensitive officers of the court given this authority and power. This paper attempts to look at the structure of probation as a societal institution and discuss some of the implications these structured relationships have for Mexican Americans brought under the influence of the court's authority.

This analysis makes use of the theory of cognitive dissonance, most articulately expressed in the works of Festinger (1956). Dissonance and consonance are relations among cognitions, fostered within an individual as he grapples with multiple opinions, beliefs, perceptions of environmental surroundings, and emotive feelings about his own conduct within those surroundings. In a society where there are multiple cultural and subcultural groups cutting across stratified segments, there is a very complex interplay of dissonance-generating social situations which are perceived by individuals and consonance-striving mechanisms which they attempt to employ. Each individual strains for a tolerable balance among the many dissonant and consonant opinions, beliefs, and social expectations.

Festinger (1956:26) outlines three ways that dissonant relations might be resolved, eliminated, or at least reduced to manageable proportions. These three alternatives are very similar to the three possible resolutions in managing socially induced strain discussed by Cohen (1959:469-70). One recourse is to change the normative demands and, consequently, the behaviors stimulated by motivational commitments made to the norms. Any perceived norms that appear to be most discordant and inconsistent with more generally accepted group or societal norms need to be altered or abandoned, if necessary, in order to bring behavior into line with more socially acceptable behavior. If the individual can perceive new norms of conduct and attain the proper motivations to implement the new norms, the more appropriate behavior patterns which result should presumably reduce the dissonance. This second alternative is a more difficult one, however, since becoming aware of new norms, trying to implement them, and trying to find them emotionally satisfying are often more distressful than sticking with the old ones, even if the latter are perceived to be inadequate.

As a third possibility, the individual can forget or try to avoid the fact that he has cognitions that are severely incompatible. Thus, the conflicts are below the surface of cognitive awareness, and the individual continues behaving as if the incompatibility did not exist. Another alternative not mentioned by Festinger would be to keep the old, unacceptable cognitions while playing the game of convincing the right people at the right times that the new, more acceptable cognitions are being mastered. Some learning might actually take place in such cases although motivations to implement the requisite behavior might not. This compartmentalization of cognitions allows the individual to consciously function in both contrasting cognitive sets--verbally, motivationally, and affectively in one and only verbally in the other.

Cognitions would be expected to be more dissonant wherever individuals have diverse multiple reference groups into which they are being socialized or anticipate being socialized (Merton 1957:265). Many of the reference group orientations which individuals have in their cognitive equipment are assymetrical; that is, individuals may sense strong internal or external pressures toward behaving according to the standards of particular reference groups, but find some of them socially and culturally more inaccessible than others. In other words, legitimate opportunity structures (Cohen 1965:10-11) which make their hopes realizable might not exist, hence, it is futile trying to behave according to reference group standards that hold so little promise of actual attainment. There may be little emotive feeling, thus there is a low level of motivation. Individuals are in a poor position to make cognitive investments in unrealizable situations. The alternatives that are left are those which provide more accessible social identities, whether or not they are congruous with the expectations of other segments of society.

In the case being presented here, the court is seen as a link between an individual and a nebulous reference group which the individual does not normally prefer but is compelled to accept by the specific terms of his probated sentence. The court aims to present an offender with a new set of norms and to provide him with a personal socializing agent in the form of a probation officer. The probation officer hopes to work toward effecting more favorable relations among the subject's cognitions in order to insure more conforming behavior to societal expectations. We need to know something of the structure of this obligatory reference group, what its norms are, what instrumentalities it employs for effecting behavioral change, and how these enter into the relations among cognitions of those implicated in the process of behavioral change.

The correctional process is a form of directed, developmental change. There is a superior planning segment (the court) and a planned-for segment (the offenders). The planning segment is aware that certain individuals need means for resolving crucial identity problems which may or may not be surmised by the individuals in the planned-for segment.

Individuals from the predominantly lower-class Mexican-American community and individuals representing the predominantly middle-class Anglo-American authority structure of the court constitute two assymetrical segments in the city. Certain specified offenses against the societal norms brings individuals representing these two segments together in a direct confrontation.

There are, of course, many assymetrical segments which constitute different kinds of social environments for the Mexican Americans in question. There are, first of all, the relative differences within the ethnic community: neighborhood differences, socio-economic differences, differences in educational backgrounds, different conceptions of appropriate interaction with the Anglo community, generational or age group differences, differences in the extent to which folk ideals prevail over "modern" ideas, etc. There is not yet a sufficient literature as to what these differences within Mexican-American communities might mean for our problem.

There are, on the other hand, mechanisms within the ethnic community which supercede these differences by providing a symbolic ethnic identity. Thus, language; physiognomy; cultural styles in foods, music, festivity, religion, and dress; and values and assumptions about life provide a basis for a "we" in contrast to "they." This ethnic identification at a more general level is assymetric with the larger Anglo community. More studies seem to be addressed at this level, where the Mexican-American and Anglo-American segments are viewed as two interacting wholes, one subordinate and the other dominant (McWilliams 1949; Saunders 1954; Tuck 1946).

There are many social assymetries in the Anglo "they" segment also. We can specifically isolate the power and authority structure of the community as one of the many differentiated segments of the Anglo community. More specifically, the criminal court operates as one institutionalized aspect of the over-all power and authority structure of the community, and within it there are relative differences as to how those involved in the activities perceive their functions and enact their roles.

All of these factors considered, the assymetry between the court segment and the lower-class Mexican-American segment is not at all surprising. How do members of the ethnic segment perceive the structure to which they have been involuntarily committed? How do they handle the stress and anxiety that the persistent confrontation with the court and its representatives initiates? In the court's attempts to reorient the subjects' cognitions and, hopefully, their behavior, what role does it actually play in creating a dissonant cognitive environment as it works toward reducing the probability of further illegal or deviant acts? Is there something about the structure of relations that can account for the apparent inability of many Mexican Americans to manage conflicting cognitions?

The Structure of the Court and the Process of Probation: A Case Example

The particular case being considered in this paper involves a probation office attached to a criminal district court in a Southwest city of 200,000, 17 percent of which are ethnically Mexican-American. The case load of the probation department for 1962 was 326 adults, of which 286 were males.[1] The number of Mexican Americans on probation constituted 23 percent of the total caseload in 1962.

The court is presided over by an elected district judge. A staff of probation officers are directly responsible to the judge, the district commissioners, and the general public interest. Probation officers ideally have the primary responsibility of seeing to it that the terms of probation are unconditionally followed. Depending upon the dispositions and training of the probation officers, however, there is usually a commitment toward helping the probationer to understand the conditions of probation and to implement them to his own best advantage, such as keeping himself out of prison and reasonably adjusted to the larger society. The work of the probation officers is essentially that of acting as intermediary between court demands and the subject's needs and problems.

An individual establishes a relationship with a probation officer through a definite process. It would, incidentally, be of great value to investigate how Mexican-American subjects perceive the whole process of arrest, prosecution, conviction, and sentencing. I know of no one who has undertaken this problem. An offense against the laws of the state introduces the alleged violator to a complicated process involving arrest, questioning, making incriminating statements, facing a grand jury, and preparing for prosecution in court. The Mexican-American subject, by the time he is placed on probation, has been through an array of interactions with local police, jailers, bondsmen, attorneys, district attorneys, etc.

Let us now look at some of the structural hang-ups that make it extremely difficult for individuals of Mexican-American descent to anticipate completing a successful probation sentence. Incidentally, these hang-ups also cause difficulties for the conscientious and sensitive probation officer as well. There are structural features of the system that are particularly inconsistent with certain core values in the Mexican-American community, and the constant reminders by the probation officer about the importance of observing certain court rules intensify the dissonance in values by keeping the awareness of cultural differences at the conscious surface.

The conditions of probation stipulated in every probated sentence embody new normative orientations for the majority of the Mexican Americans who end up in court. First, the subject is ordered "not to drink any intoxicating beverages of any kind or character or enter any establishment where the same are sold or served." The court has very obvious reasons for making such an order an important term of probation, considering the extent to which drinking is involved in so many of the cases. There is no intention to discriminate against cultural or subcultural norms, per se. From the point of view of the Mexican-American subject, however, this is a rather burdensome demand in most cases. Since this order is consistently held before the probationer, it progressively intensifies anxieties precisely because customary cognitions and habit patterns remain essentially the same, and they are incompatible with the new normative requirements. The cantina or tavern is a haven for male and female associations, where males can pursue those masculine activities essential to their sense of "maleness." An order of the court to stay away from such places has rather severe cognitive consequences. How does the Mexican American decide between the alternative norms that are available? Is he to dispense with the norms which orient him toward male associations in drinking groups at the usual favorite spots? Or if he does see a temporary need for dispensing with the norms, can he be motivated into doing so? He first has to be socialized into understanding and accepting the new norms. Then he has to anticipate sufficient emotional rewards in return for his effort to behave in the ways called for by the new norms. He finds, however, that his usual reference group relationships already provide more social identity and emotional reward than any vague set of transplanted norms. It is highly unlikely that the gross behavioral changes demanded will occur since such changes would involve a complete restructuring of basic cognitive, affective, and motivational patterns relative to the norms that are operating in drinking behavior. This is not to argue that a new norm could not be effectively used to reorient behavior from a potentially dangerous behavioral pattern. It only contends that a court order, backed by coercive legal threats, makes normal culturally-accepted drinking patterns a source of dissonance in the new context.

To drink in a customary social setting with friends is culturally valued but such patterns can now be used to inflict a severe personal penalty, hence the normal behavior must now be disvalued. The individual has to deal with his drinking patterns in a new way. He must now give his behavior more conscious thought in order to determine the social costs he might have to pay, in terms of some intimate reference group or the personal cost he would have to pay in a prison sentence.

Next, the probationer is ordered to avoid "harmful or disreputable characters," usually defined by the court as individuals with criminal records or considered to be bad influences because of their reputations in the community. This order is often very specific in terms of definite "undesirable" individuals, who are frequently life-long friends of the subject. Once again, the order is not a vicious attempt to deny the individual a personal network of close acquaintances. But it does give the court power to actually define what it considers to be appropriate or inappropriate reference groups. For Mexican Americans these are frequently their very closest amigos de confianzas or those in the palomillas. This is probably one of the most difficult demands made on a subject by the court, and probations are frequently revoked when the individual persists in maintaining associations with those in this "disreputable" category, even if no laws have been violated. I have known of many instances where Mexican-American young men would prefer to serve time than to be compelled to break these relationships.

The possibilities for a build-up of dissonance in cognitive relations are considerably increased when the order restricting friendship associations is added to the restrictions placed on drinking patterns. To purposely avoid social drinking with court-defined taboo individuals who are actually close friends or to stay away from a pool hall occupied by a number of labeled "undesirables" who are a vital source for meaningful behavioral cues, constitute extremely difficult cognitive tasks.

Another term of probation orders the individual "to seek and to maintain steady employment" that is defined by the court as suitable. When the number and range of possible legitimate opportunities for steady work available for a school dropout are considered; when we think of the community attitudes that are held toward people in trouble with the law; when we consider that Mexican Americans, by virtue of their ethnic position in the community, are already victims of the community stereotypes as to positions suitable for Mexicans--we can have some appreciation for the stress and anxiety that an individual might begin to feel when confronted by the reality that he must keep employed at "suitable" work if he wants to keep out of prison.

The court also orders the individual to permit the probation officer to visit his home and to permit him to confront other members of the family with any inquiry deemed necessary. Norms operating in

139

the context of kin are frequently foreign to the intruder and, conversely, the intruder's intentions are foreign to the subject's kin. The stress and the anxiety of the individual on probation are now extended to members of his family circle. Because of language problems and due to differences in attitudes and values regarding proper behavior, these interactions usually promote a high level of anxiety, suspicion, and confusion for the family. The order seems to assume, falsely, that the visiting probation officer knows the structures and functions of the lower-class Mexican-American family network and that he is, therefore, gifted in dealing with members of the family in some kind of helping relationship. In reality, the officer's anxiety is likely comparable to the anxiety that the subject experiences when he is required to report to the office of his probation officer. Both zones are far from neutral.

The court also orders the offender to support his family and his dependents. These responsibilities are frequently seen only in the most parochial of terms. Neither the court nor its officers has the requisite knowledge of the roles of women, the responsibilities of older offspring to parents, the kinds of provisional networks that may be operating to insure a culturally defined responsibility to one's own, the patterns of sharing and distributing available resources, the consumptive habits, etc., in lower-class Mexican-American families. The duty a man must have to his wife is defined in terms of the middle-class ideal, and these demands frequently prompt both the Mexican-American male and his complaining spouse considerable anxiety as to how to bend to these court expectations. For example, a man may be required to turn over part of his check to a domestic court in order to insure a "proper" distribution of goods and services to his family. After a while, the person may cease to pay as ordered and the wife may not protest. There are other kinds of habits that are found more operative and satisfactory to both partners, and it is only when those customary habits, and not the court-ordered pattern, break down that the complaints are once again registered. There are, of course, Mexican-American women who are socialized into the Anglo institutional patterns and they may hold their husbands to the court's standards rather than depend on less reliable customary habits. The whole domestic issue that frequently gets involved in the court's authoritative dealings with a probationer is very distressing to powerless people. These cognitive imcompatibilities provide further examples of how a social structure can function to maximize distressful cognitive relations.

Minor ordinance violations (i.e., convictions for loitering, drunkenness, fighting, disturbing the peace, wife-beating, etc.) also have reference group implications for the Mexican American and are probation violations. The court also requires the subject to seek permission before he leaves the county or state. For a people with migratory labor patterns and geographical mobility networks of long standing, a structured requirement of this kind presents many additional problems.

Conclusions

An attempt has been made to enumerate a few critical features
of one kind of structured social relations operating in a Southwest
city and to indicate how these structured relations have considerable
bearing upon Mexican-American and Anglo-American relations. The
original title of my paper suggests that the successes and failures
of the correctional system are frequently explained in terms of the
abilities or inabilities of Mexican Americans to conform to societal
expectations and to find some satisfaction in these conformities.
Hence, from the viewpoint of the Anglo Americans, the correctional
process involves socializing a certain group of Mexican Americans
away from old cognitions, thought to be distressing and vexing if
not socially harmful, toward new cognitions which will bring more
contentment and greater harmony in their life styles. When the subjects fail to be motivated toward accepting these more "consonant"
behaviors, they are seen willfully to prefer some less satisfying
state which is full of anxiety, confusion, and social distress. Thus,
they return to their less socially acceptable behavior and their unhappy, unrewarding surroundings. In Anglo eyes, they prefer a state
of dissonance to that of consonance, which the court has been gratuitously trying to offer them. Looking at it from this perspective,
the Mexican Americans whose probations are revoked have rejected an
opportunity to put their cognitive and behavioral houses in order.

I would now like to rephrase my title by altering the ordering
of the words to read: "From Consonance to Dissonance and Back Again:
Mexican Americans and Their Conceptions of Correctional Processes
in a Southwest City." An ethnocentric point of view argues that
people from other ethnic groups are more apt to experience severe
dissonance that often leads to deviant behavior which, in turn, merits
correction. It is less often seen that certain behavior is called
upon because it offers alternative cognitive resolutions that are
means of reducing dissonance. I would like to argue that individuals
of Mexican-American background may be more cognitively consonant before probation than they are immediately after being placed on pro-
bationary supervision. The confrontation with the court's orders
presents the individual with new values for which he must learn to
be cognitively aware. Many of these cognitions are quite contradictory to those meaningful cognitions which have been a part of the
person's life style and for which he has a great deal of motivational
affect. Hence, if he does not survive his probation it is because
he wishes to restore or to maintain a more consonant set of cognitive
relations. Getting the probation off his back may send him to prison
or to jail, but that is the price he is willing to pay for being able
to persist in his more familiar cognitive style. The Mexican American
finds that so many of the demands made upon him are inappropriate for

the style of life with which he has come to feel comfortable.

Considering the various alternatives for reducing cognitive strain, my data permit me to abstract what I see as the avenue most frequently taken by the Mexican American for resolving the disparity of cognitions invoked by the probation. The majority of the court demands are incongruous with so much of modal Mexican-American behavior that very few seemed willing or able to give up old cognitions, even temporarily. Their social relations were intimately tied up in reference groups of kin folks, age-peer groups, close alliances with one or two other individuals, etc., that the new orders of the court could do nothing but heighten the anxiety, which usually became more intolerable the longer the person was under supervision. During this period of increased cognitive stress, I noted an even greater dependence upon familiar reference groups whose usual patterns were apt to lead to complications for the individual on probation although the behavior per se was normal cultural behavior and not particularly deviant. This increasing dependence on cultural reference groups was even more necessary because the individual was, more than ever, in need of being motivated to obtain support from his peers due to the pressure of the court to alter patterns and to take on meaningless and socially unrewarding new behaviors. They did not particularly want to go to prison, but they especially did not wish to abandon meaningful group identities, behavior patterns, and existing conceptions of self for the many anticipated uncertainties that conformity to a new set of behavioral rules would induce.

Festinger's first alternative for managing dissonance, that of abandoning familiar cognitions which are dissonant with the new situations (ceasing to drink, staying away from cantinas, avoiding old patterns of companionship, etc.), was the most improbable one.

The second alternative, that of learning new cognitions, was a more plausible alternative. During the initial phases of probation there was personal contact with socializing agents who occasionally reminded subjects of a prison sentence if they failed to abide by the orders of the court. There is, of course, always the question of just how well the conditions of probation were communicated in ways understood by the individual. Even when the norms are communicated well, it does not mean that once the rules were known conforming behavior necessarily followed. Cognitive consonance is more than paying lip service to rules if behavior remains largely unaltered.

The third alternative, that of evading the issue and employing defense mechanisms to hide the problems from one's self (i.e., putting on a personal facade that there were no major problems, that all was well understood, and that there was no need to worry about the terms of probation since that was just normal behavior anyway, etc.), might have been operative for Mexican Americans but I could not detect it. This seems to be a syndrome of Anglos, who are usually more aware of the importance of these norms to middle-class Anglo society. It was more difficult for Anglo individuals to cognitively face up to the fact that their behavior was in violation of these accepted values. I detected little of this in the Mexican Americans, although they were capable of acknowledging the convenience in abiding by the terms of probation for the duration.

The most frequently employed alternative for Mexican Americans was that of taking a chance with a probation, trying to learn the rules in order to be able to verbally satisfy the probation officer that the rules were being followed, but keeping this attitude cognitively compartmentalized so that it could be strategically used in making office reports without it interfering with the existing reference group patterns. As the contacts with the probation office persisted or when any specific instance of violation was observed by the officer, there was usually a more serious confrontation with the rules, and dissonance momentarily increased. At this point, the individual turned toward his reference groups to receive the affect that would compensate for the heightened dissonance. Thus, at certain times, compartmentalizing behavior was a particularly poor alternative.

Of course, none of these are uniquely Mexican-American behavior. However, the particular norms operating in different segments of society make the handling of dissonance quite different in the different social segments. There are some more acculturated Mexican-American families that are also affected by these processes, hence the court's norms are closer to the norms of the families involved. In these cases, there will be more intense family concern and the supportive interests of the family may provide ways for the offender to manage the dissonance. On the other hand, dissonance is often greater in cases in which there are overriding reference group loyalties.

Finally, I think probations often failed because individuals could not handle the dissonance that probation promoted, and cognitive consonance was more readily available in potentially harmful reference groups even if these identities increased the likelihood of a prison sentence.

The intention has not been to criticize either the structure of a legitimate societal institution or its personnel. But it must be acknowledged that our understanding of the cognitive processes of people of ethnic groups who interact with these Anglo-dominated institutions are very poorly known and understood. Anthropologists might find within the structure of our courts and the social relations which they create a very fruitful field for ethnographic research.

NOTE

1. An individual is considered subject to prosecution as an adult if he is 17 years of age for males and 18 for females in the

particular state. Juvenile records in the same city reveal that Mexican-American juveniles make up 43 percent of the caseload. There is a large rate of recidivism in juvenile offenses where the boys are sent to the state school. Of the adult figure, the largest number of Mexican-Americans are between 17 and 21, and it is in this group that the most revoked probations occur. The most frequent crimes of these young men are burglary, driving without owner's consent, and theft; and the probations are most frequently revoked due to the same offenses or due to breaking rules of the probation. As age increases, the kinds of offenses seem to change considerably.

REFERENCES

Cohen, A. K.
   1959   The Study of Social Disorganization and Deviant Behavior. In Sociology Today. Robert Merton, Leonard Broom, and Leonard Cottrell, eds. New York, Basic Books, Inc. Pp. 461-484.
   1965   The Sociology of the Deviant Act: Anomic Theory and Beyond. American Sociological Review 30:5-14.
Festinger, Leon, Henry Riecken and Stanley Schachter
   1956   When Prophecy Fails. New York, Harper and Row.
McWilliams, Carey
   1949   North from Mexico, the Spanish-speaking People of the United States. New York, J. B. Lippincott Co.
Merton, Robert
   1957   Social Theory and Social Structure. Glencoe, The Free Press.
Saunders, Lyle
   1954   Cultural Differences and Medical Care, The Case of the Spanish-speaking People of the Southwest. New York, Russell Sage Foundation.
Tuck, Ruth
   1946   Not with a Fist: Mexican-Americans in a Southwest City. New York, Harcourt, Brace and Co.

A TRI-ETHNIC TRAP: THE SPANISH AMERICANS IN TAOS

John J. Bodine
Marquette University

This paper will examine certain of the factors of acculturation that define the relationships established between three ethnically separable populations in the New Mexico community of Taos. Crucially important is the documentation of the value of ethnocentrism. For each group this has required the adherence to certain attitudes that are apparent in the interactions that occur.

There is ample demonstration in the literature of acculturation that bi-ethnic communities are complex subjects for study and the variability they display have frustrated many anthropologists who have attempted to construct a meaningful typology of acculturational models (Lurie 1967). The examination of a tri-ethnic situation poses even more difficulties. However I feel that such investigation can provide very fruitful insights into the nature of culture contact.

With the appearance of summary studies of the history of relations, like Edward Spicer's _Cycles of Conquest_, we are in a much better position to investigate the realities of interaction that occur in the many tri-ethnic communities of the Southwest. One such community that can be considered archtypical in terms of the intensity of tri-ethnic contact is Taos, New Mexico. For the purposes of this paper, the spotlight will be turned on the Spanish Americans of this mountain valley town to illuminate their special position in the complex web of acculturational forces that bear heavily on them in 1968.

Taos is home for the Taos Pueblo Indians, a sizeable colony of Anglo-American artists and tourist entrepreneurs, and a numerically dominant group of Spanish Americans. First it is important to summarize briefly certain historical facts that laid the groundwork for the present set of relationships. We know that effective Anglo-American control of this region began with the usurpation of political domination in the late 1840's. Until then Taos and her sister communities along the upper Rio Grande were governed, if tenuously, by Spain and briefly by Mexico. The people of Hispanic culture were politically and economically the dictators of their fate. They shared the resources of the region with the indigenous Indian populations and had established, more or less successfully, a working set of relationships between themselves and the Indians. There never seems to have been a serious question in the Spanish mind that their cultural system was superior to that of the persistently pagan Pueblos. Until

145

the arrival of members of the special Anglo-American colony around the turn of the 20th century there was comparatively little reason for them to doubt their superiority.

In 1898 the first Taos artists took up residence in this small "Mexican" town and soon afterward ethnicity-seekers, led by a former empress of Greenwich Village and the salons of Florence, Mabel Dodge, arrived in Taos. When Taos was "discovered" the Spanish, tucked away in their small and relatively isolated mountain communities, were perpetuating a life-way akin to peasant settlements elsewhere in the Southwest and in Mexico. They were people of the land for whom life was difficult and inevitably so. Stoicism made its harsh reality a bit more bearable. Of course this is a value they share with their cultural peers elsewhere in the Hispanic world. I feel it is probably an important factor limiting their frustration and possible rebellion against the injustices they received from Anglo society.

The reasons for the attraction of Taos for artists and ethnicity-seekers alike are vitally important in determining the present position of the Spanish. These Anglos were drawn to this valley by the presence of the Taos Indians and what they conceived to be their immutably mysterious culture. They came as well because Taos offered a remarkably beautiful environment and a rather effective degree of isolation wherein they could develop their artistic and intellectual talents. Finally, in order of importance, they could savor certain elements of Hispanic culture so markedly imprinted on New Mexico. All of these factors convinced them that they were residents of an area that was different and quite foreign by comparison with most other U. S. communities. Therefore they emphasized and attempted to preserve those elements of ethnic difference which fed their special mental appetites. They did not consciously attempt to disturb the tenor of relationships established between the Indians and the Spanish.

On a formal and quite vocal level the Anglos expressed, and still do, an attitude of tolerance and acceptance of both individual as well as cultural idiosyncracy. While they sought from the two other ethnic groups proof of cultural difference which they found quaint, charming, mysterious and psychically satisfying, they never relinquished their claim to their own cultural superiority. As bearers of the civilization of the now dominant society, they made it crystally clear to both the Indians and the Spanish that they were the representatives of the new order that inevitably would be established. This points up again that the value of ethnocentrism is the base on which interaction can so often be interpreted. If other values and attitudes had not developed Taos would be more similar to other bi- or tri-ethnic communities.

One would expect, as elsewhere, that the members of the two European derived groups would jockey for first place in the status structure, but there would be little question that the Indians occupied the position at the bottom. However the Taos Anglos in weighing the elements of ethnic attraction have consistently placed the Spanish Americans on the lowest rung of the ladder. The reasons are clear. The Anglo of Taos tenaciously holds the belief that this community is a kind of Utopia. It is transformed into a never-never land by the rather constant employment of a kind of mental gymnastic in which imagination reigns supreme. From the Anglo point of view one can legitimately speak of the "mystique" of Taos. In its creation the Anglos glorified Taos Indian culture and relegated the Spanish American to the bottom of the prestige structure.

With these facts in mind we can proceed to examine in a more concrete manner the realities of interaction. We are faced with a cultural triangulation which demands daily and face-to-face contact by members of each ethnic group. Today the Anglos firmly control the one important commodity that Taos sells: ethnicity. Tourism is the only industry that matters and no one is unaffected by its operation. The Spanish have been able to improve their economic lot by finding employment in the many Anglo owned tourist businesses. They provide the Anglos with a pool of cheap labor from which waitresses, service station attendants, store clerks, domestics and all manner of menials can be drawn. Some Indians also serve in these capacities, but Anglos have frequently found them to be less dependable in terms of faithfully reporting for work. The Spanish are more attuned than the Indians to the Anglo-American attitudes toward work (Bodine 1964). By and large the Spanish need steady employment more than many Indians. They often do not have the extended family to fall back on if they lose a job. This has greatly increased their reliability as employees, but it has created a certain amount of resentment toward Anglos as well. The Spanish have learned that if they do not closely follow Anglo orders they can be quite quickly and easily replaced. The Anglos demand and receive faithful service due to this usually subtle form of coercion. Many Taos domestics, for example, are willing to work for 75 cents an hour. Of course there are only so many positions available. The significant decrease in agricultural production in the valley and the general increase in the Spanish-American population have thrown great numbers of Spanish into the unskilled labor market. Taos cannot support them all, so many are forced to leave each year to seek either permanent or seasonal work elsewhere. Many are absorbed into the produce centers of the West and follow the harvests from Colorado sugar beets to Washington apples.

However it should be noted that in spite of the substandard wages for many jobs, there has been a gradual increase in affluence among the Spanish Americans who remain in the area. Never as protected by the government as the Indians, the Spanish have nevertheless managed slowly to raise their standard of living. The great amount of truly desperate poverty that was certainly characteristic before World War II has diminished. An increase in various kinds of welfare programs has been important in helping many, particularly the physically unfit and the aged. These aids are relieving the younger generations of the responsibility for total support. However the Spanish are far from having achieved an economically comfortable status by national standards, as all recent government surveys have demonstrated.

The change which led to this slow road toward economic betterment began during the Second World War in which great numbers of Spanish Americans served. Men in the armed forces sent home more cash than many of their families had ever seen and in their absence this money usually went into the purses of the women. Spanish-American women had rarely been in such a position. Cultural patterns decreed that the husband was the acknowledged head of the household and controlled all strategic income. There had been little opportunity for the women to rise above their position of economic subservience. Suddenly they were in control. At first many were totally irresponsible in handling this money, but gradually most learned to direct the financial affairs of their families and they came to enjoy their new position of responsibility.

Many men returned from the War to find their wives were not only capable of handling their own affairs but determined to preserve their new-found independence. In many cases the traditional structure of husband-wife status and role playing was broken. The women refused to remain at home as long suffering "servants" of the men. If the men proved to be poor providers, the women left the home to find work. Such a move would have been improper under the traditional system. The Spanish-American male came back from service to face the problems of adjustment that hit many veterans and frequently to find that the family he left was not the same. Alcoholism increased as did the divorce rate. A major factor preventing even more widespread chaos was the maintenance of the traditional family relations by the older generation--the parents of the veterans and their wives. Their conservatism tended to hold in check the rebellious nature of the younger women and the confusion of their sons.

To a much greater extent than with the Indians, the War succeeded in implanting new needs and desires in the minds of the Spanish. They are now significantly directed toward attaining the economic standing of the Anglo American and many have dedicated themselves to that aim with an almost fanatic zeal. However in Taos they are consistently frustrated in their attempts to achieve their goals. The Anglos still consider them lower class citizens. The Spanish represent the poverty ridden masses who lost control of their town as Anglo settlers and businessmen poured in and took over the reins of economic exploitation. Naturally the Anglos have no intention of relinquishing their hold on these operations, which they often worked very hard to develop. Therefore the Spanish find themselves victims of a system which demands attitudes of accommodation in decided contrast to their personal goals of achievement, but which has so far offered them no real avenue of escape. They are trapped.

The economic structure is not the only aspect of life in Taos through which the Spanish have suffered prestige and status deprivation.

Religion constitutes another if somewhat different force. The majority of the Spanish Americans of Taos are practitioners of the brand of Hispanic folk Catholicism found elsewhere in the United States and in Mexico. The details need not be repeated here since they have been admirably reported by others (e.g., Madsen 1964). One special aspect of their religious system does need mentioning.

Due partly to the rather effective isolation from their cultural peers, the Spanish Americans of this region kept alive a religious cult that largely disappeared elsewhere. This is the penitente movement, which is still operative although considerably slowed down. Excessive self-flagellation and crucifixion are not as characteristic as in the past. The official wrath of the Church was felt by these people in a blanket decree of excommunication imposed by the Archbishop of Santa Fe. It resulted in the penitentes surrounding their devotion with utmost secrecy so that now, although the decree is lifted, it is very difficult to obtain accurate information on this practice. However the attitudes held by most Anglos can be easily summarized.

One would suppose that the mysterious nature of penitente activity would have been a factor to intrigue and enflame the imaginations of the ethnic-seeking Anglos. Indeed Anglo Americans were fascinated by the macabre processions and crucifixions that took place each year in the valley. But their fascination was not accompanied by respect for these customs. Catholicism generally and the penitente cult in particular engendered more prejudice than admiration. The majority of Anglos were either Protestants or non-practitioners of religion. Settling themselves in a sea of papists only tended to reify their anti-Catholic feelings. Even Anglo Catholics found the excesses of penitente custom incomprehensible. So this spectacular ethnic difference figured rather unimportantly in the attractions of the area. On the other hand, Indian religion was lauded by most Anglos as being beautiful in its symbolism and majestic in its performance.

This has been a very hard thing for the Spanish to swallow. Regardless of whether as individuals they were loyal members of the Church, certainly Catholicism or at least Christianity was the only road to salvation. For generations the priests had worked to convert the pagan Indians to the True Faith. Their reluctance to accept this core aspect of civilization was taken as proof of their inferiority. Most Spanish are still very derogatory in their remarks about the nominal adherence to the Church of most Indians. To discover that the Anglos heaped praise on the Indian religion, while either ignoring or belittling their own, increased not only their resentment toward Anglos but toward the Indians as well. Yet the Spanish are forced to pay lip-service to the importance and beauty of Indian culture since they are painfully aware that most tourists come to Taos not to see them but to see the Indians and their famed four and five storied pueblos. Again they are forced into the background and have been unable to convince anyone that their cultural system is more advanced, more respectable and far more worthy of emulation than that

149

of the Taos Indians. I strongly suspect, but have no means of measuring it, that a certain amount of Spanish resistance to acculturation is prompted by their need to demonstrate cultural superiority. Any number display definite signs of social paranoia.

One rather small victory the bearers of Hispanic culture have achieved is to insist on the term "Spanish American." They point out rather vehemently that they are the pure and direct descendants of the Spanish Conquistadores. They are Spanish, not Mexican. Use of the term "Mexican" is definitely derogatory in Taos. Significantly the Indians insist on calling them just that, although not too openly anymore.

It is true that certain families of Taos can trace their genealogies back to the time of the de Vargas reconquest in 1692. At least there were Bacas, Lujans and so forth on the expedition, some of whom settled in Taos Valley. But today there are very few, if any, "pure" line families left. The majority possess a very mixed background. Intermixture with persons of Indian ancestry has produced a population that can hardly be categorized as Spanish, let alone Castilian as a few insist they are. In fact, if you establish sufficient rapport, most Spanish Americans at Taos will tell you of the Indians they know in their ancestry.

Anglos willingly employ the term Spanish. Their motives again seem to be linked with their desire to consider all aspects of Taos as being different and special. By acceding that their darker neighbors are indeed Spanish effectively separates them from the vast sea of lower-class Mexican Americans found elsewhere in the southwestern United States. Actually the Spanish Americans of Taos have never been totally successful in this mild effort to distort reality, although certainly there are not the very real ties with Mexico that one finds farther south. And as a small element of the Taos "mystique" the term Spanish-American, which does not mean simply Spanish speaking, is appropriately accepted.

There is an area of Taos life in which the Spanish have succeeded in maintaining control. They rather effectively dominate the local political scene and become deeply involved in small town politics. They can elect to office Spanish-American candidates because their superior numbers permit them to control the vote. Until recently no Anglo American had any interest in being an elected official in Taos town or county. Anglos relished their enclaved minority status in this "foreign" community and were quite willing to allow the local inhabitants to run the petty affairs of government. Salaries are substandard anyway, so few Anglos were tempted.

The Spanish-American mayors and their councils have frequently used their positions of authority to try and thwart attempts by the Indians to gain any more prestige within the Taos social milieu. They can always be counted on to oppose the claims of the Indians to grazing, water, a right of way or even a cash settlement for past land grabs by either the Spanish or the Anglos. The Spanish Americans

are easily aroused over such issues and become the staunchest supporters of the cause against the Indians. I feel there is little
question that the Spanish suffer most from the injustices of the past.
Naturally their ire is raised when they see the Indians, who have received so many benefits from the Federal government, attempt to obtain
even more. However I believe that a good part of their resentment is
the result of the discrimination emanating from Anglo-American society.
They try to retaliate by any means available and they certainly cannot
accept further blessings bestowed on the Taos Indians regardless of
whether those blessings will affect them directly or not.

Among the many other factors that could be employed to document
the position of Spanish Taoseños, one stands out as crucial in helping to formulate Anglo attitudes. Whenever anything happens in Taos
of a criminal nature the finger is pointed first at the Spanish-American community. Vandalism, theft and physical violence are frequent.
Anglo women have been raped on occasion. Such behavior, including
rather rampant juvenile delinquency, is readily understandable and
for many of the same reasons that such problems occur in similar
populations in other communities. Since most of the Spanish are
economically lower class, they bear many of the problems that such a
predicament so frequently creates. High unemployment and consequent
idleness often leads to frustration. Moreover there still exists the
value of _machismo_ in the Spanish community, even though it has declined
since the Second World War. But fighting was long an established
mechanism through which _machismo_ was expressed. The weekly brawls at
"Old Martinez Hall" in Ranchos de Taos became almost legendary. The
lower-class Spanish still have their own _cantinas_ where physical
violence often occurs. The Anglos have little patience with such behavior. They imperfectly understand the stresses and strains facing
many of the Spanish and most have never heard of the term _machismo_.
This issue however greatly increases their distrust of the Spanish
Americans and is partly responsible for the very real degree of
social separation that exists in Taos.

Only in the past few years has there been any significant inva-
sion by Spanish Americans into the clubs, restaurants and bars patronized by the Anglos. Even today few Spanish venture into these places
and those who do must be the more affluent since the prices are
pitched to snare the tourist dollar. Moreover most Spanish Americans
still feel out of place and Anglos do little to help them overcome
their self consciousness. Indeed many Anglos would prefer that
large numbers did not invade their places of enjoyment. There are
Anglos who resent the fact that some of the Spanish are now in an
economic position to measure up to them. Token acceptance is often
reflected in hearing an Anglo refer to a particular Spanish American
or family by saying, "He is a _nice_ Spanish boy" or "I have always
liked María and José. They are quite different from most of the
others."

It is obvious that many of the well known signs of prejudice and discrimination are characteristic of Taos. They are perhaps more subtly expressed there due to the special set of attitudes that has created the Taos "mystique." Significantly both the Indians and the Spanish have been affected by the creation of this somewhat imaginary environment. Indeed as I have shown in another study, Indian culture has been decidedly influenced by the special breed of Anglo who settled Taos (Bodine 1967). Everything should be so beautiful and serene. It is not, of course, but the idea is sufficiently attractive that nearly everyone is infected with it. A member of any of the three ethnic groups is apt to make the plea at a time of community crisis, "Let's not allow this issue to destroy the marvelous harmony that we three peoples of Taos have achieved." Verbalization of the possibility of such destruction rather pointedly demonstrates that harmony in Taos is rather superficial. If harmony is destroyed I am confident that the push will come from the Spanish Americans, as perhaps other papers in this symposium will support. After all it is they who find themselves firmly held by the tri-ethnic trap of Taos, New Mexico.

REFERENCES

Altus, William D.
    1949   American Mexican: The Survival of a Culture. Journal of Social Psychology 29:211-220.
Bodine, John J.
    1964   Symbiosis at Taos: The Impact of Tourism on the Pueblo. Paper presented at the Central States Anthropological Society Meetings. Milwaukee.
    1967   Attitudes and Institutions of Taos, New Mexico: Indices for Value System Expression. Unpublished Ph.D. dissertation. New Orleans, Tulane University.
Coke, Van Deren
    1963   Taos and Santa Fe: The Artists' Environment 1882-1942. Albuquerque, University of New Mexico Press.
Dozier, Edward P.
    1961   Rio Grande Pueblos. In Perspectives in American Indian Culture Change, Edward H. Spicer, ed. Chicago, University of Chicago Press.
Edmonson, Munro S.
    1957   Los Manitos. New Orleans, Middle American Research Institute.
Fechin, Alexandra
    1951   European Aspects of Cosmopolitan Taos. New Mexico Quarterly 21:158-161.
Gillin, John
    1942   Acquired Drives in Culture Contact. American Anthropologist 44:545-554.
Luhan, Mabel Dodge

1937   Edge of the Taos Desert. New York, Harcourt.

Lurie, Nancy O.
    1967   Culture Change. <u>In</u> Introduction of Cultural Anthropology, James Clifton, ed. Boston, Houghton Mifflin.

Madsen, William
    1964   The Mexican-Americans of South Texas. New York, Holt, Rinehart and Winston.

McWilliams, Carey
    1948   North From Mexico: The Spanish-Speaking People of the United States. Philadelphia, J. B. Lippincott Company.

Parsons, Elsie Clews
    1936   Taos Pueblo. General Series in Anthropology No. 2. Menasha, Wisconsin, George Banta Publishing Co.

Sanchez, George I.
    1940   The Forgotten People. Albuquerque, University of New Mexico Press.

Senter, Donovan
    1945   Acculturation among New Mexican Villagers in Comparison to Adjustment Patterns of Other Spanish-Speaking Americans. Rural Sociology 10:31-47.

Siegel, Bernard J.
    1952   Suggested Factors of Culture Change at Taos Pueblo. International Congress of Americanists 29:133-140.

Spicer, Edward
    1954   Spanish-Indian Acculturation in the Southwest. American Anthropologist 56:663-678.
    1962   Cycles of Conquest. Tucson, University of Arizona Press.

FACTIONALISM AND FUTILITY: A CASE STUDY OF POLITICAL AND ECONOMIC REFORM IN NEW MEXICO

Thomas Maloney
Ripon College

At least since the time Lewis so drastically revised Redfield's view of Mexican rural life, factionalism and a prickly individualism have been assumed as normal aspects of Latin American culture. If one considers the Hispano Americans of northern New Mexico and southern Colorado as the northernmost contiguous extension of Latin America, then it may come as no surprise that factionalism is an important part of the political life of at least parts of northern New Mexico. While bearing in mind the dangers of generalizations about national character, this paper recounts and attempts to analyze some of the events of the period 1964-1967 in San Miguel County of New Mexico, in the Democratic party of the county, and in the two adjacent municipalities of the county, the City of Las Vegas and the Town of Las Vegas. The City and the Town have been separate political units since the late 19th century.

The population of the county, according to the 1960 U. S. Census of Population, is 23,468. Hispano Americans are the dominant ethnic group, with Spanish-surnamed white persons in this population numbering 16,077 or 68.3% of the total. The latter figure is essentially the same as the Hispano population for this county. With this dominance and the typical regional pattern of Hispano political activism and Anglo passivism, county political organizations and offices of both parties are nearly completely manned by Hispanos. However, effective control of the Democratic party, dominant in the county since the 1930's, has usually been by an economically dominant Anglo minority. Anglos also control the state Democratic organization. In large part the factionalism in the local Democratic party in recent years has been an attempt to break loose from this traditional "outside" and Anglo power.

Paradoxically, among the groups encouraging the formation of what might be called a truly "grassroots" faction has been the local chapter of a reform-minded Anglo liberal splinter group of state Democrats, the so-called Grassroots movement, officially the New Mexico Democratic Council. This group, during the period under study, had gained control of the party in metropolitan Albuquerque, where a quarter of the state's population resides. This organization is thus a power to be considered in state politics. The San

Miguel Grassrooters were twelve residents of the City of Las Vegas, all but one of them members or wives of members of the faculty of a small local state college and all Anglo Americans. While this group had no political weight of its own, it did provide a link with one important group of state Democrats and rebellious local Democrats. It also gave local prestige to these dissidents, who soon broke away from the local regular Democrats and formed a predominantly Hispano faction. Although this Anglo group worked closely with the rebel faction, no Hispanos joined the group or regularly attended its meetings, preferring to remain outside it and utilize it in specific political situations. Since most of the college faculty and par- ticularly the college administration were identified with the regu- lar, Anglo-dominated organization, there was considerable suspicion of these faculty Grassrooters, both because they were Anglo and be- cause they were transient college faculty. There seem always to have been one or two Anglo college faculty who were sympathetic to and helpful in political and economic changes in the region, always only a small handful at best. By mid-1967 all the original Grassrooters except the one non-college member had moved out of the county.

The major political developments around which factionalism evolved in 1964-1968 were these:

a. Primary contest for the Democratic nomination for the Congressional seat vacated by Joseph Montoya when he decided to run for the U. S. Senate in 1964.

b. Attempts to consolidate the Town and City of Las Vegas, either by action of the state legislature or by local bilateral municipal action.

c. Control of the Community Action Program of the county, and the attempted discharge of the CAP Director.

d. Primary contest for the Democratic nomination for the office of Governor of the state, and the general elec- tion for state offices that followed, 1966.

e. Control of the municipal council of the City of Las Vegas, also in early 1966.

There were several other issues intertwined with these in the county, including the possibility of consolidation of the two major Public School districts, in one of which the Town is located, in the other the City. Local offices, including the important ones of District Attorney and District Court Judge were also involved. Only a few key incidents will be recounted in this paper.

Behind all these issues, loomed, and still does, the control of the county Democratic organization and representation in state Democratic bodies, especially the nominating conventions. This con- flict centered around three experienced politicians, all Hispano Americans, although the eminence grise of the local Anglo-American "power elite," personified in the county's conservative Anglo State Senator, now deceased, could never be forgotten. The three politi- cians were the District Attorney, who also was chairman of the Town

School Board, the Town Mayor, a local mortician and former State Representative, and the leader of the Anglo-backed county organization, a man who has, in combination with his wife, derived his entire livelihood from appointed and elected local and state positions for most of his adult life.

By way of background, the ethnic and economic composition of the two municipalities must be considered. The Town is overwhelmingly Hispano, probably about 90%, although census figures are not available for this. The City is approximately 40% Hispano. The Town is the poorer of the two communities, by any economic evaluation. All the major retail stores of the area are in the City, as are most of the commercial and industrial establishments. Although the populations of the two municipalities are about the same, the Town 6,028 and the City 7,790 according to the 1960 Census, the City is far more affluent in terms of personal income and conditions of housing. Since the retail sales tax and real estate taxes are the major sources of municipal income in New Mexico, the City and its school district has much more income than do the Town and its district. This has been a constant smoldering cause of Town resentment of the City, and particularly resentment of City resistance to consolidation of the municipalities and the school districts. On the other hand, the superior general status of the City has made the City a status symbol for upwardly-mobile Hispano Town residents, moving when they "make it." It also has affirmed most Anglos in their sense of innate superiority to Town residents. Needless to add, the Hispano leader of the Anglo-allied Democratic faction has long been a resident of the City.

The first recent open rupture of the organization of the County Democratic party during the period under study occurred during the County pre-primary convention in the spring of 1964, when delegates to the state pre-primary convention were selected. This county meeting was preceded by one week by precinct meetings to select delegates for the county convention. Anyone willing to sign up for this duty was allowed to do so, and was voted a delegate. Five members of the local Anglo Grassroots organization attended the 29th precinct meeting, a large unit of virtually the whole City except one "suburban" area where the Anglo-Democrat power leaders lived. This last area, the 18th precinct of the county, came to be known as "Goldwater country" after the 1964 Presidential election. In all precincts but the 18th, participation has been almost entirely by Hispano Americans. At the county convention the five Grassrooters were the only Anglos present on the floor of the meeting. The meeting was conducted entirely in Spanish, with a brief English summary provided by an Hispano translator. The 29th precinct meeting was conducted entirely in English as were all smaller political meetings in which this participant observer took part. English was also the sole language heard at election victory celebrations. Spanish appears to be a political ritual language, adhered to for many reasons, but not because

156

delegates to county conventions (and political rallies) do not understand English at least as well.

In the course of the 1964 pre-primary county convention, the District Attorney arose and moved that all persons who wished to be delegates to the state convention be allowed to submit their names for election. The County Chairman, the Hispano leader of the Anglo-dominated group, the third politician cited above, was so disturbed by this motion that he immediately answered in English. The translator, having just finished giving the English version of the motion, quickly translated the chairman's remarks into Spanish and the whole convention, excepting the chairman, burst into laughter. The motion was duly seconded and voted upon affirmatively. People could then nominate themselves as possible state delegates, an important change from usual practice. But no one mentioned when, where, or how this was to be done. Within a short time the Chairman announced that the nominating committee had made a list of delegates to the State Convention and he called for a vote. Through all this various people had attempted to object, but to no avail. A hand-picked delegation, predominantly friendly to the Chairman and the state party leaders, was elected. Open conflict between the Chairman on the one hand, and the District Attorney and the Mayor of the Town on the other began.

Without reconstructing the whole history of the Democratic party in the county, one must mention that these factions had some base in recent political events, two years before. The political organization of the nationally liberal U. S. Senator Dennis Chavez had backed a conservative Albuquerque businessman as candidate for the Democratic nomination for governor in 1962. This man was defeated and Jack Campbell, who became something of a liberal governor, was nominated and won the 1962 election. Senator Chavez died late in 1962 and the defeated Republican governor, Edward Mechem, was appointed to this unexpired term before Campbell became governor. The County Chairman had backed Campbell in the primary fight, while the District Attorney and Town Mayor had backed Ed Mead, the defeated conservative Democratic candidate. The County Chairman was rewarded with a $10,000 a year job in the state government in Santa Fe and was running the party in the county on weekend trips home from the capital 65 miles away in Santa Fe. Since the governor was soon in firm control of the entire state party, and became known for liberal activities, he had the backing of the State Grassroots organization. This made for a very peculiar situation in San Miguel County, where the rebellious faction was dominated by self-proclaimed political liberals and reformers such as the District Attorney, and the party regulars were die-hard conservatives.

Aside from this confusion of liberal-conservative loyalties as a practical political lesson to the local Grassrooters, this point is stressed to show that ideological factors were not basic to the formation of factions in the county. The District Attorney was clearly affronted by the complete ignoring of his successful motion

157

for an open delegation. Himself a political liberal, he had at least in part proposed democratic selection of delegates as a move for popular control of the party. He was already the chief leader of people of the Town, an elected spokesman of the poor. His own family was clearly of aristocratic, even patrón background, his maternal grandfather having been elected an early governor of the state of New Mexico. If a personal rivalry with the Chairman had not existed before the District Attorney's humiliation in the 1964 convention, it certainly began at that time. Later events only increased his dislike, hatred of, and refusal to work with the Chairman. This animosity extended to those in the state organization who backed the Chairman, including the Governor. The county's Anglo Grassrooters were caught in the middle, between local agents capable of and willing to make needed political and economic reforms and the state "liberals," chiefly from Albuquerque, who saw the District Attorney as a patronage-oriented, reactionary opponent of standard liberal and impersonal solutions to the problems of poverty, disease, and lack of education, all matters that have plagued the northern counties of New Mexico at least since the turn of the century.

With occasional lapses, the rebel faction had remained a solidified group. The Town Mayor and the District Attorney worked together for practical political reasons, not for friendship or kinship or ethnic solidarity. These two men gathered nightly with a few political friends, usually including the Town Superintendent of Schools, in a local restaurant called "Mama Lucy's," and were known, to their enemies at least, as the "Mama Lucy Gang." This daily congregation demonstrates the personalism of politics in this county and much of the rest of the region. Face-to-face, frequent, and informal relationships are the order, with friendship, or at least acceptance, as a requirement for prolonged alliance. This was in contrast to the more formal relationships of the "Establishment," the regular county Democrats, which tended toward manipulative, covert, even elitist operations. Anyone could walk into Mama Lucy's and join the discussion. The door was open, and there were no secrets.

To show the element of personalism more clearly, mention must be made of the problems of the Community Action Program of the county in the spring of 1966. These centered around the Hispano Director and the Board of the Program. The Board had repeatedly in the fall of 1965 warned the Director that he was not performing his duties satisfactorily. Early in 1966 a special Evaluation Committee of the Board reported its recommendation of non-reappointment together with its criticisms of the Director's work. Both Hispano and Anglo members served on this committee and were in agreement. The C. A. P. Board was not at this time dominated by any political faction, with City, Town, County, and a few general members on it. When the report of the Evaluation Committee was made public, to the full board in an open meeting, an interesting situation arose. One of the Hispano Board members who had been passive in his work on the Board arose to attack critics of the C. A. P. Director, saying the committee, particularly the Anglo members, were criticizing the Director only because they did not like him. This man clearly stated that you do not criticize people you like, at least certainly not in a public or official manner. This personalization of the situation eventually led to the resignation or removal from the C. A. P. Board of all the current Anglo members, who along with some Hispano members had been dissatisfied with the Director's work. The Hispano members remained on the Board but made no further overt criticisms of the Director.

Personalism was not the only element in this controversy. The ubiquitous District Attorney was a part of it, too. Through a former teacher-coach of the C. A. P. Director he was asked to intervene, to help the Director. By 1966 his faction had control of not only the Town and the Town school system, but also the County Commissioners. Since each of these political units had representation on the C. A. P. Board, and only the City and the City school system had delegates not under his control, his protection of the Director was effective. Further, the C. A. P. Director was convinced that the main reason for opposition to him was prejudice of the Anglo members against Hispanos. He was able to exploit this alleged prejudice and ethnic solidarity to silence Hispano critics of his work. He kept his job, with Regional O. E. O. office in Austin, Texas, confirming his reappointment. Given the political realities of the county, the O. E. O. investigators had little choice. They had either accept the power situation of the county and recognize as Director a man who was doing mediocre work at best, or abandon C. A. P. in the county. That important economic and social reforms would not likely come from the C. A. P. was a tragic by-product, and, I believe, unintended. It was the very result conservative elements in the county wanted. Here personalism and ethnic solidarity led to effective neutralization of C. A. P. as an agent of change. Not that some Anglo conservatives were not afraid the Director might propose radical changes, for the element of prejudice and fear of change were not absent. But the end result was that the rebel "liberal" faction acted to keep in control of the C. A. P. a man who did not, or could not, bring about programs of radical change. This incident illustrates the often self-defeating activities of the reform element of the county, haunted by the spectre of Anglo domination of local affairs, and thus self-immobilized from bringing about changes the reformers agree are needed, even when the reformers have control of the situation.

One could write at length about the frustrations of liberal political reforms and of the even more complex economic reforms that result from personalized factions in the county. After five years of both participation and observation in reform attempts, I must confess a sense of futility is stronger than any sense of hope of eventual unity of all the people of the area, or even of the Hispano majority. Recently the people of the Town and City voted to consolidate into a single municipality, an act overdue by eighty years. There is then perhaps more hope than any experiences led me to expect. San Miguel County and its sister northern county, Rio Arriba, remain notorious hot-beds of political factionalism that thwarts real progress in the direction of changes the people may want and need.

Even as a good anthropologist I have difficulty explaining this personalism and accompanying factionalism in terms of a generalized Latin American culture. The concept of "machismo" has been, I think, overworked, used as a blanket explanation for wide areas of adult male conduct. I suspect that personalism and factionalism might also be found in a demographically similar region of the Anglo-American West, such as Idaho or Montana, or rural Colorado. Kiev (1968:72-78), who certainly utilizes the "machismo" idea beyond overt sexual behavior, has said recently that Hispano (in his case Mexican-American, although he has also worked in northern New Mexico) male behavior may be very similar to Anglo behavior in similar circumstances. We are faced with an old problem, that national character may really be an ethnic stereotype, a "scientific" prejudice. One final comment on this. When I lived in Las Vegas I believed that the dominant Hispano group there acted as it did to me and my family because we were Anglo Americans and they were Hispano Americans. Having lived a year now in a small Anglo community in Wisconsin, I am convinced that the phenomenon is general, not ethnic. "Strangers," regardless of pigmentation or language, are discriminated against, and in turn discriminate. My ethnic identity is now with a tiny island of faculty families. The difference is that the majority are not, at least on the surface, victims of injustice, exploitation, prejudice, and poverty, and I do not suffer from trying to identify with them, to work with them, to help them as a social scientist with a social conscience.

Factionalism exists in the life of northern New Mexico. Whether its cause can be traced to rural poverty, or to a Latin American "personality" type, or to deliberate "divide and conquer" tactics of state and national political parties, particularly the Democrats, or to some combination of these factors and perhaps others not mentioned here, factionalism exists. Changes in the political order toward greater democratic control, changes in the economic order toward adequate income and conditions of living continue to be slow. There is no unity among the Hispano people in efforts for political and economic reform. Only occasionally, on a specific issue, does effective cultural or ethnic solidarity develop. Pressures for assimilation into Anglo culture only add to the problem. Factionalism and individualism remain important aspects of the region, retarding reform and preventing unity. In many ways the situation seems ripe for drastic, revolutionary changes, but aside from Reies Tijerina's Land Grant movement, which is gaining appeal and strength, no organized activity has arisen in recent years to question or challenge the status quo. The District Attorney's faction could be an agent for change, but to date changes have been slow, and as we have seen in this paper, often self-defeating. The people are accustomed to working within the existing political structure. Radical movements have not attracted enough support to weather the defensive reactions of the existing socio-political structure. The Hispano people of northern New Mexico and southern Colorado have shown elephantine patience through over a hundred years of Anglo exploitation, abetted by assimilated Hispano local leaders. With the rise of effective protest by Blacks and Mexican Americans in equally desparate situations, it is doubtful that the frustrations of the Hispano people of the region will continue to be accepted as what life is or should be.

REFERENCES

Kiev, Ari
　　1968　　Curanderismo: Mexican-American Folk Psychiatry. New York, Free Press. Pp. 72-78.

THE ALIANZA MOVEMENT: CATALYST
FOR SOCIAL CHANGE IN NEW MEXICO[1]

Frances L. Swadesh
Albuquerque, New Mexico

A series of dramatic incidents, set in the spectacular surroundings of some tiny mountain communities of northern New Mexico, have made familiar to countless people in the United States, Mexico and other countries such terms as "Tierra Amarilla," "Canjilon," "Coyote," "The Alianza" and "Reies Lopez Tijerina."

These terms first burst into front-page headlines on June 5, 1967, when some twenty men entered the Rio Arriba County courthouse at Tierra Amarilla, bent on making a "citizens' arrest" of Alfonso Sanchez, district attorney of New Mexico's first judicial district. Grounds for the attempted arrest were that Sanchez had banned a public meeting at Coyote, where land-grant heirs were gathering for a fresh assertion of their claims to lands granted their ancestors by the governments of Colonial Spain and Mexico. Sanchez had arrested a number of leaders and members of the Alianza (renamed "Confederation of Free City States" but still better known by the original name), which is the main organization of land-grant heirs. He had arrested these people both in Coyote and on the highway, and had seized Alianza records and called Alianza leaders "Communists."

Alfonso Sanchez was not found in the courthouse at Tierra Amarilla, but the wrathful men who sought him held the courthouse for two hours. They shot and wounded a state policeman and a jailor, drove a judge and various county employees into closed rooms and shot out many of the courthouse windows before they departed. The last men to leave loaded two hostages into a police car and made a spectacular getaway.

That same day, 350 New Mexico Guardsmen, 250 State Policemen, 35 members of the Mounted Patrol, with horses, tanks and helicopters, mobilized for a historic manhunt. Eventually, thirty people were charged with crimes, including kidnaping, a capital offense. At preliminary hearings on these charges in early 1968, charges were dropped against all but eleven and the kidnaping charge was reduced to "false arrest," a fourth degree felony.

The accused, however, were not all rounded up for a number of months. The first targets of the manhunt were women, children and elderly members of the Alianza, who were camped out near Canjilon. They were seized and held overnight at the point of bayonets, under conditions of physical hardship and personal indignity.

News photographs of mothers with babies in their arms, teenagers and elderly cripples being herded by the National Guardsmen drew swift intervention by the Human Rights Commission and by the New Mexico Civil Liberties Union. Liberal Anglos became uncomfortably aware that the Spanish-speaking people of their state might have some cause for feeling rebellious.

Behind the sensational headlines of June, 1967, and the even more sensational headlines which have announced subsequent events in northern New Mexico, there is an ongoing process of social change, constantly accelerating, of which the Alianza is the chief catalyst. This process has been described as a "movement fully within the category of those described elsewhere as nativistic cult movements" by Nancie Gonzalez (1967:71). This interpretation follows the analysis of revitalization movements made by Anthony Wallace in his 1956 article of that title. Dr. Gonzalez, throughout her report, refers to Reies Tijerina as the "prophet" of the nativistic movement and stresses all revelational and dream-inspired aspects of his rise to leadership among the grant heirs.

The Problem

The question is, does the Alianza actually fit within Wallace's revitalization concept? It is my contention that, despite many early developments in the organization which lend themselves to that interpretation and the strikingly charismatic nature of its leader, the answer is no, on the following grounds:

(1) Revitalization movements described by Wallace share with other movements for social change such a characteristic as deliberate innovation functioning as their principal motor force, rather than the chain reaction effect of evolution, drift, diffusion, historical change or acculturation (Wallace 1956:265).

(2) On the other hand, the principal goal of a revitalization movement is to transform the culture, to make it more satisfying (Wallace 1956:267). Such a process is largely internal, whereas other movements for innovative change strive to change the conditions of existence of subordinated groups by directly challenging the controls exercised by the dominant group. Such a process is largely external.

For instance although the Ghost Dance Religion had the expressed goal among others, of causing the White Man to disappear, the focus of the movement was internal and the steps taken to achieve the above goal were symbolic rather than practical. On the other hand, the mystique of the American Revolution was not unlike that of a re-vitalization movement, yet its main objective was to challenge control exercised by the British Empire.

(3) The dynamics of revitalization movements, their directional processes vary from those of other innovative movements. Even Christianity, one of the most widely influential movements cited by

163

Wallace, involved a process of cultural divergence, the splitting off of the first Christians from the Judaic tradition. The Alianza, on the other hand, while originally a movement of divergence, early embraced principles and organizational methods which changed its direction, and brought it into participation in a much larger movement.

(4) The principal revitalization movements cited by Wallace were religious movements. In assessing the Alianza, the pervasive religiosity of New Mexico's Hispanos is evident. In the Alianza, however, religion does not affect the motor force for change, in fact the dynamic for change, as I shall demonstrate in a later paragraph, operates <u>despite</u> religious factors.

(5) Finally, Wallace lists six revitalization types: Nativistic, Revivalistic, Cargo, Vitalistic, Millenarian and Messianic (Wallace 1956:267). If the Alianza really is a nativistic cult movement or any other revitalization type, how is it possible to explain its vital part in a new cross-ethnic alignment of subordinated groups in the United States whose declared intention is to challenge domination by the "White-Anglo-Saxon-Protestant" system? It should be added that this is not a movement of cultural or racial exclusiveness, as many "WASPS" are a part of it.

Below is a documentation of the innovative characteristics of the Alianza as they have emerged in its brief history. Each is linked with the problems they have been forced to solve and with the results of the innovative experience.

Introduction: Changes Desired by Hispanos

The Alianza was founded to deal with grievances which are widespread and deep-seated among the Hispanos[2] of New Mexico. Specifically, these grievances stem from alleged violations of the Treaty of Guadalupe Hidalgo. Under that treaty, signed in 1848, Hispanos became citizens of the United States, but citizens with special rights acquired through previous governments, such as the right to their grant lands. Historical evidence supports the allegation that citizenship has been only nominal and that deprivation of the grant lands has forced a large percentage of Hispanos into chronic poverty. Economic loss has been accompanied by loss of cultural rights, especially the right to use the Spanish language in the environment of the school and the State Legislature.

The grievances are founded on facts, and many interested observers of the early 1960's conceded that something ought to be done about them. The prevailing opinion about the Alianza in its formative years, however, was: "Those people won't get anywhere."

The reason for this scepticism was the isolated and rustic character of the Hispano communities. New Mexico's 269,000 Hispanos constitute only 30% of the total state population, and are the most isolated and atypical of the more than four million Spanish-speaking people dwelling in five southwestern states. Despite occasional published opinions that the Hispanos are politically the most active of all Spanish-speaking groups and that, in the counties where they constitute a majority, they have "complete control of the power structure" (Samora [ed.] 1966:210), the reverse is more nearly the case.

What passes for "Hispano Political activity" is largely the activity of a handful of precinct leaders and henchmen who are deeply involved in the power structure but are far from controlling it. Any small base of power, in a social setting where so many are impoverished and powerless, can be used to control voting and other political behavior with a minimum of promises, bribes, threats and sanctions.

This is an attenuated continuation of the semi-colonial system originated during New Mexico's prolonged Territorial period. Handpicked Hispanos served in the Legislature as junior partners to those who really held the reins. Their official task was to represent the overwhelming majority of the population, but in practice they helped keep this majority under control.

Control is still maintained, much as in the late Nineteenth Century, by garbling as much as possible the information which reaches Hispano communities and by taking advantage of the extended kin system to control entire groups by controlling their key members. This system is today the foundation of precinct politics in Albuquerque, a city of some 300,000, in every precinct with a high percentage of Hispano residents. Leaders and candidates build their influence through their relatives, affines and compadres and win support of other kin groups by extending small favors or handing a few dollars to key members.

In communities where the tendency for social enclavement is strong, the plea of ethnicity is useful as a last resort. Of many a Hispano incumbent who has proven himself incompetent or worse, the saying goes, "He's a bastard, but he's our bastard," since it is assumed that any Anglo in his place would be worse. To satisfy this sentiment, the New Mexico power structure allots certain slots to Hispanos whom they can control.

Along with this system goes widespread factionalism, dividing the smallest as well as the largest communities, mainly into rival kin groups. While this system can decide the vote in counties where the Hispanos constitute a majority, and is important in counties where their united vote can constitute a balance of power, it provides them with little say on the issues and with very narrow choice in candidates. Political lag will continue in New Mexico, along with its regressive system of taxation upon the backs of the poor, until Hispanos learn to form coalitions around issues of common concern with other ethnic groups.

Schedule of Innovative Changes

The Alianza has existed as a formal organization since 1963, but its organizational roots go back somewhat further:

1. 1959

Reies Tijerina was invited to give his views on the land-grant problem to a meeting of the Abiquiu Corporation of Tierra Amarilla Grant heirs. The meeting was broken up by fighting between factions of the Corporation, some insisting that non-members had no right to speak. Tijerina, assisted from time to time by his brothers and other supporters, spent much time during the next five years collecting data on the Spanish and Mexican land grants of the Southwest in the National Archives of Mexico.

2. 1963

Having completed his researches in Mexico, Tijerina returned to New Mexico and promptly founded the Alianza Federal de Mercedes (Federated Alliance of Land Grants), whose first annual convention held during the Labor Day weekend, was attended by some 800 delegates. The Alianza was incorporated under Federal and State laws as a non-profit, non-political organization. Its constitution, adopted by the convention, represented a new approach to the grievances of the Hispanos (AFDM 1963).

a) United Action: Most previous efforts to press land grant claims had been initiated on behalf of individuals, families or factions on a single grant, often in opposition to other heirs. Never before had representatives of many grants united to press their claims.

b) The Common Lands: Common, or "ejido," lands constituted the greatest acreage by far of all community land grants. The principle of "ejido" has been no less dynamic in New Mexico than in Post-Revolutionary Mexico, where it continues to serve as the basis for land reform and the establishment of producers' cooperatives. Until the Alianza raised the issue, however, the very existence of ejido lands in the southwest had been obscured.

A large percentage of the New Mexico ejido lands had been assigned to the Public Domain by the Surveyors General of the period 1854-1880, because they paid no attention to claims other than those made on behalf of individuals. Some of the ejido lands were later opened up for Homestead entry, but a much larger acreage was incorporated into National Forest lands in the early years of the Twentieth Century.

The heirs were largely unaware of these transactions, due to isolation and the language barrier, and only reacted when fences were erected on these lands, cutting off their access to grazing and firewood. The history of violence in New Mexico is closely linked with the fencing off of ejido lands, from the Lincoln County outbreaks in

1876 to those on the Sangre de Cristo Grant at the Colorado-New Mexico border in 1963.

c) New Legal Strategy: Previous to the formation of the Alianza, heirs had repeatedly sought relief through the courts. There, case after case had been lost while the lawyers reaped fortunes. For instance, the lawyer who represented the heirs of the Canyon de San Diego in 1904, managed to get confirmation of 80% of the original 110,000 acres, then took half the acreage as his fee (USDA 1937:5-8). A quiet-title suit on behalf of some Tierra Amarilla heirs undertaken by Alfonso Sanchez shortly before he became district attorney won nothing for the heirs but brought Sanchez into ownership of some Tierra Amarilla real estate.

The Alianza took the position that no competent legal decision on the grant lands could be made below the level of the Supreme Court. Early efforts were made to persuade the Attorney General of the United States and the New Mexico Senators to work for a Congressional bill to investigate the facts. In case this tactic should fail, recourse to the United Nations was mentioned in the Constitution of the Alianza (AFDM 1963:2). The Constitution also invited the moral support of all individuals and organizations with a disinterested concern for human rights (AFDM 1963:3).

3. 1964

By the time of its second annual convention, the Alianza claimed a membership of 6,000 land grant heirs from the five states of New Mexico, Colorado, California, Texas and Utah. Some out-of-state delegates attended the convention, giving New Mexicans the sense of a common cause beyond their individual and community problems.

a) Contact with Indians: Friendly contact with members of several Indian Pueblos developed following the 1964 convention. The potential for joint efforts with the Pueblos began to be considered, since the documentary basis for both Hispano and Pueblo land claims was the Spanish and Mexican Archives. With this thought in mind, when Taos Pueblo began to press its claim to the Blue Lake area, the Alianza voiced its support. By so doing, it lost potential supporters among the Hispano population of the Taos area, due to the attitude of envy which has characterized the Hispano view of Indian gains in this century. Having once taken this position, the Alianza has continued to seek further for friendly relations with Indians, and the number of Pueblos represented has risen with each annual convention.

b) Direct Action: Some Alianza members had scant hope that Congressional action would be taken, despite continuing efforts toward the introduction of a bill. Some Tierra Amarilla Grant heirs began posting notices against "trespassers" on what used to be the Tierra Amarilla ejido lands, by which they meant Anglo ranchers who had bought tracts, built ranches and claimed ownership of these lands. A new "Mano Negra" scare was born.

Ever since 1912, when fencing was begun on the Tierra Amarilla common lands, a vigilante organization called the "Mano Negra" (Black Hand) had intermittently cut fences, slashed livestock and set fire to barns and haystacks. Lately, it has been rumored that some ranchers have set fire to their own premises so that they could whip up sentiment against the Mano Negra and, by implication, the Alianza, while collecting insurance on the damages.

Hispanos have had to resort to vigilante action whenever they have lost hope of securing justice through the government or the courts. Most Hispanos will not condone vigilante action, neither will they condemn it under certain circumstances.

4. 1966

This was a year of accelerated change for the Alianza. Many of the older members were hesitant about making the changes, but in this year the total membership claimed for the Alianza rose to 20,000.

a) New Leadership-Membership Relations: One of the reasons the Alianza has been described as the core of a Hispano nativistic movement is the personality and background of its founder and leader, Reies Lopez Tijerina. His charisma, rhetoric and visionary references to dreams all fit neatly into Wallace's portrayal of the "prophet" of such a movement. His background as a travelling preacher of the Assembly of God sect, during his years as a migrant worker, only adds to the image for the outside observer.

Focussing on the attitude of the Alianza membership toward their leader, one is forced to a differing view. This point first came to attention when Tijerina went to Spain in the spring of 1966, to study colonial archives in Seville. Long before he was due to return, many members began to be so fearful that he had taken his travel money and disappeared for good that they went to Alianza headquarters every day to check on the news. In view of the fact that Tijerina's bride of a few months had been left at home, such a likelihood appeared remote.

Conversation with some of the members revealed that, since Tijerina was Texas-born and a Protestant to boot, many of his Catholic New Mexico followers accorded him the distrust with which they meet "outsiders." Even his rhetoric, while greatly admired, was often not fully believed. Distrust was so deep that the Alianza membership had voted to put Tijerina on a very slim budget which often failed to cover expenses. Sometimes, a concerned member would buy his groceries.

When Tijerina returned from Spain in the early summer of 1966, he assessed the mood of the membership and resolved to build confidence by deeds rather than by words. He turned to a program of action and participation which placed him in the position of a participant-leader and began to develop leadership skills among the more promising members.

This tactic was productive. While no other Alianza leader compares with Tijerina as a public speaker, the pace of work continues during his increasingly lengthy absenses, whether out of state or in jail. The Alianza has become a functioning organization, although its style of work is too spontaneous to impress outsiders as anything but chaotic.

b) <u>Self-Identity</u>: Over the 1966 Fourth of July weekend, a large delegation of Alianza members marched from Albuquerque to Santa Fe, many camping by the roadside at night and 125 assembling in Santa Fe to seek an audience with Governor Campbell. After a long wait, the delegation was able to present the Governor a petition asking his support for a Congressional bill to investigate their land-grant grievances. On this occasion, the inaction of Senator Montoya was criticized openly for the first time. For many Alianza members, this was their first taste of group demonstrative action.

Although the official purpose of the march fell short of accomplishment, in that no substantial help came from the Governor, its enduring effect on the membership was to change their perception of themselves. Through the public action they had jointly taken, they affirmed their identity as members of "La Raza," or what Reies Tijerina calls "a new breed," the people of New World Hispanic culture with its many increments from indigenous sources.

This broadening and firming-up of group self-identity gave Alianza members pride and tranquil self-confidence to a degree which is uncommon among Hispanos of today. Like members of other groups who are subject to lifelong social discrimination, maddeningly covert when it is not blatantly overt, Hispanos have tended to feel painfully ambivalent about themselves. Questionnaires which they have to fill in our prevalently racist land leave them wondering whether they are "white" or "other non-white." The language question is a constant thorn, since few of today's adults have escaped the ordeal of initiation into a school system where the use of English is forced upon pupils who can often barely understand it, let alone speak it. Such situations feed feelings of inadequacy and timidity--and also burning resentment against the dominant Anglos.

c) <u>Changing Role of Women</u>: Women, from the start, had been devoted members of the Alianza. The fund-raising dinners they prepared and served were vital supporting activities, yet no women had assumed a public role in the organization until the march to Santa Fe. Since then, their activist role has unfolded, sharpened by the experience of arrest, of the jailing of their husbands for weeks at a time and of visits by FBI agents. More and more women have taken these events in their stride and have emerged as fluent spokesmen for their organization.

d) <u>Youth Roles</u>: No formal youth group has been formed in the Alianza yet, informally, the teenage and young adult sons and daughters of active Alianza members have made a place for themselves in the organization. Many of them participated in the July, 1966, march to

169

Santa Fe and an increasing number have participated in subsequent activities of the organization. In addition to the arrests which followed the Tierra Amarilla uprising, some very young people were charged in the original indictment. Perhaps because of the stresses voluntarily incorporated into their lives, these young people appear more poised and purposeful than is common for their age-group. Despite the police surveillance with which they are surrounded, none of these youth have been mentioned in the records of pick-ups for marihuana and drug use which are constant among youth of their income level. Disorder and brawling at Alianza dances are unknown.

e) <u>Renewal</u> <u>of</u> <u>Community</u> <u>Ethic</u>: In October, 1966, convinced that only by direct acts of civil disobedience could they force official attention to the land issue, Alianza members began to spend weekends in a National Forest campground located on ejido land of the San Joaquin del Rio de Chama (or Chama Canyon) Grant. Its area totalled some one-half million acres bestowed upon a group of settlers in 1806. The land shark, Thomas Burns, won his claim to the entire grant in the Court of Private Land Claims in 1904, but Congressional confirmation was denied because the Carson National Forest was created at this time and included the San Joaquin Grant area.

The heirs to the grant continued to live there, mainly in Canjilon at the northeast corner. For years, they were unaware that their grant had been taken away from them.

The Alianza campers took possession of the campground in the name of the San Joaquin Corporation, whose legal existence as the governing body they proclaimed. They refused to buy the required camping permits, cut a few trees for firewood and forbade the Forest Rangers to trespass on their grant.

Not all the campers were heirs to this particular grant. Some had come from as far away as California to participate in the "test case." On the other hand, the San Joaquin Corporation was real enough. This corporation had been re-activated under a constitution dated February 9, 1940, and for twenty-seven years had been dedicated to the following goals:

> ...to protect the society which is encompassed by said
> Corporation against the injustices and tricks of tyrants
> and despots, of those who insult us and seize our lands;
> to seek Law and Justice; to initiate lawsuits; to acquire,
> hold, possess and distribute through proper legal chan-
> nels the rights, privileges, tracts of land, wood, water
> and minerals which were deeded to, and bequeathed by our
> ancestors, the heirs and assigns of the Grant of the Cor-
> poration of San Joaquin del Rio de Chama (ms, translation
> by F. L. S.).

On October 26, the Forest Service proceeded against the Alianza by placing a stop sign at the campground entrance and stationing uniformed personnel there. When the Alianza caravan drove into the campground without stopping, the Rangers followed them and demanded that they pay up or vacate. At this point, the Rangers were seized, their trucks and radios were impounded and a mock trial was conducted, in which they were charged with violation of the laws of the grant.

Participants in these proceedings who came from nearby communities and had deep-seated personal resentments against the Rangers would have preferred to carry matters much farther, but they were restrained by leading Alianza members. The Forest Service trucks and radios were returned and the Rangers were instructed to depart.

One year later, Reies and Cristobal Tijerina and three others were convicted in Federal Court of having "assaulted" Forest Rangers and of expropriating Government equipment. The verdict is being appealed.

The experience of living together under the community legal code and customary rules of their ancestors, often wistfully recollected by their grandparents, revived among Alianza members a sense of the vitality of their traditional value system. The feeling for solidary relations of the community, reaching beyond the ties of the extended kin group, was expressed by many Alianza members after the San Joaquin experience, and has become crystallized in strong ties of loyalty and affection among the members. These sentiments bring to mind the theme of Lope de Vega's great drama, "Fuente Ovejuna."

f) Quest for an Alliance with Negroes: While Alianza leaders had, in the past, stated that they did not intend to adopt the militant direct action methods of the Negro movement, their admiration for the organizational strength and effectiveness of this movement had grown with time and experience. Dr. Martin Luther King was invited to be a featured speaker at the 1966 annual convention of the Alianza. When he declined on the grounds of a previous commitment, Stokely Carmichael was invited. Carmichael accepted but was called elsewhere at the last moment.

A young Negro staff member of the local Poverty Program agreed to pinch hit. Despite his hastily prepared speech, delivered in broken Spanish, he was cordially thanked for his expression of Negro sympathy for Hispano aspirations.

Alianza members had hitherto been trying to win the sympathy of people in power for their slogan, "The land is our heritage. Justice our credo." Now they had come to realize that they would not be heard until they had the strength to force a hearing and that, to have this strength, they must seek allies among other subordinated peoples.

5. 1967

The "uprising" at Tierra Amarilla has been described in the opening paragraphs of this report. What remains to be discussed are the innovative changes it produced:

a) Recognition by Other Spanish-Speaking Groups: Since June, 1967, "Tierra Amarilla" has become a rallying cry as well as a place name. From Denver came Rodolfo "Corky" Gonzales, leader of the Crusade for Justice, to hail the Alianza members for having "had the guts" to take their stand. A few weeks later, Bert Corona, leader of the Los Angeles Mexican-American Political Association ("MAPA"), made a like pilgrimage to Albuquerque. Cesar Chavez, leader of the migrant farm workers of the Southwest, was invited to Albuquerque to address liberal organizations, but took time out to attend a regular meeting of the Alianza. There, after an effusive greeting by the membership and a public embrace with Tijerina, Chavez announced that, if he were a New Mexico resident, he would sure be an Alianza member. He hoped all Hispanos of New Mexico would join, because the issue of the land is crucial to rural Mejicanos and reflects the cruel injustices to which they have been subjected. Chavez predicted no early victories, but spoke soulfully of the road of sacrifice that would have to be travelled by those who are committed to the struggle, sacrifice in atonement for the sins of others. The membership responded with heartfelt "Amens," for Chavez had touched the well-spring of Penitente thought which is still so alive in northern New Mexico.

b) <u>Partnership</u> <u>with</u> <u>Negroes</u>: The 1967 annual convention of the Alianza was attended by a busload of Mejicano and Negro activists from Los Angeles. The culminating point of the convention was a "Treaty of Peace, Harmony and Mutual Assistance" jointly signed by the Alianza leaders and leaders of SNCC, CORE, Black Panthers and other Black Power organizations. The members of the Alianza, with the ringing approval of all present at the convention, thus identified their movement with the objectives of Black Power, no longer on the basis of temporary and conditional "mutual self-interest," but in the context of "full brotherhood" (see center-page spread in <u>La</u> <u>Raza</u>, Los Angeles newspaper, 10/20/67).

6. <u>1968</u>

a) <u>Impact</u> <u>on</u> <u>Youth</u>: Partly inspired by the "Black Beret" and "Brown Beret" movement of Los Angeles activist Negro and Mejicano youth, the Alianza youth are starting to move out in new directions. In Albuquerque, it will be hard to build unity between "Black and Brown," as the two groups are now identified, because of the record of poor communication between the groups and of clashes between their youth. The coolness is partly the product of conservative trends in the local Negro leadership which, in the future, is likely to be stimulated to new trends or else to be replaced.

On April 22, 1968, students of an Albuquerque junior high school called a strike. Under the slogan, "We want Education, not Contempt," the students charged that the educational curriculum of the school was adequate only for its few Anglo students, no effort being made to compensate for the educational handicaps of the Hispano majority and the Negro minority. Other student demands were an end to hitting the students, punishing them for speaking Spanish on school premises and displaying prejudice against Hispanos and Negroes. Forty of the students were arrested while marching to recruit students from other junior high and high schools to form a joint delegation to the School Board. Among those charged with "littering," "loitering" and "truancy" were two Tijerina offspring.

An ambitious plan has been written for a free summer workshop for fifty Spanish-speaking youth, to provide them with a background in all the knowledge of the world of today that they will need in order to become effective leaders. Included in the proposed curriculum are history, philosophy and the arts. Sponsorship and funding for the project are being sought.

b) <u>Leadership</u> <u>Role</u> <u>of</u> <u>the</u> <u>Alianza</u>: Paradoxical as it may seem, the relatively small Alianza with its widely scattered and largely rural membership occupies a central place in the regionwide united movement of minority groups. As such, the Alianza has become significant on a nationwide scale. The Tierra Amarilla episode so stirred the imagination that the Alianza has become standardbearer for the entire Southwest.

The authentic leadership of the Alianza in the ranks of the poor caused Dr. Martin Luther King to invite Reies Tijerina to the planning conference for the Poor People's March, held shortly before his assassination. King also chose Tijerina to be mobilization director for New Mexico and to be one of three leaders representing Mejicano-Chicano-Hispano demands in Washington.

Predictably, the implementation of these decisions produced hostile editorials in the New Mexico press and anguished wails from some liberals. While the mobilization commanded strong support from poor people and many middle-class liberals, measures to paralyze Tijerina's leadership were promptly taken.

On April 27, Reies and Cristobal Tijerina were arrested and warrants were out for the arrest of eleven other Alianza members on an indictment issued by the Rio Arriba County Grand Jury. The indictment reversed the decisions of the preliminary hearing on the "Tierra Amarilla Uprising" and reinstated the kidnapping and other charges which had been reduced or thrown out of the case by judicial decision. No new evidence was cited. Bond for most of the defendants was set at $24,500.

The national leaders of the Poor People's March expressed their conviction that these arrests were an attack on the March itself. They demanded through the Justice Department's intervention release of the accused by writ of Habeas Corpus.

The State Attorney General and District Attorney Alfonso Sanchez, however, cling to the expressed belief that, once the Alianza leaders are behind bars for a long stay, the Hispanos will once more relapse into apathy. The State Attorney General has taken the position that the Alianza is part of a Communist plot and that elements at the University of New Mexico and in the Poverty Programs are in league with the plot. The State OEO director was dismissed as a result of the allegations, and covert investigations have been made of a number of Community Action programs. It is not known whether the recent firing of several University deans is connected in any way with the State Attorney General's campaign.

   d) <u>Progress</u>: Despite the storm of controversy and accusation which surrounds the Alianza, it is considered a real political force in the upcoming elections. While no direct, overt concessions may be made on issues which the Alianza has raised, behind-the-scenes promises are expected, as in the gubernatorial elections of 1966. Very quietly, action is being taken to soften Hispano grievances and to still the protests. It is said that the Forest Service has opened grazing facilities to Hispanos to a greater extent than at any time since the 1930's. In addition, projects funded both publicly and privately are centering on the economic problems of the northern counties. Producers' cooperatives have been established in several communities, with promising results. Whether or not these concessions will still Hispano demands remains to be seen.

Summary and Conclusions

   The development of the Alianza in less than five years since its foundation in 1963 is notable for the changes in the very process of change itself which can be traced. At the start, the organization had many of the characteristics of a nativistic cult; the charismatic leader, the goal of restoration of socio-economic forms to a prior state, the search for ethnic identity and the renewal of the traditional community ethic. Had these been the only characteristics of the organization, the Alianza might have become a revitalization movement according to the definition of Anthony Wallace.

   The main direction of such a process of change is toward cultural divergence or, in the evolutionary theory of Sahlins and Service (1960), "Specific Evolution." This apparently, is the main direction of many nativistic, cargo, messianic, etc. cults.

   The Alianza, on the other hand, included from its inception innovative changes such as unity of purpose and action on a scale long unfamiliar to Hispanos, the linking of human, ethnic and political rights with those of property and, finally, the transformation of the action program from a base in traditional vigilantism to active participation in today's major national sweep for social change.

   Here, I think, is an example of deliberate innovation that does not fit the revitalization concept. As an analogy, the emergence of a divergent sect of "Christian" Jews with a revitalized religious concept can be compared with the early Christian Church and its relation to the transformations between the time of the late Roman Empire and the emergence of the Medieval State. The latter changes seem to fit the stagewise advance to a higher level which Sahlins and Service call "General Evolution" (1960:50-52).

The Alianza movement is as yet very young, yet the changes it has stimulated make possible a new direction for the Hispano rural communities. Presently under severe stress of rapid acculturation and forced emigration for livelihood, they could restabilize if the conditions of existence for which the Alianza presses were met. It has already been noted that some avenues of economic development have been opened as a result of the Alianza's campaign. It should be added that those Hispano communities which have the resources for self-support (Chimayo, for example) possess both cultural stability and the flexibility to incorporate elements of the majority culture which are compatible with Hispano values.

Can it be said that cultural revitalization and social revolution are alternative aspects of the same process of deliberate innovative change? If so, it is logical that a revitalization movement may develop into a revolution, and that an aborted or detoured revolution may become a revitalization movement.

In setting criteria for predicting the success or failure of a revitalization movement, Anthony Wallace (1956:279) implies that "success" might be equivalent to social revolution:

> While a great deal of doctrine in every movement (and, indeed, in every person's mazeway) is extremely unrealistic in that predictions of events made on the basis of its assumptions will prove to be more or less in error, there is only one sphere of behavior in which such error is fatal to the success of a revitalization movement: prediction of the outcome of conflict situations. If the organization cannot predict successfully the consequences of its own mores and of its opponents' mores in a power struggle, its demise is very likely. If, on the other hand, it is canny about conflict, or if the amount of resistance is low, it can be extremely "unrealistic" or extremely unconventional in other matters without running much risk of early collapse.

While cultural change was not an objective of the Alianza, some cultural changes are occurring due to the easing of the cultural enclavement of the rural communities. This, then, is a by-product of the past struggles. Yet, within the movement that is sweeping the country, the greatest cultural change that is sought is one in the dominant culture. As Dr. Martin Luther King (1968:25) stated shortly before his death:

> The American people are infected with racism--that is the peril. Paradoxically, they are also infected with democratic ideals--that is the hope. While doing wrong, they have the potential to do right. But they do not have a millenium to make changes.

It is in the light of this national perspective that the social changes of which the Alianza is the catalyst should be viewed.

NOTES

1. Background for this report is field and archival research conducted in 1960-1964. Results are incorporated into a doctoral dissertation entitled "Hispanic Americans of the Ute Frontier" (University of Colorado, 1966). To this background have been added news items, conversations with Alianza members and attendance at open meetings and annual conventions of the Alianza. Because more recent data are informal and undigested, and because of the rapid acceleration of changes since 1966, conclusions stated and implied in this report are tentative and incomplete.

Thanks are due to Anselmo Tijerina for verifying the factual material of the report and to Peter Nabokov for letting me examine some of his unpublished data.

2. The term "Hispano" is used to mean Spanish-speaking people of northern New Mexico and their relatives living in other states. From Albuquerque northward, virtually all Spanish-speaking people are descendants of the colonial families of New Mexico, starting with the group of less than one thousand souls who accompanied De Vargas on his "Reconquest" in 1694. As new emigrants came in but a thin trickle until the latter Nineteenth Century, the present Hispano population is somewhat like an oversized kin-group. When perfect strangers met, they check their genealogies and generally are able to find a kin link.

The Territorial Government, which remained under the control of the Military from the time of the United States takeover in 1846 until late in the Nineteenth Century, abolished the previous form of municipal government and caused Church administration to fall into the hands of prelates foreign to the Hispanic tradition. For this reason, the only native, non-familial, institutions remaining operative in the Hispano communities are the Ditch Associations and the Penitente Brotherhood. Both of these institutions have lost ground in recent years, leaving the extended kin group as the most binding force in village life. The great stability of these groups is presently threatened with dissolution due to forced emigration from communities where land loss had destroyed the economic base.

REFERENCES

AFDM
   1963   Alianza Federal de Mercedes: Constitucion Nacional
           adopted September 21, 1963.
Gonzales, Nancie L.
   1967   The Spanish American of New Mexico: A Distinctive Heritage. Advance Report #9. Mexican-American Study Project. Los Angeles, University of California Graduate School of Business Administration.

King, Martin Luther
    1968   Showdown for Non-Violence. Look Magazine 32/8:23-25.
Sahlins, Marshall D. and Elman R. Service
    1960   Evolution of Culture. Ann Arbor, University of Michigan Press.
Samora, Julian, ed.
    1966   La Raza: Forgotten Americans. Notre Dame, University of Notre Dame Press.
USDA
    1937   Notes on Community Owned Land Grants in New Mexico. United States Department of Agriculture Soil Conservation Service Region 8. Albuquerque, New Mexico. Section of Human Surveys.
Wallace, Anthony F. C.
    1956   Revitalization Movements. American Anthropologist 58: 264-283.

THE ANGLO SIDE OF ACCULTURATION

Paul Kutsche
Colorado College

It takes at least two cultures for acculturation to take place.
Anthropology has proceeded for the most part on the tacit assumption
that the only system which requires examination is the one undergo-
ing acculturation. Particularly, we have avoided a critical examination of Anglo culture in the United States as the acculturating
force. Martin Luther King, in the article from which Frances Swadesh
quotes in the preceding paper, asserts that

> The American people are infected with racism....
> Paradoxically, they are also infected with democratic
> ideals.... To end poverty, to extirpate prejudice, to
> free a tormented conscience, to make a tomorrow of
> justice, fair play and creativity--all these are worthy
> of the American ideal (King 1968).

I. The Problem

The task I set myself, in this last paper of the symposium, is
to examine the history of certain portions of the Anglo-American
ideal in relation to our treatment of minority groups, in particular
the Spanish Americans. I do so conscious that every generation
writes its own history, and that our own discipline, as Cora DuBois
recently reminded us, is ethnocentric, has always been, and inevitably will continue to be (DuBois 1967).

As participants in the intellectual atmosphere of our times,
American anthropologists started in the nineteenth century with the
assumption, shared with other Americans with the possible exception
of the Quakers, that inside the boundaries of the United States
American Indians and other minorities were destined to oblivion.
(Vivid documentation of this assumption, drawn from school textbooks,
is to be found in Elson 1964:71-81.) We have come not much faster
than the rest of the population to realize that our non-Anglo ethnic
groups show remarkable persistence, both culturally and demographically (e.g., Hallowell 1946; Hadley 1957).

Until very recently, anthropologists like other Americans have
assumed that the aim of efforts to deal practically with minority
groups was to bring them into the mainstream of American life.

Anthropologists along with other liberals have spoken of giving minority peoples the right to choose whether to stay in their cultural enclaves or move into the mainstream, with the assumption that most would choose to move.

We are now beginning to understand that perhaps a majority of non-Anglo minorities have not moved and have no intention of moving. Glazer and Moynihan argued this point vociferously, if not always elegantly or with ideal documentation, concerning Irish, Italians, Jews, Puerto Ricans, and Negroes in Beyond the Melting Pot (1963). Some Negroes, we now know, prefer some kind of cultural pluralism to the perfect integration of their race into Anglo society (cf. Lincoln 1961; Essien-Udom 1961). Even American Indians are at last fighting back, not just by figurative retreats further back onto their reservations, but through more aggressive measures to protect their cultural separateness which at least on book dustjackets is being called the "Red Power Movement" (Steiner 1968).

In the context of considerable Negro violence, and occasional shows of weapons among American Indians which have stopped just short of violence (e.g., Steiner 1968:1-5), it is very interesting but not surprising that Spanish Americans are using guns to protect their way of life. Spanish culture on both sides of the Atlantic Ocean is marked by emphasis on bravado shows of maleness, including force, and skill in the use of force. If we are to be amazed, it is that Spanish villagers have withheld from violence so often and have inflicted so little damage to their enemies.

After Dr. Swadesh's thorough review of the Alianza as a relatively non-violent channel for the frustrations and the hopes for continued cultural existence of Spanish Americans, I do not propose to add more detail on how and why Spanish Americans are trying to preserve themselves, although the question will be a major part of the report of my own field research from New Mexico.[1]

Instead, I return deliberately to the ethnocentrism of American anthropology at a moment in American intellectual development when self-doubt and the analysis of American national goals are major themes of American discussion, to pose the following questions: Why has Anglo America insisted on the assimilation of minority groups, most particularly in the use of the English language? What elements or forces in Anglo-American culture history make valid the pressure to treat every citizen as an equal before the law or, to put the statement on its head, to apply the same standard of values, as expressed in the law and elsewhere, to every American regardless of his cultural differences? And how have these pressures to uniformity and equality affected Spanish Americans? Our discipline has always assumed that the values of non-Western cultures are logical portions of the non-Western cultures we study. I proceed on the same assumption concerning Anglo-American culture. The hypothesis I want to test is that an important element in American pressure to cultural conformity has been fear that the nation could not survive otherwise, that encouraging the separate identity of non-Anglo minorities would tear the nation apart.

II. Methodological Apologia

A humble acknowledgment of the superficial methodology employed in this paper is in order before plunging into the data of American intellectual history. Historians, as the great medievalist Helen Maud Cam used to proclaim, are artists and humanists, not scientists. Their summaries of intellectual and other history, consequently, are artistic productions, and their methods of choosing and arranging data are not open to the same kinds of criticism as those of scientists. Rarely, an historian will make a systematic quantitative, or quasi-quantitative survey of all of the relevant data on a topic, such as Ruth Miller Elson did in her history of American school textbooks (1964).

This paper is methodologically historical, in the sense above. My sources have been intellectual histories of the United States.[2] This effort is open to the criticism made by Honigmann of national character studies which read, he says, "like a historian's account of the temper of an age, or like Hogarth's pictorial representations of eighteenth-century London types" (Honigmann 1967:99). In a short paper I can hope to do no more than to make a hypothesis and ask a few questions about the history of certain aspects of modern American culture which have impact upon minority groups. A thorough test of these or related questions would require sophisticated techniques of sampling and handling data, probably using computers. B. N. Colby (1966) has been experimenting with similar techniques in handling American Indian texts. If this paper incites another anthropologist to test my questions in such a manner, I shall be content.

III. Anglo-American Attitudes toward Minorities

The themes in American intellectual history which I find particularly relevant to our treatment of minorities are egalitarianism, self-conscious nationalism, and racism.

Before examining the first of these recurring themes, perhaps we should remind ourselves briefly, what all of us as comparative ethnographers know: that to ignore the existence of ethnic groups in the law is only one way of constructing a complex society. Carleton Coon in Caravan labels the antithesis the "mosaic" society, and finds its extreme in the Indian caste system, with other examples in the Aztec Empire and the Middle East (Coon 1958:2-4). Thus far I regard Coon's assertion as unexceptionable. But he goes on to describe nationalism as incompatible with a mosaic society:

> Nationalism demands that every person living permanently
> in a country become a citizen and feel himself a member
> of the nation with rights and responsibilities equal to

those of all other members (1958:5).

This is not necessarily true. Great Britain has flourished for several centuries with unequal rights and responsibilities, and so has every other nation with hereditary monarchy and nobility. Examples of horizontal rather than vertical inequality are rarer, but still characteristic of Renaissance and modern European regionalism. Egalitarianism is, of course, not absolutely peculiar to the United States, but it seems to have flourished here more vigorously than in any other major country of the world--even more than in its intellectual birthplace, France.

American culture is qualitatively different from European in a number of respects. Perhaps the most unique aspect of Americanism is its early and deliberate self-consciousness. One of the first and best foreign chroniclers of our nation, de Crevecoeur, asked in 1782 in Letters from an American Farmer, "What then is an American, this new man? He is either an European, or the descendant of an European; hence that strange mixture of blood, which you will find in no other country" (quoted in Curti 1943:3). "Individuals of all nations are melted into a new race of men," both by blood and because of the exchange of old prejudices for "new ones from the new mode of life he has embraced, the new government he obeys, and the new rank he holds" (quoted in Curti 1943:11).

Noah Webster two years later predicted of his nascent culture that

> this country must, at some future time, be as distinguished
> by the superiority of her literary improvements as she is
> already by the liberality of her civil and ecclesiastical
> institutions. Europe is grown old in folly, corruption,
> and tyranny--in that country laws are perverted, manners
> are licentious, literature is declining, and human nature
> is debased. For America in her infancy to adopt the pre-
> sent maxims of the old world would be to stamp the wrinkle
> of decrepit age upon the bloom of youth, and to plant the
> seed of decay in a vigorous constitution (quoted in Curti
> 1943:148).

This theme of pure young America set as counterpoise to sinful and febrile Europe was often to be repeated in nineteenth and even twentieth century American history and literature. Webster and other cultural nationalists advocated simplified spelling and arithmetic, universal education, even for women and even in music, the printing of books in America, the growth of the country's own geography, its own aesthetics of the wilderness, and the writing of its own culture history. Many of them not only advocated, but worked out some of the first details of this nationalism (Curti 1943:138-53). The first great American historian, George Bancroft, echoed Noah Webster in the 1860's in this eulogy to his nation:

> In the fullness of time a republic rose in the wilder-
> ness of America. Thousands of years had passed away

before this child of the ages could be born. From
whatever there was of good in the systems of the former
centuries she drew her nourishment; the wrecks of the
past were her warnings.... The fame of this only
daughter of freedom went out into all the lands of the
earth; from her the human race drew hope (quoted in
Gabriel 1956:316).

The deliberate invention of cultural nationalism in the late
eighteenth century served several purposes at once. First was an
attempt to experience the American colonial world, for which so many
migrants had given up so much in Europe, as worth the struggle.
Second was the conflict between British and other European patterns
of living for ascendancy in the New World. For the most part English
culture won unconsciously, although a few sour notes were struck like
DeWitt Clinton's complaint that the language was "melting us down into one people" (Gleason 1964:22). In the framing of our formal docu-
ments, particularly the Declaration of Independence and the Constitution, strong French intellectual influence overlay but seldom contra-
dicted the powerful stream of British legal custom. A third conscious
product of cultural nationalism was egalitarianism, which both produced and was promoted by Thomas Jefferson's Declaration that "all
men are created equal." The aim of simplifications in spelling and
arithmetic, including the choice of the decimal system, was that
every freeman might participate in the benefits of American life.
As we shall see, the only major price which Homo americanus was asked
to pay for these benefits was to abandon, in the melting, virtually
all cultural backgrounds which might not jibe perfectly with North-
western European patterns.

By the third decade of the nineteenth century egalitarianism
had become the most remarkable feature of American national life,
according to the cultural historian's reliable friend, Alexis de
Tocqueville, whose first words in the introduction to Democracy in
America are,

Among the novel objects that attracted my attention
during my stay in the United States, nothing struck me
more forcibly than the general equality of condition among
the people. I readily discovered the prodigious influence
that this primary fact exercises on the whole course of
society; it gives a peculiar direction to public opinion
and a peculiar tenor to the laws; it imparts new maxims
to the governing authorities and peculiar habits to the
governed....

The more I advanced in the study of American Society,
the more I perceived that this equality of condition is
the fundamental fact from which all others seem to be
derived and the central point at which all my observations constantly terminated (de Tocqueville 1945:v.1,3).

A nation of equal freemen, convinced that their peculiar institutions were purified from the wrecks of Europe, were not far removed from regarding themselves as chosen of God, and the extension of their political rule as an extension of God's virtue. Indeed, even in the absence of religious sanction, one of the nation's founding fathers had already advocated territorial expansion. Benjamin Franklin extolled the political leader "that acquires new Territory, if he finds it vacant, or removes the Natives to give his own People room" (quoted in Stourzh 1954:61). The ideology of Manifest Destiny was a logical consequence, and Mexico was the first to feel its impact. The Yale historian Ralph Henry Gabriel tells us that,

> Save for an angry minority that looked upon the Mexican War
> as an undertaking to open up new territory for slavery,
> citizens of the Republic found justification for expansion
> in the mission of America to extend the principles and
> practices of democracy, as [General Stephen] Kearny had
> so promptly done, into the virtually empty Western wil-
> derness (1956:73).

Kearny did not, of course, bring much of anything to New Mexico except the American flag, and it was not until after the United States recovered sufficiently from the Civil War that the nation turned its attention seriously to the Americanization of the only continental territory it ever conquered which already contained a strongly resistant European culture.

The Civil War interrupted the steady flow of the American nation toward its Manifest Destiny in a variety of ways, one of which, I suggest from the vantage of hindsight, it never quite recovered from. This was the serious challenge to the assumption that all Americans are equal. Although the positive position in the debate won its unequivocal victory on the battlefield, later developments in American thought suggest that one of the scars of the War was a niggling doubt whether it would in the end turn out to be possible for all Americans to be like all other Americans.

The immediate and overt intellectual result of the War contained no doubts at all. From perhaps 1870 to 1900 the doctrine of Manifest Destiny overcame all important opposition and wedded itself to the cult of the individual and the Gospel of Wealth. Even men of science were converted, and two of anthropology's own founding fathers, John Wesley Powell and Lewis Henry Morgan, stated that "republicanism is the ultimate in social evolution" (Powell, quoted in Gabriel 1956: 180).

At a less scientific level, the success of the success cult was phenomenal. Horatio Alger wrote 119 books, almost all of which were best sellers. William Makepeace Thayer wrote biographies which were virtually manuals on how any poor boy might become rich and successful (Gabriel 1956:646-47). In his famous essay Acres of Diamonds, Russell Conwell firmly linked the Gospel of Wealth to the Gospel of Puritanism and the older Biblical gospel. Curti tells us that

Conwell believed that material riches were a mark of God's
approval.... It undoubtedly encouraged many to strive for
success by the old-fashioned and "divinely sanctioned"
methods of personal effort, and bolstered their support
of the prevailing economic and social order in which such
individual success was possible "right where you are"
(Curti 1943:649).

Racism mixed itself more strongly with American destiny during
the last quarter of the nineteenth century than it did even in the
antebellum South. The Yankee Congregationalist preacher Josiah
Strong held in 1885,

It is manifest that the Anglo-Saxon holds in his hands
the destinies of mankind, and it is evident that the
United States is to become the home of this race, the
principal seat of his power, the great center of his
influence (quoted in Gabriel 1956:369).

If I read not amiss, this powerful race will move down
upon Mexico, down upon Central and South America, out
upon the islands of the sea, over upon Africa and beyond (quoted in Gabriel 1956:370).

Strong's divine imperialism evokes a better-known statement, in
which President William McKinley confesses to visiting Methodists
during the Spanish-American War:

I walked the floor of the White House night after night
until midnight, and I am not ashamed to tell you, gen-
tlemen, that I went down on my knees and prayed Almighty
God for light and guidance more than one night. And one
night late it came to me this way--I don't know how it
was, but it came...that there was nothing left for us
to do but to take them all, and to educate the Filipinos,
and uplift them and civilize and Christianize them, and
by God's grace do the very best we could by them, as our
fellow-men for whom Christ also died. And then I went
to bed, and went to sleep, and slept soundly, and the
next morning I sent for the chief engineer of the War
Department...and I told him to put the Philippines on
the map of the United States, and there they are, and
there they will stay while I am President (Leech 1959:
345)!

McKinley's successor seems to have escaped such agonies of in-
decision in the small hours of the White House night. Roosevelt's
Winning of the West is a clear-eyed defense of Anglo expansion,
which was inevitable

unless we were willing to see the American continent
fall into the hands of some other strong power; and
even had we adopted such lucicrous policy, the Indians
themselves would have made war upon us (Roosevelt 1891:
v.1,331).

Although acknowledging several specific injustices done to Indian tribes,

> As a nation, our Indian policy is to be blamed, because
> of the weakness it displayed...and its occasional lean-
> ing to the policy of the sentimental humanitarians...
> (1891:v.1,333).

Imperialist though he was, Roosevelt avoided the racist excesses which dominated respectable intellectual circles of his day. In the same volume, he describes both the English and the American people as more racially heterogeneous, and the Americans as having been more heterogeneous for the previous century, than other European nations. "But all were being rapidly fused into one people" (1891:v.1,21), he proudly asserts, and he is at some pains to correct the error of those who claim that trans-Appalachian settlement by Whites was pre-dominantly Anglo-Saxon.

Not long after Roosevelt wrote his account of American conquest, an explicitly anti-racist document appeared which raised the old theme of egalitarianism back into predominance. Israel Zangwill produced The Melting Pot in 1908, and the phrase, already anticipated in remarks quoted from de Crevecoeur and Clinton, caught on immediately and generally, as an apt metaphor to express the American equalizing process. Most Americans using the phrase, according to a recent review of the term (Gleason 1964), seemed to share Henry Ford's assumption that into the melting pot went the European immigrant and out of it came an assembly-line product monolingual in the American tongue, with behavior and values invented in England and adapted to American needs. The view that any degree of ethnic pluralism could characterize a healthy modern nation was never expressed by more than a small minority of social critics. A more serious flaw in what we might call the "melting pot ethos" is its blind eye to pheno-type. Zangwill himself was only concerned about Jews, but the term is used in a general context supposedly to include the Americaniza-tion of all contributors to the demographic scene. No one, so far as I know, has ever criticized the ethos on the basis of the un-meltability of people who do not look like Anglo Americans. The criticism is particularly, but not exclusively, relevant to Negroes. I believe it is with the melting pot idea that anxiety over egali-tarianism, first acutely felt in the United States during the Civil War, surfaces again. While the positive side of the melting pot ethos is the belief that America is large-hearted enough to take any human being and raise him up to American status, the underside is that America is not able to cope with cultural strains which threaten the domination of the Northern European. It was the negative side which was expressed in the Immigration Act of 1924, which set the quota for each country at "two percent of the number born in each country resident in the United States at the time of the 1890 census" (Encyclopedia Britannica). The recipe for the pot was not merely to be kept static, but turned back a generation to the good old brew of mother's kitchen.

This is a convenient chronological point at which to return to Northern New Mexico. For the United States showed little interest in New Mexico for several decades after Kearny's conquest, until the Santa Fe Railroad opened up the Territory in the 1870's. Although the Surveyor General began filing claims in 1854, interest in Spanish land on the part of Anglos became active after about 1875. According to the state archives of New Mexico, the grants of the village of "Ritos" which I studied during 1966-67 were filed in 1878 and action was taken on them between 1879 and 1886. It is customary among historians sympathetic to Spanish Americans to lay considerable personal blame on a number of lawyers known pejoratively as the "Santa Fe Ring" for despoiling the original holders of land, during this period and for the first decade or two of the twentieth century. While I have no intention of absolving any of them of personal responsibility, in the light of the foregoing synopsis of Anglo-American intellectual history it makes better cultural sense to regard the lawyers as typical representatives of Anglo America, bringing capitalist civilization to the wilderness. If they read Conwell's _Acres of Diamonds_, they certainly found their success right in their own back yards--or at least in the back yards to which the Atchison Topeka and the Santa Fe brought them. And if after a few rounds in court a good deal of the land shifted from the hands of the original grantees to those of Protestant Anglos, what was the difference between this process and the concentration of wealth and power farther East to the hands of industrialists whom we afflict with the equally pejorative sobriquet "Robber Barons?" From the point of view of the most respectable contemporary American thought, both sets of men were equally virtuous. The fact that robber barons often grew rich off men of their own ethnic background, while the Santa Fe Ring fleeced people of a different heritage was not of any particular importance.

Racism is still a very live part of American culture, as the riot commission report has just sharply reminded us (National Advisory Commission 1968). But I do not think it was ever virulent in the part of Spanish-speaking America with which I am particularly concerned--Northern New Mexico--and it is not particularly evident today. Both Anglos and Anglicized Spaniards point with pride at the present time to their integration. They serve together, often harmoniously, in state and local government bodies, on the boards of charitable societies, and in chambers of commerce.[3] Anglo pressure on the remnant of Spanish Americans who are still settled on their land grants is of cultural patterns and not of genetic origin. The Anglos and the Anglicized Spaniards of New Mexico today both represent the American values of the equality of the individual before the law, with its consequent impersonality, even depersonalization, of individual responsibility for advancement up the ladder of success, of mobility, and perhaps in a residual and unconscious form of the divine sanction for the man who can make something of himself. Both together pose the same threat to the village Spaniard, who still living on his own land makes his choices in terms of the Spanish values of respect for authority and age, of the unwritten personal obligation of political authorities as more important than the written law, of the responsibility of the individual to his family for the welfare of the whole group, of permanent attachment to a specific piece of land, and of divine sanction for the man who acts con vergüenza, (a term which among many other things, means action with a due regard to the good opinion of one's fellow villagers). The use of the Spanish language is an important part of cultural preservation, but one about which many Spaniards feel ambivalent.

One of the fascinating confusions of present-day New Mexico is that just as there are Anglos and Spaniards who epitomize the Anglo-American values, so there are both ethnic groups found to a certain extent on the side of the Spanish values. The dramatis personae of the events following the raid on the courthouse at Tierra Amarilla in June, 1967, illustrate the confusion nicely. Members of the Alianza invaded the courthouse in order to make a citizen's arrest upon district attorney Alfonso Sanchez. Every one of those wounded or taken to Canjilon as hostage was Spanish-American with the exception of an Anglo journalist. After the raid, individuals working frantically out of Santa Fe to avert more widespread strife were, in addition to a number of Spanish-American officials, Anglo Governor David Cargo, Anglo sociologist Clark Knowlton, and Peter Nabokov, Anglo journalist.

IV. Choices Concerning Pluralism

While picking out values from the intellectual history of a prolifically verbal modern nation is in some ways capricious and arbitrary, the identification of national decisions made in terms of these values can be firmer. Kluckhohn's definition of the term value implies decision-making:

> A value is a conception...of the desirable which influences the selection from available modes, means and ends of action (Kluckhohn and others 1951:395).

It may be useful, in terms of this definition, to examine a few points in American history when the choice was made whether the nation was to be pluralistic or culturally uniform.

A. Indians

The first set of choices to be mentioned are those concerning American Indians. The first treaty contracted between the new nation and an Indian tribe (the Delaware, 1778), contains the following provision in Article VI:

And it is further agreed on between the contracting parties should it for the future be found conducive for the
mutual interest of both parties to invite any othe tribes
who have been friends to the interest of the United
States, to join the present confederation, and to form
a state whereof the Delaware nation shall be the head,
and have a representation in Congress (U. S. Senate
1903:3).

Whether the term "state" is to be understood in the sense of "one of
the United States" is open to question, but it must have meant some
kind of legally recognized cultural entity. Whether the United
States Commissioners, representing a nation at war and anxious to
gain allies where they could, meant anything at all by the promise
is equally open to question. In any event, most of the Delaware
sided with the British, so this choice for pluralism was lost.

The opposite choice was written into law in treaties fostered
by President Washington to close hostilities with a number of Indian
tribes at the end of the Revolutionary War. Article XIV of the
Treaty of Holston (1791) is a good example:

That the Cherokee nation may be led to a greater degree
of civilization, and to become herdsmen and cultivators,
instead of remaining in a state of hunters, the United
States will from time to time furnish gratuitously the
said nation with useful implements of husbandry...
(U. S. Senate 1903:25).

The United States abundantly carried out this promise. The Cherokee
Nation, partly in consequence of adopting modern agricultural
methods, became prosperous by the second decade of the nineteenth
century although they gave up neither their language nor much else
of their aboriginal culture. In 1827, having already become literate
as a result of Sequoyah's syllabary, the Cherokee adopted a constitution modeled for the most part on the U. S. Constitution, but with
provision for retention of Cherokee land and culture (Mooney 1900:
112-113). It is reasonable to speculate that such a successful Indian government might have petitioned later for admission into the
United States as the State of Cherokee. The Cherokee had made
their choice, but the United States chose the opposite position
during the next decade, under the leadership of the State of Georgia
and Andrew Jackson, and by the end of 1838 all but a few outlaws had
been driven to Indian Territory and the Nation in the Southeast was
destroyed. Anecdotes from other tribes could be added, but the pattern was similar everywhere east of the Mississippi.

These decisions of the United States against Indian tribes were
imperialist, racist and not egalitarian. The reservation system,
which is the American compromise with pluralism in the Indian direction, is still uneasy and awkward for Anglos to accept, and of course
legal difficulties and confusions are as rife in the 1960's as during the nineteenth century.

B. <u>Language</u>

Competitors for English as legal languages have included German in Pennsylvania, French in Louisiana, and Spanish in New Mexico. German was never legally recognized in Pennsylvania,[4] although German dialects continue to the present day to be used by the Amish and Mennonites, whose battle to preserve their non-Anglo culture is still occasionally <u>sub judice</u>.

French in Louisiana is unrecognized by the state constitution, which requires that "The general exercises in the public schools shall be conducted in the English language" (Article XII, Sec. 12 in Abrahamson 1962:v.1).[5] Apparently English has been all too successful in that state, for according to a current news story "...legislators from this area are campaigning for...French [to be] taught in schools" (Denver Post 1968).

In New Mexico, the law still supports bilingualism. Article XII of the state constitution requires that all teachers in public schools be "proficient in both the English and Spanish languages...." Laws are to be published in both languages for the first twenty years of the state (i.e., to 1932), but amendments to the constitution are to be published in both languages without regard to time. The educational rights of children of Spanish descent, and the right to franchise in terms of linguistic ability, <u>int. al</u>., are protected by special provisions, amendment to which is more difficult than amendments to other portions of the constitution.[6] To the best of my knowledge, the franchise and law-publication provisions are adhered to. But the bilingual requirement for public school teachers is disregarded.

The position of the Spanish language in New Mexico is in fact curious and somewhat pathetic. The village of "Ritos" speaks Spanish, only about half the citizens being reasonably fluent in English, yet written notices of dances and other events of local interest are always printed in English, because almost no one reads Spanish. Formal instruction in Spanish is not available below the high school level, and those who take the subject in high school gain little reading fluency. The State Department of Public Instruction began in 1965 a demonstration project to teach Spanish from the first grade to native Spanish speakers, and also a demonstration using linguistic methods developed in Miami for Cuban refugees, to teach English from the same age-level. Both projects started with about equal support, and with equal encouragement to local school districts to adopt them. The Miami program for teaching English has subsequently been adopted by many school boards. Instruction in Spanish has been adopted by very few. Members of the board of education in the district containing "Ritos" (a majority of whom are native Spanish speakers), like board members elsewhere, have been so fully sold on the importance of speaking English well with an Anglo accent that they are suspicious of programs which, they fear, will keep their children at a disadvantage in economic competition with Anglos. This seems to be a case of "oversell," in which Anglo pressure to conform to the value of competition and to the monolingual mode of the country at large (although unsuccessful at the home and village level), is defeating a relatively inexpensive program which would aid Spanish Americans in retaining their own culture and establishing contact with other Spanish-speaking countries. As a result Spanish culture in New Mexico is totally local, feeding on itself, and slowly shrinks.

It would be an exaggeration to claim that monolingualism as an Anglo value has swept other languages away before it, either in the instances mentioned, or among American Indian tribes. In the home, languages other than English have shown amazing persistence. But the trend has been constant and in one direction, until conscious efforts began to be made within the past four or five years to use formal education to help retain native languages (e.g., the New Mexican example cited above, a Carnegie-supported campaign to re-introduce the Sequoyah syllabary into daily use in Oklahoma, the Rough Rock Project to use Navajo as a language of instruction in school).

C. Legal Institutions

French, Spanish, and American Indian cultures have provided alternatives to English common law.

French custom, in the Napoleonic Code, forms the basis for the legal system of Louisiana, but "even in Louisiana there has occurred a partial fusion of English and French doctrines, particularly in criminal law" (Grant and Nixon 1968:388).

Spanish (i.e., Mexican) legal concepts were to determine ownership of land in the territory ceded to the United States by Mexico, according to Articles VIII and IX of the Treaty of Guadalupe Hidalgo. In fact, according to most students of land problems in New Mexico, Mexican precedent has not been followed (e.g., Leonard 1943:80-89; Knowlton 1964). The formal legal code of the State of New Mexico is now based on the United States Constitution and on English common law. It is slightly modified in practise in Spanish-American counties by personalism, mutual responsibility within family groups, and differential enforcement of laws depending on how well they fit Spanish-American values. (These modifications are labelled "favoritism," "nepotism," and "corruption" by Anglo critics.)

Laws controlling the behavior of American Indians are in perhaps a greater mess today than previously, with tribal, county, state and Federal jurisdictions almost never clearly separated (author's field notes, 1961, recording interview with Frank M. Parker, former attorney to the Eastern Band of the Cherokee). The Federal Government itself has difficulty deciding whether to handle Indians separately or by the same standards as all other Americans. As this paper is written, Congress is debating whether to extend the provisions of the latest civil rights bill to American Indians on reservations.

V. Conclusions

Anglo-American insistence upon cultural homogeneity I have documented, I think, as much as one can within the limitations of this symposium. The pressure in American history to treat citizens as a consciously new breed, who have cut their ties with all political and most cultural traditions in other countries, extends in time at least as far back as the American Revolution. Non-acceptance of Anglo culture by American minorities, and the unwillingness of the Anglo majority to offer equality to various minorities, have at different times been swept under the rug or defended under the banners of Manifest Destiny and of racism.

The hypothesis that one of the principal forces urging Anglos to make minorities conform has been fear, remains to be tested by a more searching investigation. I see the high degree of self-consciousness in the start of American nationalism, the anxieties resulting from the Civil War, blatant insistence on Anglo-Saxon superiority in the late nineteenth century, and the dull uniformity of the supposed product of the melting pot as consistent with the fear hypothesis, but by no means conclusive demonstrations.

The forces in the acculturating nation which require acculturating minorities to take on Anglo behavior at the expense of their own are at least as deeply rooted in history as the forces for persistence among the minorities. In the climate of accommodation which the United States has achieved in the mid-twentieth century, one of the contributions which anthropology can make toward solving ethnic problems is the deliberate and systematic investigation of those aspects of the dominant culture which stand in the way of harmony between groups. The anthropologist has always urged that policy changes concerning subordinate cultures be made on the basis of thorough understanding of the whole culture, and of the impact of change on the entire range of cultural institutions. If, as now seems evident, the dominant American culture must change to permit other patterns to enjoy their own fulfillment unharrassed, the dominant culture deserves no less thorough an understanding.

NOTES

1. Field ethnography was carried on during 1966 and 1967 in a New Mexican village to which I give the pseudonym "Ritos," under grant GS 1313 from the National Science Foundation.

2. My guides in American history are Louis Geiger, Frank Tucker, and Tom K. Barton, all of the Department of History, Colorado College. Geiger has been particularly generous with references and discussion of themes. Van B. Shaw, Department of Sociology, has helped me with sources on the Black Muslims, and Rudolph Gomez,

Department of Political Science, with sources in government.

3. This statement is only apparently contradictory to Bodine's description of discrimination against the Spanish in Taos in a preceding paper in this volume. The part of Northern New Mexico which I know best has few tourists, and discrimination by resident Anglos against Spaniards would be suicidal. Santa Fe, which I also know, is the state capital, and here too Anglos must get along with Spaniards. It is true, however, that Anglos have financial and other ties with the rest of the United States which the Spanish generally lack, and are able to educate their children better and to gain better jobs. It is also true that many Anglos and Spaniards who work harmoniously together do not socialize outside of business.

4. Because of time pressure, I have not followed up leads given me by Tom K. Barton concerning a dispute between Benjamin Franklin and Gottlieb Mittelberger on the language question, and by Arnold Pilling concerning an attempt to make German an official language at the time of the Civil War.

5. For the same reason, I have not checked previous Louisiana constitutions. The one quoted from was approved in 1921.

6. Sections of the New Mexico constitution dealing with language are as follows:

Article VII, Elective Franchise.

Sec. 3. _Religious_ _and_ _racial_ _equality_ _protected_; _restrictions_ _on_ _amendments_. The right of any citizen of the State to vote, hold office, or sit upon juries, shall never be restricted, abridged or impaired on account of religion, race, language or color, or inability to speak, read or write the English or Spanish languages except as may be otherwise provided in this Constitution; and the provisions of this section...shall never be amended except upon a vote of the people of this state in an election at which at least three-fourths of the electors voting in the whole State, and at least two-thirds of those voting in each county of the State, shall vote for such amendment.

Article XII, Education.

Sec. 8. _Teachers_ _to_ _learn_ _English_ _and_ _Spanish_. The legislature shall provide for the training of teachers in the normal schools or otherwise so that they may become proficient in both the English and Spanish languages, to qualify them to teach Spanish-speaking pupils and students in the public schools and educational institutions of the State, and shall provide proper means and methods to facilitate the teaching of the English language and other branches of learning to such pupils and students.

Sec. 10. _Educational_ _Rights_ _of_ _children_ _of_ _Spanish_ _descent_. Children of Spanish descent in the State of New Mexico shall never be denied the right and privilege of admission and attendance in the public schools or other public educational institutions of the State, and they shall never be classed in separate schools, but shall forever enjoy perfect equality with other children in all public schools and educational institutions of the State. This section shall never be amended except upon a vote of the people of this State, in an election at which at least three-fourths of the electors voting in the whole State and at least two-thirds of those voting in each county in the State shall vote for such amendment.

But the procedure for amendments to other portions of the constitution, as spelled out in Article XIX, Sec. 1, requires only a majority in each house of the legislature, followed by vote of a majority of all the voters of the state.

Article XX. Miscellaneous.
Sec. 12. <u>Publication of laws in English and Spanish</u>. For the first twenty years after this Constitution goes into effect all laws passed by the legislature shall be published in both the English and Spanish languages and thereafter such publication shall be made as the legislature may provide.

Publication of Amendments to the constitution, however, is handled separately in Article XIX, Sec. 1, as follows:

The Secretary of State shall cause any such amendment or amendments to be published in at least one newspaper in every county of the State, where a newspaper is published once each week, for four consecutive weeks, in English and Spanish when newspapers in both of said languages are published in such counties....

(All quotes from Abrahamson 1962:v.2.)

REFERENCES

Abrahamson, Shirley S., ed.
    1962   Constitution of the United States. (3 vols.) Dobbs Ferry, N. Y., Oceana Publications, Inc.
Colby, Benjamin N.
    1966   The Analysis of Culture Content and the Patterning of Narrative Concern in Texts. American Anthropologist 68:374-88.
Coon, Carleton S.
    1958   Caravan: The Story of the Middle East. (Revised ed.) New York, Henry Holt & Co., Inc.
Curti, Merle
    1943   The Growth of American Thought. New York, Harper & Brothers.
Denver Post
    1968   Required French Sought for Cajuns. May 8, Associated Press dispatch from Lafayette, Louisiana.
DuBois, Cora
    1967   Is Anthropology Culture-Bound? Paper delivered at 66th annual meeting, American Anthropological Association,

Washington.

Elson, Ruth Miller
1964   Guardians of Tradition: American Schoolbooks of the
        Nineteenth Century. Lincoln, University of Nebraska
        Press.

Essien-Udom, E. U.
1961   Black Nationalism: A Search for Identity in America.
        Chicago, University of Chicago Press.

Gabriel, Ralph Henry
1956   The Course of American Democratic Thought. (Second
        ed.) New York, The Ronald Press Co.

Glazer, Nathan and Daniel Patrick Moynihan
1963   Beyond the Melting Pot. Cambridge, Mass., M. I. T.
        Press.

Gleason, Philip
1964   The Melting Pot: Symbol of Fusion or Confusion?
        American Quarterly 16:20-46.

Grant, Daniel R. and H. C. Nixon
1968   State and Local Government in America. (Second ed.)
        Boston, Allyn & Bacon, Inc.

Hadley, J. Nixon
1957   Demography of the American Indians. In American Indians
        and American Life, G. E. Simpson and J. M. Yinger, eds.
        (The Annals of the American Academy of Political and
        Social Science, v. 311. May.) Philadelphia, The
        American Academy. Pp. 23-30.

Hallowell, A. Irving
1946   Some Psychological Characteristics of the Northeastern
        Indians. In Man in Northeasteastern North America,
        Frederick Johnson, ed. (Papers of the Robert S. Pea-
        body Foundation in Archaeology, vol. 3.) Andover,
        Phillips Academy. Pp. 330-75.

Honigmann, John J.
1967   Personality in Culture. New York, Harper & Row.

King, Martin Luther
1968   Showdown for Non-Violence. Look 32, No. 8:23-25.

Kluckhohn, Clyde and others
1951   Values and Value-Orientations in the Theory of Action:
        An Exploration in Definition and Classification. In
        Toward a General Theory of Action, T. Parsons and E. A.
        Shils, eds. Cambridge, Mass., Harvard University Press.
        Pp. 388-433.

Knowlton, Clark S.
1964   One Approach to the Economic and Social Problems of
        Northern New Mexico. New Mexico Business (September) 3:
        15-22.

Leech, Margaret
1959   In the Days of McKinley. New York, Harper & Row.

Leonard, Olen E.
    1943   The Role of the Land Grant in the Social Organization
            and Social Processes of a Spanish-American Village in
            New Mexico. Ann Arbor, Edwards Bros., Inc.

Lincoln, C. Eric
    1961   The Black Muslims in America. Boston, Beacon Press.

Mooney, James
    1900   Myths of the Cherokee. (Nineteenth Annual Report of
            the Bureau of American Ethnology, Part 1.) Washington,
            Government Printing Office.

National Advisory Commission of Civil Disorders
    1968   Report of the National Advisory Commission on Civil
            Disorders. New York, Bantam Books, Inc.

Roosevelt, Theodore
    1891-96 The Winning of the West. (4 vols.) New York, George
            P. Putnam's Sons.

Steiner, Stan
    1968   The New Indians. New York, Harper & Row.

Stourzh, Gerald
    1954   Benjamin Franklin and American Foreign Policy. Chicago,
            The University of Chicago Press.

Tocqueville, Alexis de
    1945   Democracy in America. (2 vols.) New York, Vintage
            Books.

U. S. Senate
    1903   Indian Affairs. Laws and Treaties. V. 2 (Treaties).
            (57th Congress, Document No. 452.) Washington, Govern-
            ment Printing Office.

Student Paper: Winner of the Elsie Clews Parsons Prize

ECONOMICS, HOUSEHOLD COMPOSITION, AND THE
FAMILY CYCLE: THE BLACKFEET CASE

Lynn A. Robbins
University of Oregon

In this paper I accomplish two objects: first, I explicate
and measure the relationships between economic variables and types
of household composition within an essentially rural sample of 73
households in the Blackfeet (Piegan Branch) Indian Reservation in
northern Montana.[1] Second, I explain the cycle through which modern
Blackfeet families pass.

Like most western American Indian tribes, the Blackfeet live
under conditions of oppression, discrimination and economic isolation. Few studies have been made of the ways in which reservation
Indian families have adapted to harsh and uncertain economic conditions. To my knowledge only Munsell (1967), working among the Pima-
Papago in Arizona, has specifically addressed himself to this problem.

The question asked here is what kinds of empirical generalizations can be derived from a detailed statistical analysis of Blackfeet family adjustments to impoverished conditions? My results add
some information to the meagerly reported social and economic circumstances of western American reservation tribes. Hopefully this
study will also contribute to the growing theoretical and empirical
literature on the relationships among household composition, the
family cycle, and economic variables.

The Sample

Fifty-two of the 73 sample households are from the small rural
Blackfeet community of Heart Butte, 16 are located along major
drainages in the central and southeast sections of the Reservation,
and five are from Browning, Montana, an urban Reservation community
of 2,200 persons. Ninety-six percent of all households in the entire
Heart Butte community are accounted for; the remaining rural and
Browning cases have been selected on the basis of availability. The
total sample is largely rural and probably not representative of the
entire Reservation.

196

Household Typology

There are six household types, the names and compositions of which follow:

1. <u>Independent Nuclear Family Household</u>. Husband and wife, or spouseless husband or spouseless wife along with one or more off-spring; in some instances they include miscellaneous relatives of the wife or husband, (i.e., nieces, nephews, grandchildren, grand-mother, mother, mother-in-law, father, father-in-law, foster chil-dren, and step-children) or even non-kin.

2. <u>Grandparent-Grandchild Household</u>. One or more grandparents, or step-grandparents as household heads with one or more grandchil-dren or step-grandchildren. This family unit is functionally in-distinguishable from independent nuclear family households. Nearly all grandparents in this category have raised their dependent grand-children from infancy, serving as parent surrogates in all respects. They have passed or at least plan to pass property, i.e., land and dwelling, to the grandchildren. The latter is the expected mode of inheritance from parent to dependent offspring. Of the seven house-holds of this type, only one has another type of member outside the grandparent-grandchild or step-grandparent and step-grandchild cate-gories; this lone example is a disabled male sibling of a male house-hold head.

3. <u>Purely Conjugal Pair Household</u>. Conjugal pair with or with-out miscellaneous spouseless and childless kinsmen.

4. <u>Single Person Household</u>. Spouseless, lone individual main-taining a separate household.

5. <u>Joint Family Household</u>. Married siblings and their off-spring. Spouses may or may not be present. Only one such household is recorded. It consists of two sisters, one spouseless but with offspring, the other with spouse and offspring.

6. <u>Extended Family Household</u>. Parents or spouseless parent with married or separated children and their offspring. The house-hold head is one of the parents in the ascending generation. By head is meant principal decision-maker, owner of land and/or dwelling. No extended household consists of more than two nuclear families, although 14 such households occur in the sample. The following is a frequency distribution of each household type:

TABLE I

HOUSEHOLD TYPE	NUMBER
Independent Nuclear	44
Extended	14
Grandparent-grandchild	7
Purely Conjugal Pair	5
Single Person	2
Joint	1
TOTAL HOUSEHOLDS	73

Economic data reveal that most of the households comprising the
sample are impoverished, or nearly so. The median cash income per
household is $3,550 per year. Approximately 50% of the total income
of the households is derived from earnings (mainly seasonal employment), 30% from county, state, and federal welfare funds, and 20%
from individually owned reservation land leased to others for grazing
and farming.

I hypothesize that when family income is relatively high and
stable, single families will constitute single households. On the
other hand, when family income is low and unstable families will
unite in single households to pool available resources (income, land,
housing). Stable income means that income is dependable throughout
the year regardless of its source (welfare, earnings, or lease income) and unstable income, of course, means just the reverse.

Stability of income, though it by no means insures a sizable
income, nonetheless provides an economic prediction for the household. The residents of stable income households can rely on their
resources and adjust to them while residents of households without
a stable income must go through periodic uncertainty and privation.
The hardships of such privation are lessened somewhat through consolidation of resources (transportation, housing, utility costs,
food, fuel, etc.) with other families so as to reduce per capita
expenses. Comparison of stable income households with unstable income households reveals the marginal nature of Blackfeet economic
adaptation and suggests the processes by which income is distributed
and subsistence is maintained.

Table II suggests strong associations between unstable income
and multiple-family households. No multiple-family household has
more than two families. In the single instance of the joint family
household, mentioned above, there are two sisters, their offspring,
and the spouse of one of the sisters. Each extended family household consists of two families, one in the ascending generation and
one (a dependent nuclear family) in the descending generation. Of
the 14 dependent nuclear families (one in each of the 14 extended
family households) only three have stable income throughout the
year, while 11 have unstable cash resources. With these additional
figures in mind, Table II has been revised so as to compare types
of income with types of families. In Table III, I assess the stability of income for each family type.

Again strong relationships are suggested between stable income
and single family households and unstable income and multiple-
family households. The relationships between stability of income
and household and family types are tested in the following 2 x 2
contingency tables.[2] These results demonstrate a very strong relationship between income type and household composition, and they
closely parallel the findings of Munsell (1967) among the Pima-Papago

TABLE II

PERCENTAGES OF HOUSEHOLD TYPES BY STABILITY OF INCOME,
73 BLACKFEET RESERVATION INDIAN HOUSEHOLDS, 1967

HOUSEHOLD TYPE	INCOME TYPE				Total	Percent of Total of Households
	Stable	%	Unstable	%		
Single Families						
Independent nuclear	(31)	71	(13)	29	(44)	60
Grandparent-grandchild	(5)	62	(2)	38	(7)	10
Non-families						
Purely conjugal pair	(3)	60	(2)	40	(5)	7
Single person	(1)	50	(1)	50	(2)	3
Dual-families						
Extended	(4)	29	(10)	71	(14)	19
Joint	(0)	0	(1)	100	(1)	1
TOTALS	(44)		(29)		(73)	100

TABLE III

PERCENTAGES OF FAMILY TYPES BY STABILITY OF INCOME,
88 BLACKFEET RESERVATION INDIAN FAMILIES, 1967

FAMILY TYPE	INCOME TYPE				Total	Percent of Total Families
	Stable	%	Unstable	%		
Single Families						
Independent nuclear	(31)	71	(13)	29	(44)	50
Grandparent-grandchild	(5)	62	(2)	38	(7)	8
Non-families						
Purely conjugal pair	(3)	60	(2)	40	(5)	6
Single person	(1)	50	(1)	50	(2)	2
Dual-families						
Extended (28 families)	(7)	25	(21)	75	(28)	32
Joint (2 families)	(0)	0	(2)	100	(2)	2
TOTALS	(47)		(41)		(88)	100

TABLE IV

HOUSEHOLD

	Single or Non-family	Dual Family	
Stable Income	40	4	44
Unstable Income	18	11	29
	58	15	73

$$Q = .72, \quad \chi^2 = 8.72, \quad p < .01$$

TABLE V

FAMILY

(Includes dependent Nuclear
Families and Non-families)

	Single or Non-family	Dual Family	
Stable Income	40	7	47
Unstable Income	18	23	41
	58	30	88

$$Q = .76, \quad \chi^2 = 16.45, \quad p < .001$$

of the Salt River Reservation on the urban fringe of Phoenix, Arizona. Munsell discovered that stability as well as amount of income are critical economic factors common to single-family households. Amount of income, explained below, is also crucial in the formation and maintenance of single-family Blackfeet households.

In my sample of 73 households the median for all income is $3,550, whereas the median for unstable households is $2,370. It is interesting that the annual median income for extended family households is $3,700, or only $150 above the over-all median. In these households the head of the dependent nuclear family and his spouse contribute an average of 45% ($1,650), whereas the head of the family in the ascending generation contributes 55% ($2,050). The latter, then, contributes the dominant share of the total income for the extended family household. What is striking is that neither family brings in a sum comparable with the over-all median; the 45-55% ratio of contribution to the total household income and the moderate total of $3,700 suggest mutual economic dependencies between the families. These data also point to the importance of dual-family consolidation of expenses and income. The hypothesis regarding the relationship between amount of income and the formation of single-family households is tested in Table VI. The predicted one-way relationship is positive, strong, and significant.

TABLE VI

FAMILY

(Includes Dependent Nuclear
Families and Non-Families)

Annual Family Income	In Single or Non-Family Households	In Dual-Family Households	
Above $3,800	27	1	28
Below $3,800	31	29	60
	58	30	88

$$Q = .92, \quad \chi^2 = 14.8, \quad p < .001$$

As further confirmation of this hypothesis, I have arranged all types of families according to income. In Correlation Diagram I, η^2 is used to test the prediction that family type will change with amount of family income. The obtained value of .53 is high. The hypothesis is strongly supported. The .53 value means that 53% of the variation in family type is "explained" by variation in amount of income. The 47% unexplained variation is explained below along with exceptions present in the 2 x 2 tables. The distribution of cases shows that the mean incomes for the three types of families found in multiple-family households are conspicuously lower than for other types of families. The only exceptions to this generalization are the two Single Person households. These two cases are elderly males who subsist on low welfare assistance incomes. η^2, a powerful, rigorous statistic, has been used to demonstrate the strength of association between the variation in family type and variation in income.

My impression about the need to pool cash and services is also supported by the figure for the median number of persons in multiple-family households, 7.4. This figure compares very closely with the median number of persons per household in the entire sample, 7.3.

CORRELATION DIAGRAM I

CORRELATION RATIO OF FAMILY TYPE AND AMOUNT OF FAMILY INCOME, 88 BLACKFEET INDIAN FAMILIES, 1967

Family Type (Y)	300/1299	1300/2299	2300/3299	3300/4299	4300/5299	5300/6299	6300/7299	7300/8299	8300/9299	9300/10299	10300/11299	11300/12299	Mean Income Per Family Type
Independent Nuclear	1	10	11	4	7	6	1	1		1		1	4460
Purely Conjugal Pair (Household)		2	2	1	1			1					3950
Grandparent-Grandchild		3	1	2	1		1						2907
Head Nuclear Family in Extended Family Household	2	6	3	2	1	1							2300
Dependent Nuclear Family in Extended Family Household	7	2	5										1657
Joint	1	1											1300
Single Person (Household)	2												1050
Income Amount													

X (Income)

Annual Family Income in Intervals of $1000

$\eta^2_{xy} = .53$

- - - = Trend line

The remarkable similarity between multiple-family household incomes and incomes for the entire sample and the median number of persons per multiple-family household and the total sample seem to constitute the tolerable and achievable limits in income and density of household population. It is clearly advantageous for families with unstable incomes to consolidate their resources to sustain themselves throughout the year on a collective rather than an individual basis. But it is equally clear that nuclear families prefer privacy and space. Whenever it is economically possible to establish an independent household this is precisely what happens. My Blackfeet informants barely tolerate the crowded and emotionally taxing atmosphere of a multiple-family household. It is necessity which forces families to cluster under a single roof.

Unstable, low incomes do not account for all instances of multiple-family households. There are exceptions, as Tables IV, V, VI, and Correlation Diagram I show. Of the 18 households in Tables IV and V that are not multiple and do not have a stable income, seven cannot in any way be extended or joint regardless of economic resources because the members of these households have no kinsmen with whom they can form multiple-family households. Eleven of the 18 form cooperative economic units of 2 to 3 households each. These consist of separate dwellings located on land owned by a male or female in the parental generation. Married sons or daughters of the land-owner live in separate dwellings near the land-owner. Economically these families form single households and many of them were, in fact, single households prior to the development and increased availability of houses which are federally-sponsored. This accounts for all 18 cases in the lower left quadrant of Tables IV and V.

Of the four stable income, multiple-family households, there is one case in which extension is the result of a recent marital split; extension in this instance is not the result of economic necessity. Of the two remaining cases, one is temporary--a young man with his spouse and one offspring living with the man's parents until his earnings reach an amount sufficient for the establishment of a separate household. In the third case, a young couple with one offspring reside with the female spouse's infirm and elderly parents to assist the male parent. The fourth case involves a stable income dependent nuclear family and an elderly household head who also receives a stable income. The dependent nuclear family in this instance is headed by a Blood Blackfeet from Canada who owns no land or dwelling; furthermore, his father-in-law, the head of the extended family household, is infirm and requires the aid of his daughter.

As for the 31 cases in the lower left quadrant of Table VI, 18 are the unstable income households and families explained for Tables IV and V. Of the remaining 13 households, all receive stable incomes. Nine of these could not be in extended or joint family households because they have no kinsmen with whom they could share a dwelling; three are purely conjugal pairs whose incomes are apparently sufficient to obviate the need for substantial help from kinsmen. One of the remaining two cases is a young woman with her small son living on stable Aid to Dependent Children funds, funds which permit the maintenance of a separate household. The final case is a young couple with a single offspring living in a dwelling provided by the wife's father. The male head of this independent nuclear family household is a fully employed clerk who receives periodic financial assistance from affines.

The Family Cycle

The relationships between economics and household structure have been explicated. The economic conditions operative in the formation of single- and multiple-family households are specified. The economic variables that contribute most to the establishment and maintenance of single-family households are stability and amount of income. Conversely, unstable, low income contribute most to the formation of multiple-family households. With these generalizations in mind, I now wish to discuss the family cycle.

By using synchronic data I have constructed a cycle based on the ages of family heads. The first step in explaining changes in the family through time is to set up a η^2 correlation diagram. Correlation Diagram II shows the mean age of the heads of each type of family. The η^2 coefficient is a modest .29. That is, 29% of the variation in types of families is "explained" by variation in age of the household heads. The mean age of heads of each family type shown along the right hand side of the Correlation Diagram are helpful in putting into perspective the changes in families through time.

The families are grouped into four stages corresponding with age of family heads. Each stage is characterized by the predominance of a particular family type. The predominance of family types at various stages is explained below.

Stage I (Age of Heads, 20-34, 26 Families; Dependent Nuclear Families Predominate)

Stage I is the earliest phase of the family cycle. Dependent nuclear families predominate over all the other family types as Figure I shows. Young, newly-formed nuclear families will or will not be with related families in a single dwelling depending almost exclusively on stability and amount of family income as Tables VII and VIII show. The exceptions present in the upper right and lower left quadrants in these and other tables that are to follow are the same exceptions explained for Tables IV, V, and VI; it would only be redundant to reiterate the explanations already given.

The five youngest families, those whose heads are 20-24 years of age, as Correlation Diagram II shows, are all dependent nuclear families. Of the 11 families in the 25-29 age interval, six are

CORRELATION DIAGRAM II

CORRELATION RATIO OF FAMILY TYPE AND AGE
OF FAMILY HEADS, 88 BLACKFEET FAMILIES, 1967

Y (Family Type)

Family Type	20-24	25-29	30-34	35-39	40-44	45-49	50-54	55-59	60-64	65-69	70+	Mean Age of Family Heads
Grandparent-Grandchild							1		2	1	3	65.6
Single Person (Household)									1	1		64.6
Head Nuclear Family in Extended Family Household						1	1	3	3		3	60.6
Purely Conjugal Pair (Household)				1		1	1		1		1	58.0
Independent Nuclear		5	6	7	7	4	2	6	4		3	44.9
Joint		1				1	1					34.5
Dependent Nuclear	5	6	3									27.8

Age of Family Heads in Intervals of 5 Years

X (Age)

$\eta^2 xy = .29$

- - - = Trend line

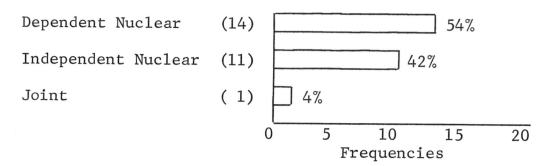

	Frequencies	
Dependent Nuclear	(14)	54%
Independent Nuclear	(11)	42%
Joint	(1)	4%

FIGURE I.   BAR CHART, RAW FREQUENCIES AND PERCENTAGES OF FAMILY TYPES; AGE OF HEADS 20-34, 26 BLACKFEET FAMILIES, 1967

TABLE VII

STAGE I FAMILIES

	In Dual Family Household	In Single Family Household	
Unstable Income	14	4	18
Stable Income	1	7	8
	15	11	26

$Q = .92$, $\chi^2 = 9.29$, $p < .01$

TABLE VIII

STAGE I FAMILIES

Annual Family Income	In Dual Family Household	In Single Family Household	
Below $3,800	15	7	22
Above $3,800	0	4	4
	15	11	26

$Q = 1.00$; χ^2 not significant. The distribution in this table is significant with all exceptions explained.

206

dependent nuclear, five are independent nuclear, and one is part of a joint family household. In the final portion of Stage I, in the 30-34 age interval, six of the nine families are independent nuclear. There are no dependent nuclear families whose heads are older than 34. It is at this point that dependent nuclear families change in the cycle. By this time the erstwhile dependent families generally achieve some form of economic independence, as we shall see in Stage II of the family cycle.

Stage II (Age of Heads, 35-49, 22 Families; Independent Nuclear Families Predominate)

Figure II provides a ready impression of the frequencies and percentages of family types in this stage. Economically this is the

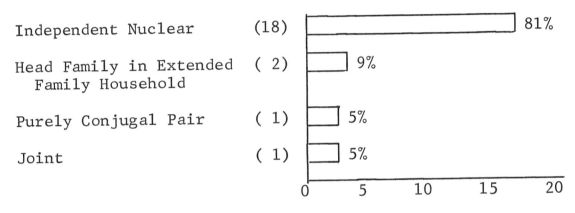

FIGURE II.   BAR CHART, RAW FREQUENCIES AND PERCENTAGES OF FAMILY TYPES: AGE OF HEADS 35-49, 22 BLACKFEET FAMILIES

most productive age group in the sample. Twelve of the heads among the 22 families earn regularly throughout the year and a total of 16 have stable incomes. So, proportionately this age group has the greatest percentage of stable income families (73%) and the highest percentage of single family households (86%). Tables IX and X both show high one-way strengths of association between single-family households and stability and amount of income.

Stage II can best be summarized as the peak earning years (median age for steady, year-round family head earners is 41.9 years) and is the period during which independent nuclear family households have the greatest probability of occurrence.

TABLE IX

	In Single Family Households	In Multiple-Family Households	
Stable Income	15	1	16
Unstable Income	4	2	6
	19	3	22

$Q = .76$, x^2 not significant, but the posited one-way relationship is strong.

TABLE X

Annual Income	In Single Family Households	In Multiple-Family Households	
Above $3,800	13	0	13
Below $3,800	6	3	9
	19	3	22

$Q = 1.00$, $x^2 = 5.02$, $p < .05$

Stage III (Age of Heads, 50-64, 25 families; Independent Nuclear Families continue to predominate; all of the late stage family types appear in this stage)

This stage shows a gradual trend from independent nuclear families toward late phase family types. Stable incomes are far more important for the continuation of single-family households than amount of income as Tables XI and XII show.

There is a shift in this stage toward stable welfare and leased land income in contrast to the predominance of stable earned incomes in Stage II of the family cycle. Of the stable income families in Stage III, five live mainly on welfare, three on leased land income, and five on stable earned income. The eight families living on welfare and on leased land income generally fall below $3,800 per annum, five of the eight, yet stability of income allows all eight to live in independent nuclear family households. This explains why there is a discrepancy between the two tables in the distribution of cases.

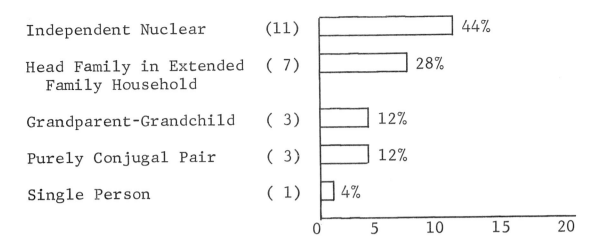

Independent Nuclear   (11)   44%

Head Family in Extended   (7)   28%
  Family Household

Grandparent-Grandchild   (3)   12%

Purely Conjugal Pair   (3)   12%

Single Person   (1)   4%

0   5   10   15   20

FIGURE III.   BAR CHART, RAW FREQUENCIES AND PERCENTAGES OF
              FAMILY TYPES; AGE OF HEADS 50-64, 25 BLACKFEET
              FAMILIES, 1967

TABLE XI

	In Single Family Households	In Multiple-Family Households	
Stable Income	12	1	13
Unstable Income	6	6	12
	18	7	25

$Q = .85$, $\chi^2 = 3.90$, $p < .05$

TABLE XII

Annual Income	In Single Family Households	In Multiple-Family Households	
Above $3,800	6	1	7
Below $3,800	12	6	18
	18	7	25

The posited one-way association is not strong or significant, the ratio of ½ between high annual income and single family households as opposed to 1/6 between high income and multiple-family households is supportive of my argument.

Stage II also shows a growing number of head families in extended family households, though there are two head families in extended family households in the 35-49 age interval. One of these cases occurs in the 40-44 age interval and the other in the 45-49 interval. Neither of them is permanently extended; one broke up while I was making my investigation and the other consists of a divorced female with two offspring in the ascending generation with a daughter and granddaughter. The daughter's spouse is in the Armed Services; he and his wife plan to establish a separate household upon his return. In short, these two cases seem to be exceptions. Permanently extended family households occur later in the family cycle as Table XIII shows.

The majority of extended family households are fluid in nature, with expected shifts toward establishment of independent nuclear family households sometime before the head of the dependent nuclear family reaches 35 years of age.

Permanently extended households are such for two obvious reasons: (1) all but one of the permanently extended households is headed by a single person whose sons stand to inherit an elderly male or female's land and dwelling; and (2), in all of these cases the elder head and the dependent nuclear family have unstable, low incomes. There seem to be few promising prospects for the dependent nuclear family's getting out on its own to establish an independent nuclear family household. The one exception is a young woman, her spouse and single offspring with the woman's infirm, stable income parents. Extension in this instance is a dual coincidence of physical and economic dependency. Likely the young woman will remain in her parents' household with her spouse and offspring.

TABLE XIII

PERMANENT AND IMPERMANENT EXTENDED FAMILY HOUSEHOLDS BY TYPE OF FAMILY
IN ASCENDING GENERATION, 14 BLACKFEET HOUSEHOLDS, 1967*

Type of Family or Non-Family in Ascending Generation	Impermanently Extended	Age of Head	Permanently Extended	Age of Head
Purely Conjugal Pair	2	67, 62	0	-
Grandparent-Grandchild	2	55, 72	0	-
Independent Nuclear	5	41, 48, 56, 58, 69	1	75
Single Person	0	-	4	53, 63 64, 72
Total	9		5	

*This table does not include the single instance of a joint family household which was the only other dual family household in the sample. The joint family household dissolved during the latter part of the summer of 1967. It was clearly an aberrant case.

Of the nine impermanently extended family households, five of the elder families are independent nuclear families, while two of the remaining four are Purely Conjugal Pairs and two are Grandparent-Grandchild families.

Of the five independent nuclear families in the elder generation, four find collectivization families under a single roof almost intolerable. The four complementary dependent nuclear families in these households are eager to move out when incomes become sufficient to maintain separate households. These families are showing definite progress toward gaining independence. In one case of the five, a young family did achieve independence while I was in the field.

As for the four remaining cases, two achieved independence during my stay in 1967; one of these dependent nuclear families was with an elderly conjugal pair and the other was with a Grandparent-Grandchild family. The former continued intensive economic cooperation with the host family after moving into a separate dwelling and the latter is a young male with his son who returned to his spouse after a year of separation. This re-united couple moved in with the female spouse's parents, a low, unstable income, formerly independent nuclear family. The third case is a 34-year-old female--a divorcée with two offspring living with her parents. The fourth and final case, as mentioned previously, is a young woman with offspring whose husband is in the U. S. Army. When the young man returns he plans to take his family to a separate dwelling.

It is seldom, then, at least so far as my sample indicates, that extension is permanent and when it does occur it involves an agnatic link (son-father, son-mother, son-parent surrogate) where mutual dependencies are chronic and when the son or son surrogate stands to inherit land and dwelling from his parent or parent surrogate.

Stage IV   (Age of Heads, 65 to 91, 15 families, slight predominance of Extended Families)

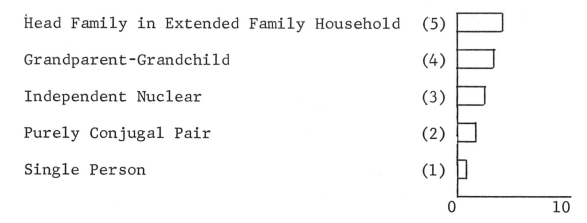

FIGURE IV.   BAR CHART, STAGE IV, 15 BLACKFEET FAMILIES; AGE OF HEADS, 65 TO 91, 1967

The final stage of the family cycle shows a slight predominance of head families in extended family households. Only one of these is permanently extended. Other final stage family types occur as well (Purely Conjugal Pair 2, Single Person 1, and Independent Nuclear 3).

The most striking feature of the late stage families is that the majority of elders continue to assist in supporting their own offspring and/or their grandchildren. This applies to 12 of the 15 families in Stage IV, or 80% of the total. The other three cases have no available dependents whom they can take into their households.

It would be redundant at this point to reiterate the effects of economic variables on household composition--a relationship which has already been fully explicated. Rather, I prefer to further explain the cases with dependents since the high percentage of dependents is the most unusual characteristic of the final stage of the sample families.

The three independent nuclear families consist of the following: (1) an elderly woman with three divorced offspring; (2) an elderly conjugal pair with two divorced sons and two grandsons (the grandsons are not the offspring of the divorced sons); and (3) an elderly conjugal pair with one son and one grandson (again the grandson is not the offspring of the son). None of the offspring owns a dwelling or any land on which he or she can build a dwelling and none contributes substantially to the household budget. All are either chronically unemployed or only very infrequently employed.

Grandparent-Grandchild Families

The presence of grandchildren in three of the seven Grandparent-Grandchild families are the result of marital separations, two children are illegitimate and one is an orphan. (I refer to illegitimate children as the offspring of persons whose union is not recognized by the community as a marriage.) In the last case the grandparents requested of their eldest son if they could raise the young man's first-born child, a request which was granted. The presence of grandchildren in their grandparents' households requires further explanation, however.

I refer now to all of the households in which grandchildren are with their grandparents. There are 22 grandchildren in 17 households. In none of these is either of the children's parents present. As noted, seven of these households are purely Grandparent-Grandchild households, the remaining 10 are independent nuclear family households. Nine children are illegitimate, five became the responsibility of their grandparents after parental separations, two children are orphans, one child came to live with his grandparents because of overcrowded conditions in his parents' home, one was taken on request by the grandparents, and the last was taken from his parents because of neglect.

Discussion and Conclusions

The complexity of households in Stage IV, and the complexity of households in general, result essentially from economic conditions, as is demonstrated above. Moreover, the kinds of households in which families are organized throughout the cycle hinges mainly on stability and amount of income. Independent nuclear family households are the most common type, statistically, and are the normative household type as well. Variations from this type are generally undesirable.

In this paper I have measured and explained the influence of economic variables on household composition and the family cycle. All exceptions to the demonstrated empirical generalizations have been explained.

Few have attempted to explicate the relationship between economics, household structure, and the family cycle. Tangentially, this paper should add to our understanding of the world-wide problem of household composition as associated with economic variables.

It is alleged that nuclear family households are the result of Western industrialization (Burgess 1933). This generalization rests upon the assumption that wage labor economics require a mobile work force, one that is unencumbered by kinsmen extending beyond the nuclear family. Recent studies have demonstrated, however, that

213

nuclear family households are by no means confined to countries where industrialization exists (Nimkoff and Middleton 1960; Greenfield 1961). Other studies have shown that nuclear family households preceded industrialization in Western Europe (Furstenberg 1966), and that stem, joint, extended, and other types of multiple-family households exist where industrialization is present (Goode 1963).

While the controversy over household structure and economics continues, it remains evident that more thorough research needs to be done. One should want to know, for example, under what conditions multiple-family households break up, or are maintained in other parts of the world. It is known that strong kin ties are sustained in urban centers through kin-linked control of available jobs (Young and Willmott 1957). And it is also known that extended families brought about by economic dependencies of young nuclear families were commonplace in the United States two decades ago. It may be that the Blackfeet sample discussed in this paper reveals a household pattern comparable perhaps with a small rural non-Indian community of the 1930's.

NOTES

1. I acknowledge my debt to the National Institutes of Health for a traineeship making possible the field work upon which this paper is based. The grant was administered by the Department of Anthropology, University of Oregon, Eugene, Oregon. I wish also to express my gratitude to Professors Joseph G. Jorgensen, David F. Aberle, and Malcom B. McFee, whose guidance in formulating the field problem and writing the results made this paper possible.

2. The one-way measure of association, Yule's Q, is employed here. The relationships predicted between stable income and single or non-family household type are strong, positive, and significant.

REFERENCES

Burgess, Ernest W. and Harvey J. Locke
    1953   The Family: From Institution to Companionship. Second
            edition. New York, American Book Company.
Furstenberg, Frank F.
    1966   Industrialization and the Family. American Sociological
            Review, Volume 31, No. 3.
Goode, William J.
    1963   World Revolution and Family Patterns. Glencoe, Illinois,
            The Free Press.
Greenfield, Sidney M.
    1961-2 Industrialization and the Family in Sociological Theory.
            American Journal of Sociology, Volume LXVII. July 1961,
            May 1962.
Munsell, Marven

1967   Land and Labor at Salt River. Unpublished Ph.D. dissertation. Eugene, Oregon, University of Oregon.

Nimkoff, M. F. and Russell Middleton
    1960   Types of Family and Types of Economy. American Journal of Sociology, Volume LXVI, No. 3. November 1960.

Young, Michael and Peter Willmott
    1957   Family and Kinship in East London. Baltimore, Maryland, Penguin Books.